Dictionary of
DESKTOP PUBLISHING

Dictionary of
DESKTOP PUBLISHING

Melody Mauldin Covington

SOLI DEO GLORIA

© Copyright 1995 by Barron's Educational Series, Inc.

All inquiries should be addressed to:
Barron's Educational Series, Inc.
250 Wireless Boulevard
Hauppauge, New York 11788

Library of Congress Catalog Card No. 95-15051

International Standard Book No. 0-8120-9084-5

Library of Congress Cataloging in Publication Data

Covington, Melody Mauldin (1958–   )
    Dictionary of desktop publishing / Melody Mauldin Covington.
        p.   cm.
    ISBN 0-8120-9084-5
    1. Desktop publishing—dictionaries.   I. Title.
Z253.53.C68   1995
686.2′2544536–dc20   95–15051
                                        CIP

Printed in the United States of America

5678 8800 987654321

PREFACE

The computers that we work with daily earn their keep; the amount of drudgery they save us from is truly immense. However, there *is* a drawback to the way we work with computers. There is a shortage of *names*. We point to things with the mouse, much in the way a two-year-old child points at what he (or she) wants. Sometimes we don't know the name of the object, or what to call the action that we are performing, or the name of the result we are trying to achieve. This can be frustrating when trying to remember a complex sequence of commands, reading a manual, or attempting to explain something to a colleague; we don't have the verbal skills to support our activities.

We are having to fight several different battles. First, we are in the middle of a technological revolution. The way all printed matter is typeset and produced has changed drastically in the last decade. The computers that brought about this great change were not systematically designed, but developed by different companies, using different hardware and different assumptions about the people who would use the machines. Because of corporate one-upmanship, or a desire to create a proprietary system, or even to dodge lawsuits, programmers have given similar commands and objects different names. In some cases, centuries-old typographic terminology from the time of Gutenberg has been ignored, creating more confusion. And, last but certainly not least, a lot of ideas are just *new* and have had to have names invented for them.

It's no wonder that the awkward feeling of not knowing something's proper name is a common phenomenon these days.

The purpose of this book is to give you command of some of the terms associated with Desktop Publishing. You will find here the basic terminology of typography and publishing, computer terminology, and technical terms used by printers. There are over 1100 terms defined in this dictionary. These brief articles are not meant to substitute for your manuals, but are meant to provide a basic level of understanding and enhancement of your existing knowledge. If your curiosity is raised about a particular subject, I hope you will pursue learning about it — either by reading about it in magazines, journals, and books, or by taking a course at a local college or trade school. Because the field of Desktop Publishing is so new and is still evolving, this continuing education will be necessary as the machines and software we use become more sophisticated.

Many of the product names and typeface names used in this book are registered trademarks. I have made no attempt to determine the legal status or ownership of each name, and this book should not be used as an authority on the status of trademarks. Obviously, you should not give your product the same name as a preexisting product unless you have determined that the name is free and clear.

I would like to gratefully acknowledge the assistance of several people:

- Mr. Paul Royster, who supervised the first months of this book's incubation.
- Ms. Mary Falcon, my editor during the final stages of manuscript preparation and production.
- Dr. Donald Nute, Director of the Artificial Intelligence Center at the University of Georgia, who granted me the privilege of being a Visiting Scholar and graciously allowed me the use of the Artificial Intelligence Lab as I prepared the manuscript.
- Dr. Douglas Downing of Seattle Pacific University and Dr. Michael Covington of the University of Georgia, co-authors of the *Dictionary of Computer Terms,* who allowed me to use some material from their dictionary as basis for my definitions. Many thanks to Michael (my husband) who provided much needed technical support with the computers and TeX, and who also lent his linguistic expertise to the articles on Accents, Foreign Languages, Punctuation, and Spelling.
- My daughters, Cathy and Sharon, who understood how busy I was and helped any way that they could.

Melody Mauldin Covington
February 1995

A

A4 an ISO standard paper size that is 210 × 297 mm, about $8\frac{1}{4}$ inches × $11\frac{3}{4}$ inches. This is the standard size of typing paper in Europe. Sizes A3, A2 and A1 are larger. American typing paper is $8\frac{1}{2}$ inches × 11 inches. *See table at* PAPER SIZES (ISO).

AA *see* AUTHOR'S ALTERATIONS.

ABORT to cancel an action or command. Most software developers currently prefer "Cancel."

ACADEMIC STANDARDS the typographic requirements for theses, dissertations, and similar scholarly work. A thesis or dissertation is no place for creative typography. The format is rigidly standardized for several reasons. The examiners' attention must be entirely on the text, not the layout; the examiners must have room to mark corrections; and the finished thesis must survive reproduction by several methods, including half-size reprints from microfilm.

Accordingly, for decades it has been traditional to type the text double-spaced with 1-inch margins. More recently, 12-point roman type has become acceptable, but universities still insist on greater than normal spacing between lines. Typography must be scrupulously correct and printout quality must be first-rate; graduate schools are not willing to lower their standards for computer users. Every university has its own specific regulations.

Academic work requires extensive documentation of the sources of ideas, and the methods for doing this vary from field to field. Organizations such as the Modern Language Association (MLA) and American Psychological Association (APA) publish style handbooks that are widely followed.

Many academic authors use the TeX word processor and LaTeX document design package (distributed free by Stanford University), and many universities have LaTeX style files that automatically enforce their layout requirements. Office-type word processors often lack needed features, such as proper handling of footnotes, foreign language character sets, and mathematical formulas.

ACCENTS marks added to letters (as in *é è ê ë*) to indicate differences of pronunciation; said to have been introduced by Aristophanes of Byzantium c. 200 B.C. to preserve the pitch accent of ancient Greek, which was dying out. The only major languages that do not require accents are English, Latin, and Dutch.

The rules for using accents vary widely from language to language. Most accents are not optional, and leaving them out, or putting in superfluous ones, constitutes a spelling error. Some American product names, such as *Béaucoup Mints* and *Village Coûrt,* are unintentionally comical because someone adorned them with accents that conflict with their actual pronunciation, thereby displaying ignorance of the language being aped (probably French). When indulging in creative typography, never assume that your audience is less knowledgeable than yourself.

The ACUTE ACCENT, as in *á*, indicates a stressed syllable (in Spanish), a specific vowel quality (as in French *é*), or a rising tone (in transcribed Chinese). In English, the acute accent is occasionally used to mark stressed syllables when scanning lines of poetry. The acute accent is not an apostrophe and must not be typeset as such; do not write *saute'* for *sauté.*

The DOUBLE ACUTE, as in *a̋,* is the Hungarian combination of acute accent and umlaut (see below).

The GRAVE ACCENT, as in *è,* indicates an open vowel sound (French *è*), a stressed syllable (in Italian), or a falling tone (in transcribed Chinese). In English poetry, the grave accent indicates that the suffix *-ed* is pronounced as a separate syllable (*blessèd, cursèd*).

The CIRCUMFLEX, as in *ê,* marks a place where a silent *s* formerly occurred in French, as in *forêt* 'forest.' In transcribed Chinese, the circumflex denotes a rising and then falling tone.

The MACRON, as in *ā,* denotes a long vowel in Latin dictionaries and textbooks and in transcriptions of some other languages. It is not normally used in running Latin text. In transcribed Chinese, the macron denotes a level tone.

The BREVE, as in *ă,* denotes a short vowel in Latin dictionaries and textbooks, and a falling and then

á
Acute accent

a̋
Double acute

è
Grave accent

ê
Circumflex

ā
Macron

ă
Breve

rising tone in transcribed Chinese. It is sometimes used to mark unstressed syllables when scanning English poetry.

The double dot, as in *ë*, has two functions. As a DIERESIS it shows that two adjacent vowels form separate syllables; thus Latin *praeësse,* French *Noël,* Spanish *lingüista,* and even English *coöperate, preëminent* (although *cooperate* and *preeminent* or *pre-eminent* are the preferred spellings).

Ö
Dieresis or umlaut

As an UMLAUT the double dot marks a German vowel that has undergone fronting (*ä, ö, ü*). In transcribed Russian, *ë* denotes an *e* that is pronounced *ya,* as in *Gorbachëv.*

The TILDE, as in *ñ,* marks a Spanish *n* that is pronounced *ny.* In Portuguese, tildes mark nasalized vowels, as in *João.*

ñ
Tilde

The CEDILLA, as in *ç,* marks a *c* that is pronounced *s* in French and Portuguese.

ç
Cedilla

The CHECK, HÁČEK, CARON, as in *š,* has several uses. In Czech, *č, š, ž, ř, ň,* and *ě* are pronounced approximately as English *ch, sh, zh, rzh, ny,* and *ye* respectively. In transcribed Chinese, the WEDGE is an alternative to the breve for indicating a falling and then rising tone.

Š
Check

Other languages use other accents. For example, Swedish, Norwegian, and Danish use *Åå* to denote an *a* that is pronounced like *o.* Norwegian and Danish *Øø* corresponds to Swedish and German *ö.* Polish *Łł* is a sound midway between English *l* and *w.*

See also FOREIGN LANGUAGES; FRENCH; GERMAN; LATIN; SPANISH.

ACCOUNT EXECUTIVE an advertising agency employee who is in charge of conducting an advertising campaign for a client. Account executives assemble a team to do market research, design and produce the advertisements, and place the ads in appropriate media (magazines, newspapers, television, billboards, etc).

ACCOUNTING SOFTWARE software designed to computerize the accounting process for a business. A complete system should include modules for the following functions: entering transaction data; posting the data to accounts at the appropriate times; presenting year-end reports, including balance sheets and income statements; and maintaining records of ACCOUNTS RECEIVABLE and ACCOUNTS PAYABLE. Because of the importance of the data included in the system, a program should have a security mechanism, such as required passwords, to prevent unauthorized users from altering the data. A system also should keep a record of transactions that have been entered (called an *audit trail*) so it is possible to trace how the figures that appear on the reports were derived.

ACCOUNTS PAYABLE bills that need to be paid.

ACCOUNTS RECEIVABLE money that is owed to your business, and can be counted as a financial asset.

ACQUIRE to obtain a file (for editing) from an *analog* source, such as a SCANNER or video input (*see* FRAME GRABBER). Similar to IMPORT, with the exception that an imported file will already be in a digital format.

ACRONYM a pronounceable word, usually set in all caps, whose letters stand for the initial letters of the title of an organization, computer program, or words in a phrase. An example would be MADD (Mothers Against Drunk Driving). Note that you do not put periods after the initials.

Sometimes very common acronyms become so widely used that they take normal case; *laser*, which originally stood for **l**ight **a**mplification by **s**timulated **e**mission of **r**adiation, and *radar* (**ra**dio **d**etection **a**nd **r**anging) are two such words.

ACTIVATE to make a window or object the active window or object. To activate a DIMMED window, click on its TITLE BAR.

ACTIVE COLOR the color currently selected. Whatever tool is being used will paint or draw in the active color.

ACTIVE WINDOW the window currently in use. Its title bar is highlighted. You can change the active window at any time by clicking the mouse pointer inside another window. There can only be one active

Venetian	AaBbCcDdEeFfGgHhIiJjKkLlMmNnOo&?") Venetian 301
Garalde	AaBbCcDdEeFfGgHhIiJjKkLlMmNnOo&?") Aldine 401
Transitional	AaBbCcDdEeFfGgHhIiJjKkLlMmNnOo&?") Kis
Didone	AaBbCcDdEeFfGgHhIiJjKkLlMmNnOo&?") Bodoni
Slab-serif	AaBbCcDdEeFfGgHhIiJjKkLlMmNn?") Clarendon
Sans-serif	AaBbCcDdEeFfGgHhIiJjKkLlMmNnOo&?") Zurich
Script	AaBbCcDdEeFfGgHhIiJjKkLlMmNnOo&?") Commercial Script
Display	ABCDEFGHIJKLMNOPQRSTUVWXYZ&?") Davida Bold
Blackletter	AaBbCcDdEeFfGgHhIiJjKkLlMmNnOo&?") Cloister Black
Symbols	✡❁✳▲♣❊✦❈✧✳★❋✰✛☉❖❉✳✛❊☆✪★✩● Zapf Dingbats

Figure 1 Adobe type classification

---

window at a time. *See* WINDOW; ACTIVATE.

ACUTE ACCENT *see* ACCENTS.

ADAPTABLE FRACTION a fraction composed of two full-size numbers separated by a forward slash. *See* FRACTION, BUILT FRACTION.

3/4
Adaptable fraction

ADD NOISE a photopaint filter that adds texture to a picture. Since the overall effect is rather unpredictable, it may be wise to save a copy of the image before applying this filter.

ADOBE TYPE CLASSIFICATION SYSTEM a type classification system used by Adobe Systems, Inc.

Adobe divides type into ten classes (*see Figure 1*), each of which has its own entry in this dictionary. Adobe's system is very similar to the BRITISH STANDARDS 2961:1967.

ADVERTISEMENT a persuasive communication that encourages consumers to buy a particular product or service. Effective advertisements provide information, enhance the reputation of the product or company, and often entertain. *See* CONCEPT.

ADVERTISING AGENCY a business that develops advertisements for clients and places the ads in appropriate media.

AGATE

1. a unit of measurement common in the newspaper industry. 14 agate lines = 1 column inch, so 1 agate = $5\frac{1}{2}$ points.

2. 5-point type in the old British nomenclature.

Airbrush

AIRBRUSH a tool available in some paint and photopaint programs that simulates the effect of a physical airbrush; the edges are soft and the colors are translucent. The softness of the edge, size of the spray pattern, and degree of opaqueness can be controlled.

In bitmap-editing programs that do not offer an airbrush tool, there is usually a SPRAYCAN TOOL, which is basically a coarser version of the airbrush.

The icon shown is from Corel PhotoPaint.

ALERT BOX *see* MESSAGE BOX.

ALIAS (Macintosh) a copy of a file icon that provides an alternate way of starting an application program or opening a file, folder, or disk. You can place the alias anywhere that's convenient—the desktop, the Apple menu, or a special folder. The title of an alias icon will be in italics.

Align

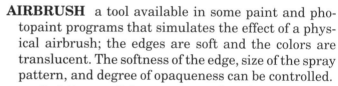

ALIGN to make things line up, either horizontally or vertically. Most drawing programs and page layout programs have specific commands to help you align objects and text.

From a design standpoint, alignment is the tension that joins elements of a design. You can play off this tension, and create an element of surprise by putting something in an unexpected place.

It is often quite tricky to align objects on screen. Use alignment aids (GRIDS, GUIDELINES) to help you. Quite often, the difference between a sharp design and a confused one is that things that should align are ever-so-slightly off.

ALPHANUMERIC alphabetic or numeric, i.e., belonging to the set of letters and digits (but not punctuation marks, mathematical symbols, or control codes).

ALTERATIONS changes or corrections. These may include AUTHOR'S ALTERATIONS (AA), EDITOR'S ALTERATIONS (EA), and PRINTER'S ERRORS (PE). These changes are marked on a proof. Clients are expected to pay for author's alterations since they represent a change from the copy that was given to be typeset.

ALT KEY a secondary shift key found on the keyboards of IBM PC compatible computers. (*Alt* stands for *alternate*.) The Alt key is used like a shift key; that is, you hold it down while pressing another key. (To type Alt-P, hold down Alt and type P.)

The Alt key gives the other key a new meaning that depends on the software being used. This gives you a quick way to give commands to an application program or a way to type special characters. For example, in WordPerfect and Lotus 123, the Alt key is used in combination with various letters to call up macros. Alt key combinations can be more than a single key: In Windows applications, Alt plus a 4-digit number gives you access to special characters. *See* MACROS, SPECIAL CHARACTERS.

The OPTION key on the Macintosh corresponds to the Alt key.

ALTS alterations.

AMPERSAND the character &, which stands for the word *and*. Although not recommended for use in a formal setting, an ampersand can provide a decorative graphic element in a layout. There is quite a bit of variation in the ampersands of different typefaces.

Ampersand

ANCHOR a nonprinting control code that marks the approximate location of a FLOATING ILLUSTRATION.

ANNOTATION an explanatory note attached to a chart or illustration.

ANNOUNCEMENT CARD a $4\frac{1}{4}$-inch × $5\frac{1}{2}$-inch (109-mm × 149-mm) card available with or without a central embossed panel. These cards are too thick to run through a laser printer; use the printer's output as camera-ready art and have the announcement cards offset printed. Ask for a sample of the stock beforehand. Make sure to leave enough room for the $\frac{1}{2}$-inch (13-mm) thick border if you are using panel cards.

I recommend using a centered layout for announcement cards. Formal scripts are the expected typeface, but an elegant roman font would also be a good choice.

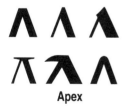

Announcement card

ANSI CHARACTER SET an extended set of characters used in Microsoft Windows and OS/2, and shown in *Table 1*. It includes all the ASCII characters plus many others. *See* ASCII; WINDOWS; IBM PC.

To type any ANSI character in Microsoft Windows, hold down the Alt key while typing 0 followed by the character code number on the numeric keypad at the right-hand side of the keyboard. For example, to type é, hold down Alt and type 0233.

ANTIALIASING a computational method of smoothing out the "jaggies," the phenomenon that causes diagonal lines to have a stair-step effect on your monitor or printout. Ordinarily, vertical and horizontal lines appear straight when drawn on computer screens, but slanted lines have a stair-step appearance because the line is drawn by turning on pixels that are arranged in a square grid. In antialiasing, the line is thought of as cutting a swath across the grid of pixels, and pixels that are only partly covered by the line are appropriately grayed. This doubles the apparent resolution of the screen.

Many of the newer NATURAL MEDIA paint programs use antialiasing to help simulate the smeared edges of chalk and watercolors. Erasures also tend to have antialiased edges, giving a very realistic effect.

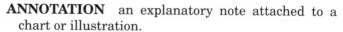

Apex

APEX the pointed top of letters like M and A. When identifying or matching typefaces, note carefully how the apex of the A is designed.

128	160	192 À	224 à
129	161 ¡	193 Á	225 á
130 ,	162 ¢	194 Â	226 â
131 *f*	163 £	195 Ã	227 ã
132 „	164 ¤	196 Ä	228 ä
133 ...	165 ¥	197 Å	229 å
134 †	166 ¦	198 Æ	230 æ
135 ‡	167 §	199 Ç	231 ç
136 ˆ	168 ¨	200 È	232 è
137 ‰	169 ©	201 É	233 é
138 Š	170 ª	202 Ê	234 ê
139 ‹	171 «	203 Ë	235 ë
140 Œ	172 ¬	204 Ì	236 ì
141	173 -	205 Í	237 í
142	174 ®	206 Î	238 î
143	175 ¯	207 Ï	239 ï
144	176 °	208 Ð	240 ð
145 '	177 ±	209 Ñ	241 ñ
146 '	178 ²	210 Ò	242 ò
147 "	179 ³	211 Ó	243 ó
148 "	180 ´	212 Ô	244 ô
149 •	181 µ	213 Õ	245 õ
150 –	182 ¶	214 Ö	246 ö
151 —	183 ·	215 ×	247 ÷
152 ˜	184 ¸	216 Ø	248 ø
153 ™	185 ¹	217 Ù	249 ù
154 š	186 º	218 Ú	250 ú
155 ›	187 »	219 Û	251 û
156 œ	188 ¼	220 Ü	252 ü
157	189 ½	221 Ý	253 ý
158	190 ¾	222 Þ	254 þ
159 Ÿ	191 ¿	223 ß	255 ÿ

Table 1 ANSI Windows Character Set

APOSTROPHE the character '. Apostrophes are used in forming possessives and contractions. *See* PUNCTUATION for more details.

'

Apostrophe

APP *see* APPLICATION PROGRAM.

APPLE one of the largest personal computer manufacturers. The company, located in Cupertino, California, was founded by Steve Jobs and Steve Wozniak, who began work in a garage. The early Apple computers were enthusiastically adopted by the educational community for computer-aided instruction. One of their most successful products, the MACINTOSH computer, is credited with starting the field of desktop publishing. The Macintosh, introduced in 1984, set the standard for word processing, graphics, and ease of use.

In 1994 Apple introduced the PowerMac, based on the PowerPC chip that was jointly developed by Apple, IBM, and Motorola.

Apple Menu icon

APPLE MENU (Macintosh) the menu at the far left of the title bar that holds desk accessories (DAs), control panels, and ALIASES of frequently used software.

APPLET a small application program that is inexpensive and designed to do a small, specific job. Most operating systems come with several applets, such as a calculator, a calendar, and a note editor.

APPLICATION MENU (Macintosh) the menu at the far right end of a window's title bar that allows you to quickly switch between open application programs. The icon for the Application Menu changes to show the active program.

A similar Windows feature is the TASK LIST.

APPLICATION PROGRAM a computer program that you use to get work done, rather than a program used to tend to the computer. Examples of application programs include word processors, charting programs, page layout, and drawing programs. *Contrast* UTILITY and OPERATING SYSTEM.

APPROVAL permission to proceed with the final production or distribution, given after the client or responsible party has thoroughly proofed the copy and layout.

ARABIC NUMERALS the characters 1, 2, 3, 4, 5, 6, 7, 8, 9, 0. These are our familiar representations for numbers in the western world. When the numerals are the same size as capital letters and do not descend below the baseline, they are called LINING FIGURES. These are best for tables and charts. When the body of the numerals is roughly equal to the X-HEIGHT of the font and have ascenders and descenders (1, 2, 3, 4, 5, 6, 7, 8, 9, 0), they are called OLD STYLE FIGURES. Old style figures do not stand out from text.

ARC part of a circle.

ARCHIVAL STORAGE storage for items (both electronic data and printouts) that must be kept for a long time but will seldom be used.

A key concept in arranging your archival storage is *organization*. Clients' files can be copied to diskettes and filed along with other papers pertaining to their job. A flat file or rack can be useful for storing large artwork. Your original program diskettes should be kept in a safe place, preferably a fireproof box that also contains the two latest backups of your hard disk drive(s). Label everything concisely and thoroughly—it will save you time in the long run.

See also BACKUP COPY, TAPE DRIVE.

ARCHIVE

1. a filing system for information that needs to be kept for a long time.

2. (DOS and Windows) a descriptive bit, associated with each file, that notes whether or not it has been backed up by copying to another disk or tape. The archive bit setting can be seen in directory listings. It is possible to back up only the files that have not already been backed up. *See* INCREMENTAL BACKUP.

ARM part of a letter that extends out horizontally, like the cross-stroke on the T.

Arm

ARRANGE

1. to organize the display of windows, program groups, and icons. In a windowed environment, you are given a considerable amount of help organizing and grouping the windows and icons. You will find commands to help you straighten the icons under the "Windows" menu in the PROGRAM MANAGER title bar (MS Windows). The CASCADE and TILE options refer to the arrangement of open windows: "Cascade" gives you a neat stack of windows with all the title bars visible; "Tile" makes the open windows fill the entire screen without overlapping. *See* TILE *and* CASCADE for picture.

If you want the computer to do most of the icon housekeeping, select "Auto Arrange" from the "Op-

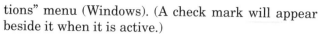

tions" menu (Windows). (A check mark will appear beside it when it is active.)

2. to place an item in relation to other items. In drawing programs, there is usually an *Arrange* menu that contains commands relating to the placement of selected objects (ALIGN, SEND TO FRONT, etc.). Objects are layered as if they were opaque pieces of paper. *See also* STACKING ORDER.

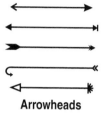

Arrowheads

ARROWHEAD the pointed triangle at the end of an arrow. This may seem trivial, but you need to remember that you have a great deal of control over the appearance of the arrowhead. Take the time to find out how to change the size and shape of the arrowhead in your software.

ARROW KEYS keys that move the cursor up, down, or to the left or right. The effect of these keys depends on the software being used; some software ignores them or handles them incorrectly. Basically, the arrow keys are an alternative to the mouse. Some drawing environments let you NUDGE the selected object with the arrow keys, giving you greater precision. Touch typists sometimes prefer the arrow keys to a mouse because it allows them to keep their hands on the keyboard. *See* NUDGE; MOUSE.

ARTICLE

1. a nonfictional written piece that is part of a larger publication.

2. the word *a, an* or *the*, used before a noun. Articles in titles are usually not capitalized unless they come at the beginning of the title. Examples: *The Scarlet Letter*; *History of the Incas*.

Ascender

ASCENDER the part of a letter that rises (ascends) above the X-HEIGHT of the letter. The letter d has an ascender and the letter o does not.

ASCII (pronounced "as-key") **A**merican **S**tandard **C**ode for **I**nformation **I**nterchange, a standard code for representing characters as binary numbers, used on most microcomputers and printers. In addition to printable characters, the ASCII code includes control characters to indicate backspace, escape, carriage return, etc. *Table 2* shows a list of ASCII printable

0	Ctrl-@	32	Space	64	@	96	'
1	Ctrl-A	33	!	65	A	97	a
2	Ctrl-B	34	"	66	B	98	b
3	Ctrl-C	35	#	67	C	99	c
4	Ctrl-D	36	$	68	D	100	d
5	Ctrl-E	37	%	69	E	101	e
6	Ctrl-F	38	&	70	F	102	f
7	Ctrl-G	39	'	71	G	103	g
8	Backspace	40	(	72	H	104	h
9	Tab	41	)	73	I	105	i
10	Ctrl-J	42	*	74	J	106	j
11	Ctrl-K	43	+	75	K	107	k
12	Ctrl-L	44	,	76	L	108	l
13	Return	45	-	77	M	109	m
14	Ctrl-N	46	.	78	N	110	n
15	Ctrl-O	47	/	79	O	111	o
16	Ctrl-P	48	0	80	P	112	p
17	Ctrl-Q	49	1	81	Q	113	q
18	Ctrl-R	50	2	82	R	114	r
19	Ctrl-S	51	3	83	S	115	s
20	Ctrl-T	52	4	84	T	116	t
21	Ctrl-U	53	5	85	U	117	u
22	Ctrl-V	54	6	86	V	118	v
23	Ctrl-W	55	7	87	W	119	w
24	Ctrl-X	56	8	88	X	120	x
25	Ctrl-Y	57	9	89	Y	121	y
26	Ctrl-Z	58	:	90	Z	122	z
27	Escape	59	;	91	[	123	{
28	Ctrl-\	60	<	92	\	124	|
29	Ctrl-]	61	=	93	]	125	}
30	Ctrl-^	62	>	94	^	126	~
31	Ctrl-_	63	?	95	_	127	Delete

Table 2 ASCII character set with decimal codes.

characters. For popular extensions of ASCII, *see* ANSI CHARACTER SET.

ASCII FILE a TEXT FILE on a computer that uses the ASCII character set. It contains no control codes to specify font or text attributes—just the text, as if it were typed on a typewriter.

ASPI *see* SCSI.

ASTERISK

Asterisk

   1. The star-shaped character *. An asterisk is usually used to mark a footnote.

   2. In DOS, OS/2, UNIX and other operating systems, an asterisk is known as a *global* file character. You use it to stand for any legal combination of characters in a file name. To see a directory listing of a certain file extension, type DIR *.cdr at the DOS prompt. This will give you a listing of all the Corel-Draw files.

ASYMMETRICAL a layout or arrangement that has more elements to one side of the center of the page. Balance is achieved by increasing the visual weight or size of an object on the less crowded side. Asymmetrical layouts are more dynamic and seem to have movement. *See also* INFORMAL, FORMAL.

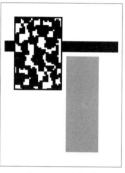
Asymmetrical

@
At sign

AT SIGN the symbol @, which stands for "at." The origins of this symbol go back to medieval times. The t has become vestigial and is left uncrossed; the circle surrounding the a is basically a decorative flourish.

AUTHORING SOFTWARE software used to produce multimedia or HYPERTEXT presentations (Multimedia encyclopedias, interactive displays). The authoring software provides ways of linking sounds, music, visuals, and text. An interactive presentation may have highlighted keywords that will lead the reader to another section of the presentation. Authoring software gives the developer the necessary tools to create these hypertext links. The possibility of creating different paths through the material is what sets authoring software apart from PRESENTATION SOFTWARE.

   Many of the layout and graphic design skills necessary for good desktop publishing carry over to these

14

new media. The common thread is good communication skills. *See* ELECTRONIC PUBLISHING.

AUTHOR'S ALTERATIONS a proofreader's abbreviation used to mark changes made to a typeset galley because of the author's error. Because they represent changes from the copy that was given to be typeset, any expenses incurred from making author's alterations are borne by the client, not the typesetter. *See also* EA, PE, PROOFREADER'S MARKS.

**Author's alterations
(proofreader's mark)**

AUTO-DIMENSIONING a CAD feature that keeps imported graphics correctly scaled as the drawing or diagram is completed.

AUTOEXEC.BAT (DOS) the name of a file that contains commands to be executed automatically whenever the computer boots up.

AUTOJOIN a feature of drawing programs that automatically joins endpoints that are within a certain distance of each other, so that you can draw a closed curve without having to come back to the exact pixel where the curve started. If you are having trouble getting curves to close so you can fill them, try increasing the autojoin setting. See your software's manual for details.

AUTOTRACE (DRAW PROGRAM) a command that instructs the computer to fit a curve to the outline of a bitmap. When the bitmap is traced (converted into VECTOR GRAPHICS), it is more easily manipulated in the drawing program.

AWARD *see* CERTIFICATE.

AXIS

   1. a line that provides a reference against which to measure a quantity or passage of time. When constructing a 2-dimensional chart, you have 2 axes, the vertical or Y-AXIS, and the horizontal or X-AXIS.

   2. an imaginary line that marks the center of rotation or symmetry.

   3. (MULTIPLE MASTER FONTS) the range of characteristics along which the intermediate designs can be generated.

B

BACKGROUND the field or color against which objects are drawn or displayed.

BACKSLANT type that is slanted to the *left* rather than to the right. Typefaces designed with a backslant are rather rare, but they may be useful for setting the occasional headline. *See also* SKEW.

Backslant

BACKSLASH \ as opposed to the forward slash /. It is important not to confuse them, especially when producing computer documentation.

BACKUP COPY a copy of working programs and related files that can be used to restore lost or damaged programs and files. You should have a full backup copy of your hard disk on diskettes or tape. It's a good idea to also make *daily* backups of work in progress. Store your backup copies in a secure place, preferably a fireproof box. Then, in case of any hardware problems, you will be able to restore your files. See also DAILY BACKUPS, ARCHIVAL STORAGE, HARD DISK MANAGEMENT.

BALLOON HELP a Macintosh System 7 help feature that identifies icons and tools as the mouse pointer is dragged over them. The speech balloon appears as close as possible to the selected object. Balloons can be very useful for novices; more advanced users can turn them off.

Ballot box

BALLOT BOXES small square outlined boxes (or circles). If you do not see a ballot box provided in your DINGBAT font, use a solid box and switch the font to OUTLINE for that character.

Bang

BANG slang for an exclamation mark. Also known as a *screamer*.

BAR CODE a printed pattern of wide and narrow bars. A computer reads the bar code by scanning it with a laser beam or with a wand that contains a light source and a photocell. The coded information can be anything from a product identification number to programming information for your VCR.

The most familiar bar code is the Universal

ISBN 0-8120-4824-5

Bar code

Product Code (*see picture*), which seems to have invaded stores of all types, allowing fast checkouts and computerized inventory systems. Magazine designers particularly detest bar codes because they have to leave a large and prominent place for the code on the magazine cover.

BAR GRAPH a type of chart that displays information by representing quantities as rectangular bars of different heights. Sometimes symbols are stacked or stretched to the appropriate heights to lend some visual interest to the chart.

Bar graphs are usually preferred for representing and contrasting data collected over a period of time.

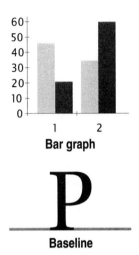

Bar graph

Baseline

BASELINE the imaginary line that letters rest upon.

BASE TO BASE the space from baseline to baseline of paragraph text. This measurement (in points) will be the total of the size of the type plus any LEADING.

BAUD the rate of serial data transmission, measured in state transitions per second. At the serial port of a computer, there are 10 state transitions per character, so a transmission rate of 9600 baud is equivalent to 960 characters per second, or 3 megabytes per hour.

Baud rate is often the factor that limits the speed of a laser printer. Suppose you are printing a full-page 300-dpi bitmap image and the printer is connected to a serial port at 9600 baud. The bitmap is about 1 megabyte in size and will take about 20 minutes to transmit to the printer. You could print it faster by using a higher baud rate or by connecting the printer to a parallel port instead of a serial port.

Baud rate also limits the speed with which you can send graphics files to a service bureau by telephone. For example, a digitized color photograph can be as large as 16 megabytes and can take hours to transmit at 9600 baud. (Some modems work as fast as 38,400 baud under ideal conditions, but that's the limit; telephone lines designed to transmit sound will not carry data at an unlimited speed.) Instead of using a modem, it may be faster and cheaper to use a utility such as PKZIP to spread the file across several diskettes, then ship the diskettes by express mail.

Baud is not quite synonymous with bits per second, because there are some communication devices in which each state transition carries more than one bit. But the baud rates you will encounter in practice all pertain to serial ports, where the equivalence holds.

BÉZIER SPLINE a curve that connects two points smoothly and is further defined by two more points that it does not pass through. Most draw programs represent curves as Bézier splines. For picture, *see* SPLINE.

A Bézier spline can be thought of as a gradual transition from one line to another. Call the four *control points* that define the curve P_1, P_2, P_3, and P_4. Then the curve starts out heading from P_1 toward P_2. But it curves around so that by the time it gets to P_4 it is approaching from the direction of P_3.

To plot a Bézier spline, let (x_1, y_1), (x_2, y_2), (x_3, y_3), and (x_4, y_4) be the coordinates of $P_1 \ldots P_4$ respectively, and let t range from 0 to 1. Then compute x and y from t as follows:

$$
\begin{aligned}
a &= -t^3 + 3t^2 - 3t + 1 \\
b &= 3t^3 - 6t^2 + 3t \\
c &= -3t^3 + 3t^2 \\
x &= ax_1 + bx_2 + cx_3 + t^3 x_4 \\
y &= ay_1 + by_2 + cy_3 + t^3 y_4
\end{aligned}
$$

Notice that as t goes from 0 to 1, a drops from 1 to 0, and t^3 rises from 0 to 1. This computation was first described by Pierre Bézier in 1970.

BIBLIOGRAPHY a listing of the sources of information available in print on a specific subject. The bibliography listing should include the author's name, title of the book or publication, date of issue, and any others details necessary to locate the reference (e.g., page numbers of the journal cited).

BILLING sending an invoice to a client requesting payment for completed work. Barring unforeseen complications, this amount should be the amount agreed upon at the start of the project. It is important to be matter-of-fact and professional. Thoroughly identify all work so that there will be no question of what the specific invoice is for. Whatever program you use to keep track of your accounting, double-check all items and totals. *See* INVOICE.

BIMONTHLY a publication that is issued once every two months.

BINDERY WORK postpress work needed to produce a finished publication. Some examples include FOLD-ING, DRILLING, STAPLING, COLLATING, CUTTING, and BINDING.

Bindery work can be time-consuming. Be sure to allow enough time for it when setting the delivery date of your project.

BINDING
1. fastening SIGNATURES into a book.
2. the covers and backing of a book.

There are many types of binding available. Budgetary concerns, the size of the book, and the number of pieces being printed will influence the choice of which one to use.

- **Edition binding.** The traditional method of binding a hardcover book. The FOLIOS are sewn together and then glued to a supporting material (called *crash*). The hardcover case is pasted on by the ENDPAPERS. Edition binding is relatively expensive, but it is the most permanent binding method.

- **Perfect binding.** Suitable for softcover books and magazines, perfect bound pages are literally glued to the spine. Best for large press runs and publications too thick for stapling.

- **Saddle stitching; saddle stapling.** The most common binding method for short books, brochures, magazines, etc. The book is opened to the middle, hung on a "saddle" and sewn or stapled. The book is trimmed *after* being bound to even up the pages. Make sure there is enough margin on the outside edge to allow for this final trim.

- **Edge stapling; side stitching.** The staples or stitches are passed through the left margin of the finished book. There should be a wide middle GUTTER because the book won't open flat.

- **Velo and spiral bindings.** The velo binding is a plastic strip along the left or top side of the book that pierces through the pages to a backing strip. Spiral bindings of plastic or metal pass through drilled holes in the left margin (or at the top). Spiral bound books will open flat (great for cookbooks and manuals). The velo binding shares many of the shortcomings of stapling the left margin: The book will not open flat, and there has to be a large middle gutter. However, velo bindings will outlast staples because they support the paper better. These two methods are best for small quantities.

BIRD'S EYE WINDOW a screen that presents the view from a high vantage point. This feature is available in CAD PROGRAMS that allow the user to change the viewing angle.

BITMAP a graphical image treated as a large array of dots (PIXELS), and drawn by specifying the color of each pixel. These images can be black and white or color. Clip art is often supplied in bitmap format.

Bitmaps can be imported into other application programs, such as word processing and page layout programs, but you will not be able to edit bitmaps in those environments. You must use a PAINT PROGRAM or PHOTOPAINT PROGRAM to change bitmaps. *Contrast* VECTOR GRAPHICS. *See also* PAINT PROGRAM and DRAW PROGRAM.

BIWEEKLY a publication that is issued once every two weeks (fortnightly).

𝖂𝖊 𝖙𝖍𝖊 𝕻𝖊𝖔𝖕𝖑𝖊...

Black letter

BLACK LETTER a typeface design based on 15th century manuscript writing. Fraktur is a good example of a black letter typeface. These typefaces are sometimes called *gothic* (a term that, confusingly, is also applied to sans-serif type). Today, we limit black letter to headlines and short texts; although monks in the Middle Ages found it easy to read, we do not.

BLACK SCREEN OF DEATH a totally blank screen that heralds a program crash so bad that the computer's operating system can't even manage an alert box. The keyboard and mouse will be dead also;

the catatonic computer will have to be rebooted. All progress made since the last "Save" command will be lost.

The phrase "Black Screen of Death" probably started among Windows users, but the term could be extended to other computers as well. *See also* CRASH, BOMB.

BLANKET the rubber-surfaced sheet that transfers the printed image from the printing plate to the paper in an offset printing press. *See Figure 17* at OFFSET PRINTING.

BLEED EDGE printing extending to the edge of the paper. There's a trick to this—printing presses *can't* print all the way to the edge of the paper. There has to be a GRIPPER ALLOWANCE for the press to grab the paper; also, if printed past the side edge of the paper, the ink would spread to the back of the page. To get a bleed edge, the piece has to be printed on oversized paper and trimmed to size after the ink has dried. The expense and time required for the extra steps should be considered at the design stage.

BLEND

1. a drawing program command that computes the intermediate shapes between two selected objects. You would use the blend command to make the smooth highlights on a rendering of a can.

Blend

In many ways, the blend command is like the *morphing* special effects we see on television commercials. You could make the letter C turn into a cat, for example. But blend has practical applications as well as the playful ones. You can use it to create equally spaced objects, such as lines for a business form. Blend *identical* objects (make sure they are aligned!), setting the intermediate blend steps to the desired number.

2. in a photopaint program, the blend filter will smooth colors, removing texture.

BLIND EMBOSSING pressing a design into the surface of paper with a metal die. In blind embossing, no inks or foils are used to enhance the embossing. Blind embossing gives the impression of a small relief sculpture, and is very elegant (good for letterheads).

Fake embossing

Because it is a fairly expensive process (embossing usually doubles the cost of a printing job), many creative souls have figured out how to fake the look of blind embossing with their drawing programs. The basic idea is to cast a very light gray shadow to one side of the design while adding a light highlight to the other. (*See picture at left.*) This effect works best if there is a printed texture being added.

BLIND FOLIO   a page without a page number on it; the bane of all modern magazine readers trying to follow an article to its conclusion.

BLOCK MOVE   the operation of moving a section of text from one place to another within a file. It is a two-step procedure. You mark the block (either with the mouse or with cursor and arrow keys) and then CUT and PASTE the copy to its new position. *See also* EDITOR.

BLOCK PROTECT   to mark a block of text so that it will not be split across pages. This is useful to prevent tables and lists from being broken up.

BLOW UP   to enlarge a photograph, illustration, or type. The resulting graphic is also called a *blowup*.

BLUR   a paint program filter that throws the image slightly out of focus. Blur can be repeated until the desired effect is achieved. *See also* MOTION BLUR.

BLURB   a brief summary or review of a book, usually placed on the book's jacket.

BMP   (Windows and OS/2) a file extension that indicates a bitmap image. *See* BITMAP.

BODY COPY   text. *Contrast* HEADLINE *and* DISPLAY TYPE.

BODY TYPE   type used to set textual material. Body type is 14 points or smaller. *Contrast* DISPLAY TYPE.

B
Bold

BOLD   a typeface that is darker and heavier than the normal weight of the type family. The entry terms in this dictionary are set in **bold.**

BOMB   to fail spectacularly (either computer programs or human performers); to CRASH. When a program bombs on a Macintosh, an alert box containing a picture of a bomb appears — the computer must be restarted and all progress made since the last "Save" will be lost. *Contrast* HANG; FREEZE.

BOOK a printed and bound publication. *See* BINDING for descriptions of the different methods of book construction.

BOOKLET a short book; sometimes called a PAMPHLET or BROCHURE.

BOOT to start a computer up. The term *boot* (earlier *bootstrap*) derives from the idea that the computer has to "pull itself up by the bootstraps," that is, load into memory a small program that enables it to load larger programs.

BORDER the area surrounding an image, which may be left plain or decorated with clip art or rules.

There are many collections of decorative borders available. *See* CLIP ART.

Keep in mind that laser printers cannot print within $\frac{1}{4}$ inch of the edge of the paper. You will need to incorporate this page border into your design or create a work-around. If the finished piece is to be offset printed, you will need to leave $\frac{1}{4}$ inch GRIPPER ALLOWANCE on the leading edge of the paper.

BOUNDING BOX the invisible box surrounding an object; the corners and midpoints of the bounding box will be marked by small black squares (HANDLES).

BOWL rounded strokes that enclose an interior space of a letter. Examples would be the P, B, and the upper part of g (the descender is called a LOOP or TAIL to distinguish it from the bowl).

BOX

1. a box is a type of window (DIALOG BOXES, MESSAGE BOXES). Generally, a box cannot be resized or moved. You have to deal with the box before going on to any other actions. For example, if you are confronted with a message box, you must click on "OK" before the computer will let you proceed.

2. a rectangle or square. All drawing programs and page layout programs have a tool for creating

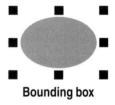

Bounding box

Bowl

boxes. You can specify the thickness of the line the box is drawn with and whether the box is filled with a color or a gray screen. For a perfect square, hold down the Ctrl (Control) key while drawing the box.

3. a text box; a special type of non-printing box that contains textual material. Also called a FRAME. Text boxes can be linked together to allow an article to be continued on a following page.

BRACES the characters { and }. These are sometimes called *curly braces*. They are not used much for setting regular text, but mathematicians really like them. You might choose to use braces as an extra outer set of parentheses like this: { ( ) }.

When setting italics, make sure to use braces from the roman rather than the italic font (you don't want them slanted).

Bracketed serif

BRACKETED SERIF a type of serif that looks as if it has a triangular or curved support holding it to the main stroke of the letter. The PANOSE SYSTEM calls these COVE SERIFS. *Contrast* SQUARE SERIF.

BRACKETS the characters [and]. Also called *square brackets*. Brackets may be used as a secondary inner set of parentheses: ([ ]). They may also be used to marks words inserted into a quotation.

As is the case with parentheses and braces, make sure to always use the brackets provided with the roman style of the typeface. The italic version is sometimes slanted and looks very odd.

BREAKS, SCHEDULING the necessary practice of allowing sufficient rest time away from the computer. Working at a computer is like playing a video game; hours can fly by, resulting in eyestrain, stiff muscles, and headaches. If needed, an inexpensive timer may be used to prompt you to get up and stretch. The Macintosh operating system has a built-in timer that may be used to let you know that it's time to get a cup of coffee.

Just remember that working harder is not the answer; you need breaks to rest your eyes, get some refreshment (mental and physical), uncramp your body, and tend to your personal needs. You will get more work done if you are not overworking yourself.

BREVE a phonetic symbol (ˇ) that is used to show that a vowel is pronounced with a short sound. The breve is also used in some mathematical formulas. *Contrast* MACRON. *See also* ACCENTS.

ă

Breve

BRIGHTNESS

1. a photopaint filter that has the same effect as turning the brightness knob on a TV or monitor; it lightens or darkens the entire area that it's applied to. Brightness may be combined with the contrast filter since the two attributes affect each other.

2. a software control normally available with scanners, which is used to adjust the overall brightness of the image.

BRING TO FRONT a command that puts an object or window in front, so that it hides other objects or windows that it overlaps. One way to hide part of an object in a drawing program is to create an object the same color as the background, then put it in front of what you want to hide.

See also OVERLAID WINDOWS; SEND TO BACK.

BRITISH STANDARDS 2961:1967 a method of classifying typefaces. Very strong on historical accuracy, this classification provides a good framework for understanding how type has developed over the past five centuries. *See Figure 2.*

Some typefaces cannot be sorted neatly into one category. It is possible to describe something as a hybrid, i.e. *Garalde / Transitional*. In fact, every classification immedialtely inspires type designers to invent something that doesn't fit in!

You can find more information about each of these type classifications at their respective entries.

BROCHURE a short book or pamphlet, usually intended for limited distribution.

BROWNOUT an extended period of insufficient power line voltage. Brownouts can damage computer equipment. *See* POWER LINE PROTECTION.

BROWSER a computer program that enables the user to retrieve information that has been made publicly available on the Internet, especially through HTTP

(**H**ypertext **T**ransfer **P**rotocol). Popular browsers include Mosaic (which includes graphics) and Lynx (which skips graphical images but runs much faster than Mosaic). *See* WORLD WIDE WEB.

B-SPLINE a smooth curve that approximately connects two points. B-splines can be joined together to make a smooth curve passing close to any number of points. For picture, *see* SPLINE.

Each segment of a B-spline curve is influenced by four points — the two that it lies between, plus one more in each direction. This makes computation of a B-spline much quicker than computation of a cubic spline, because every part of a cubic spline is influenced by all the points to be joined.

To plot a B-spline defined by four points (x_1, y_1), (x_2, y_2), (x_3, y_3), and (x_4, y_4), let t range from 0 to 1 and compute values of x and y for each t as follows:

$$
\begin{aligned}
a &= -t^3/6 + t^2/2 - t/2 + 1/6 \\
b &= t^3/2 - t^2 + 2/3 \\
c &= -t^3/2 + t^2/2 + t/2 + 1/6 \\
d &= t^3/6 \\
x &= ax_1 + bx_2 + cx_3 + dx_4 \\
y &= ay_1 + by_2 + cy_3 + dy_4
\end{aligned}
$$

That gives you a curve that lies approximately between (x_2, y_2) and (x_3, y_3). You can then advance by one point (letting the old x_4 become the new x_3, and so on) to plot the next segment. *See also* BÉZIER SPLINE; CUBIC SPLINE.

BUFFER a holding area for data. Several different things are called buffers:

1. Buffers are areas in memory that hold data being sent to a printer or received from an RS-232 port. The idea here is that the printer is much slower than the computer, and it is helpful if the computer can prepare the data all at once, then dole it out slowly from the buffer as needed. Similarly, an RS-232 port needs a buffer because data may come in when the computer is not ready to receive it.

2. An edit buffer is an area in memory that holds a file that is being edited. Some editors allow you to

Venetian	AaBbCcDdEeFfGgHhIiJjKkLlMmNnOo&?")
	Venetian 301
Garalde	AaBbCcDdEeFfGgHhIiJjKkLlMmNn&?")
	Aldine 401
Transitional	AaBbCcDdEeFfGgHhIiJjKkLlMmNn&?")
	Kis
Didone	AaBbCcDdEeFfGgHhIiJjKkLlMmNnOo&?")
	Bodoni
Slab-serif	AaBbCcDdEeFfGgHhIiJjKkLlMm?")
	Clarendon

Lineal:

Grotesque	AaBbCcDdEeFfGgHhIiJjKkLlMmNnOoPpQqRrSsTtUuVv&?")
	Alternate Gothic 2
Neo-grotesque	AaBbCcDdEeFfGgHhIiJjKkLlMmNn&?")
	Zurich
Geometric	AaBbCcDdEeFfGgHhIiJjKkLlMmNn&?")
	Euromode
Humanist	AaBbCcDdEeFfGgHhIiJjKkLlMmNnOo&?")
	Zapf Humanist
Glyphic	AaBbCcDdEeFfGgHhIiJjKkLlMmNn&?")
	Flareserif 821
Script	AaBbCcDdEeFfGgHhIiJjKkLlMmNnOo&?")
	Commecial Script
Graphic	ABCDEFGHIJKLM&?
	Decorated 035

Figure 2   British Standards 2961:1967

27

edit more than one file at once, and each file occupies its own buffer.

3. A disk buffer is an area in memory that holds data being sent to, or received from, a disk. Some operating systems allow you to adjust the size or number of disk buffers to fit the speed of your disk drive.

4. A keyboard buffer holds signals from keys that have been pressed but have not yet been accepted by the computer.

BUG an error in a computer program. An infamous example is the tendency of one major drawing program to mirror image type when fitting text to a path. The program just does not do what it is supposed to do. Most software vendors are good about supplying workarounds or updated versions to registered users. This, however, is little consolation to someone working on a deadline. There is a growing consensus in the user community that software companies need to strengthen quality control and provide better warranties for their products.

BUILT FRACTION; BUILT-UP FRACTION a fraction composed by setting the NUMERATOR and DENOMINATOR as regular numerals separated by a forward slash. Example: 15/16. Also called ADAPTABLE FRACTION. *Contrast* PIECE FRACTION, CASE FRACTION.

BULLET a graphical device used to mark items in a list. Most commonly, a bullet is a small black dot optically centered on the CAP HEIGHT of the font. Asterisks and square boxes can also be used as bullets.

A common failing of personal computer fonts is that the bullet provided will be too large in proportion to the letters. If you have software that will let you edit the character outlines (e.g. Fontmonger or Fontographer), you may want to make the bullet smaller. A quick and dirty solution is to change the font to a smaller size for just the bullet. Again, this approach has problems; the bullet may appear too low.

●

Bullet

Bull's eye

BULL'S EYE a symbol consisting of a circle with a cross superimposed. Bull's eyes are used for color separations to help the printer align the second (or third or forth) press runs to the first one. *Also called* REGISTER MARKS.

BUSINESS CARD a $3\frac{1}{2}$-inch × 2-inch card containing a person's name, title, and corporate affiliation, address, phone number, FAX number, e-mail address and any other pertinent information. It is sometimes quite a challenge to fit all of this vital information in such a small space and one of the reasons for collecting colleagues' business cards is to see how they managed it.

When preparing business cards to be offset printed, check first with the printer about how the CAMERA-READY COPY needs to be set up. There is special business card stock that comes correctly sized to print the cards FOUR-UP (*see* GANG-UP), but business cards can be printed on any COVER STOCK.

Ideally, a company's business cards should be designed at the same time as its letterheads. Try to maintain a consistent look. When designing a business card, remember that you can turn it sideways (PORTRAIT ORIENTATION). Don't forget the possibilities of using color and special effects such as embossing or foil stamping, budget permitting. If there is a lot of copy to be included on the card, consider a folding card.

There are now available specially designed preprinted papers for laser printers that are microperforated to tear apart easily into ten business cards. These are great for new employees, temporaries and businesses that wish a high degree of customization. (For example, you could have a business card emphasizing computer illustration, and another version that listed you as a desktop publisher.) There are some drawbacks to laser-printed cards: the card stock is too thin, and the edges are not perfectly clean.

BUSINESS FORMS forms such as invoices, purchase orders, employment applications and receipts.

Form *must* follow function when designing a business form. Who is going to use or see this form? Will they have to fill it out, or just mark check boxes? What can be done to make the wording clearer? Is there enough room to write?

Fortunately, there are many examples of business forms suitable for adapting to a specific purpose. Often, there are examples in clip art collections, or TEMPLATES included with word processors and page layout programs. It helps not to have to start completely from scratch. If you need help with the wording of the form, consult a reliable reference book or seek the advice of an attorney.

Try to make business forms consistent with the firm's corporate identity. Make sure the company's logo, address, and phone number are on each piece. Companies that use e-mail will want their electronic address featured.

Keep examples of good business forms in your SWIPE FILE; they can provide inspiration and examples to draw on at a later time. Be careful not to violate copyright or to imitate a competitor so closely that the result is embarrassing.

Button

BUTTON a small circle or rectangular bar within a windowed DIALOG BOX that represents a *choice* to be made. One of the buttons in a group will be HIGHLIGHTED, either by having a black circle inside of it or having a heavy black border. This represents the DEFAULT choice. You can choose any one of the buttons by CLICKING the mouse pointer on it.

There are two kinds of buttons: OPTION BUTTONS (sometimes called radio buttons) and COMMAND BUTTONS. Option buttons represent mutually exclusive settings; that is, you can only choose one. They are usually small and round, but are sometimes diamond-shaped. If you change your mind and click on another option button, your original choice will be grayed (DIMMED).

Command buttons cause something to happen immediately when you click on them. They are usually rectangular and larger than option buttons. The most familiar examples are the "OK" and "Cancel" buttons that seem to be in every dialog box. If the command button brings up another dialog box, you will see an ELLIPSIS (. . .) after its label. *See* WINDOW for illustration.

BUTTONBAR a row of small icons usually arranged across the top of the workspace on screen. Each icon represents a commonly used command; many programs allow you to customize your buttonbar to suit your personal taste. Also called a TOOLBAR.

BYLINE a credit line that appears just below the headline of a story.

BYTE A byte is the amount of memory space needed to store one character. The size of a computer's memory and disk are measured in KILOBYTES, where 1 kilobyte (K) = 1,024 bytes.

C

CAD computer aided design. A type of software that allows designers to do accurate three-dimensional drawings of objects that may be rotated and viewed from any angle. CAD programs have the ability to save drawings in formats that may be imported into page layout programs for illustrations. *See* EXPORT.

CALIBRATION adjustment of image values to ensure faithful rendering of colors and gray tones when output to a printer or imagesetter. The calibration loop should include your scanner, your monitor, your software, and the printer. The goal is to make sure that "everybody's on the same page" and that what the scanner sees as magenta, *displays* on the monitor as magenta, is *recognized* by the software as magenta, and *prints* as magenta. *See* COLOR.

Handgloves

Calligraphy

CALLIGRAPHY the art of fine handwriting, usually with an italic nib pen. Some script fonts have *calligraphic* origins.

CALLOUT the line and caption marking the specific parts of a labeled illustration. For examples, see the illustration at WINDOW.

CAMERA-READY a piece of artwork or a printed page that is ready to be photographed with a copy camera and printed. Black and white artwork is best; some colors reproduce well, but most don't. Laser printer output (300–600 DPI) is nearly ideal for many purposes. If higher resolution is needed, you can send your files to a SERVICE BUREAU and they can give you a 2400 DPI printout from their imagesetter.

The beauty of using desktop publishing technology is that often no PASTE UP is required. This means that there will be no PASTE-UP LINES, and, since the camera-ready copy doesn't have to be handled much, stray marks and smudges won't get on the original.

If you have to use some artwork that is impractical to scan, just leave a large enough area for it and paste it in. (Rubber cement works well.) Be careful. Any stray adhesive makes the toner smear and will photograph as black. Make sure the corners are down securely. Try to leave a little margin around your art-work and any ruled lines that it butts up against — you want to give the printers room to work in case they have to clean up any paste-up lines.

Use a NONREPRO BLUE pen or pencil to identify your camera-ready copy and to make any notes for the printer. This special light-blue color is invisible to the copy camera. If additional room is needed for instructions, a tissue overlay may be used.

The newest generation of printing presses skips the camera-ready artwork stage and can print directly from your computer file. *See* DIGITAL PRESS.

CANCEL to stop the execution of a command. Most dialog boxes have a "Cancel" button. This clears the dialog box from the screen *without* taking any action.

CANCEL OUT the act of canceling a command by clicking on the "Cancel" button. "Cancel out of the pen attribute box if you don't want to change the settings."

CAP HEIGHT an imaginary line that marks the height of the capital letters of a font.

Cap height

CAPITALIZATION, RULES OF the use of capital letters is part of the grammar of any written language. Practically all languages capitalize the first word of each sentence and proper names (*John, America*). German capitalizes all nouns.

The rules of capitalization in English are brief and easy to remember:

- Capitalize all proper nouns (names) and titles (Mr., Judge, Ms.), including their adjectival forms (French food, un-American).
- Capitalize the first word in a sentence or direct quote. "She asked, 'Have you got the manual?' "
- Capitalize titles of documents in one of the following ways. (Choose one and stick with it.)
    - The traditional method: capitalize the first, last, and all important words (as in "The Hummingbirds of Australia").

        An "important" word is any word that doesn't sound unnatural when you pronounce it with full emphasis. Thus *for, of, and, or, a, an,* and *the* are seldom capitalized (but cf. *Who is For Me?* where the capitalization reflects the spoken emphasis).

- The newer "sentence" method: capitalize the title exactly as if it were a sentence, as in "The hummingbirds of Australia," "Studies in mathematics."

- All capitals or small capitals: THE HUMMINGBIRDS OF AUSTRALIA or THE HUMMINGBIRDS OF AUSTRALIA. Do this only for the title at the top of your *own* document, not the titles of other documents that you refer to. Limit the amount of copy set in all caps, as it is quite tiring to read. (*See* LEGIBILITY for further discussion.)

Remember that when referring to other documents, you should italicize the titles of books and put quotation marks around titles of articles and poems. Never underline if you have italics available.

- Acronyms are set in all caps, no period in between the letters (HUD, NASA, IBM).

- Always capitalize the pronoun "I."

CAPITAL LETTERS upper case letters. Young children call them "big letters," and that is precisely what they are. Capital letters generally extend the full height of a lower case letter that has an ASCENDER. In most fonts, the capital letters do not have DESCENDERS, although occasionally the tail of the Q will descend below the baseline.

CAPS common abbreviation for capital letters. "Set the headline in all caps." *Contrast with* MIXED CASE.

CAPTION descriptive text that accompanies a figure, illustration or chart. Frequently set in a FONT different from that used for the BODY COPY.

CAPTURE to cause a picture or graphic to be saved as a bitmapped image.

Snapshots of the screen are easy to get: for Macintosh users, hold down Command and Shift, then press 3. This places a bitmapped image of the screen in a .PICT file in your root directory. In Windows, pressing the Print Screen key puts a copy of the entire screen onto the clipboard. Holding down Alt while pressing Print Screen saves a bitmap of the active window *only*.

If you have the appropriate equipment, you can use your computer to capture images from any video source. This might be a video camera or VCR. *See* FRAME GRABBER.

CARET the proofreading symbol used to mark where something should be inserted. (*Caret* is Latin for "is missing.") *See chart at* PROOFREADER'S MARKS.

Caret

CARON a v-shaped accent mark used in Slavic languages. *See* ACCENTS.

Š

Caron

CARPAL TUNNEL SYNDROME a repetitive use injury that afflicts some typists. The main symptoms are numbness and tingling in the hand. Stretching exercises and medication will help mild cases, but sometimes surgery is necessary to relieve the pain. To prevent carpal tunnel syndrome, take a break and stretch your hands frequently. Some typists find a padded wrist support to be helpful.

CARTRIDGE a self-contained, removable part of a computer, usually small and contained in a plastic case. For example, laser printers often take TONER CARTRIDGES and FONT CARTRIDGES (the latter containing memory chips with prerecorded type fonts).

CASCADED WINDOWS a method of displaying multiple windows that allows you to see all their TITLE BARS at the same time. To see the contents of any window, click anywhere in it. This will make it the active window and cause it to come to the top of the stack.

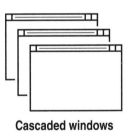

Cascaded windows

CASE the property of being a capital letter (UPPER CASE) or a small letter (LOWER CASE).

As with other typographical terms, *case* is very old and refers to how things used to be in the days of movable metal type. When the type was properly sorted and put back into the drawer (case), the capital letters went into the upper case, and the small letters went into the drawer below it.

$$\frac{1}{4}$$

Case fraction

CASE FRACTION a small fraction that is a single character in a font. *Contrast with* BUILT FRACTION.

CAST OFF to compute the length of text in order to estimate how much space it will take when typeset. Although page layout programs can do this automatically, sometimes it's useful to know how to cast off for planning purposes. You will need to know how many characters are in the text, the MEASURE of the line, the font size, and how many characters will set per line in the desired font. Using your word processor, find out how many words are in the text (the spell checker usually reports this). On the average, there are five letters for every word in English prose. Multiply 5 times the number of words to give you the number of characters. Estimate how many characters will set per line (hopefully, this is known because it was considered when setting the LINE LENGTH). Dividing the characters per line into the total characters will give you the number of lines of text. Multiply the number of lines by the font's point size to give you the height of the block of text. This number will be in POINTS; divide by 12 to convert to PICAS.

A short example: WordPerfect reports a text to be 575 words long. 575 × 5 is 2875 total characters. I am going to set this in a 10-point font that averages 50 characters per line; 2875 divided by 50 will give me 57.5 lines. Rounding up to 58 (a half line is still a line) and multiplying by 10-points gives me a total depth of 580 points, or 48.3 picas.

All in all, it's faster to mark the block, change the font, and see how much space it takes. But what if we were talking about a book-length project? It's useful to know how to cast off for planning purposes. A few minutes with a calculator will let you estimate how long a book will be when typeset.

See COPYFITTING.

CATALOG a publication that displays a company's products. Desktop publishing is nearly ideal for producing catalogs; changes can be made easily and quickly, the prices can be kept current, and production costs can be kept down.

Counter-clockwise

CCW counter-clockwise.

CD-ROM (**C**ompact **D**isk **R**ead **O**nly **M**emory) a storage medium for digital information. Compact disks, similar to audio CDs, are *read only*; the information is prerecorded and cannot be written over or erased. They are becoming increasing popular because they can hold a tremendous amount of information (approximately 600 megabytes) and are the ideal way to distribute large libraries of clip art, fonts, and software packages. A CD-ROM drive can take a lot of the load off of your computer's hard disk. You can have thousands of images at your disposal, but you don't have to provide space on the hard disk for them. Like audio CDs, computer CDs are compact to store, but are a little more fragile and should be handled carefully. In the future, it may be possible for you to WRITE to a CD with a special disk drive, but currently you can only READ the information prerecorded on the disk.

CEDILLA the accent mark placed below the c in the French word *garçon*. *See* ACCENTS.

Ç
Cedilla

CELL a unit of information that forms the building blocks for a chart, database, or spreadsheet.

CENTERED a layout in which the objects are aligned along their middle axis. Centered type is considered very formal. Poetry or short quotes look good set centered. Do not set body type all centered; it is too hard to read. *See* FORMAL.

WE
THE
PEOPLE
Centered text

CERTIFICATE a document that honors an individual's achievements. Certificates are easily produced by computer. There are many clip-art borders and typographical elements available, as well as a tremendous variety of colorful PREPRINTED papers. Color may be added to black and white certificates by the use of COLOR FOILS and foil seals. Certificates for all the individuals on a list can be created by utilizing the MERGE feature of your word processor.

CHALKING a printing problem caused when the ink doesn't bind the paper surface and flakes off, leaving the paper showing through.

CHANNEL a set of images that will compose the final image when combined. The most common use for channels is the representation of the CMYK color separations in a paint program. Each color has its own channel.

Sometimes channels can be used like LAYERS in a DRAW PROGRAM. Selected areas can be saved to a new channel, manipulated separately from the rest of the image, and later recombined with the main channel.

CHAPTER HEADS a headline that indicates the beginning of a new chapter in a book. Select a typeface and style that contrasts strongly with the body copy so the reader will recognize the new chapter. Most book designers prefer to start each new chapter at the top of a page.

CHARACTER any symbol that can be stored and processed by a computer.

CHARACTER SET the set of all characters available in a single font. Surprisingly, this is *not* a standard set. *See* ANSI, ASCII. Some fonts have just the upper and lower case alphabets and the more common punctuation marks. Some fonts have a great deal more. These extra characters may include accented vowels, special symbols, LIGATURES, alternate characters, and fractions. Such a font is called an EXPERT SET, and it requires some special know-how to be able to set the special characters.

CHARACTER SPACING *see* LETTER SPACING.

CHART a graphical display of information, designed to make it easier for the reader to interpret and understand numerical data. There are many different types of charts. You'll need to know enough about them to decide which will suit your purposes best. *See Figure 3.*

- **Bar chart** Displays information by representing quantities as rectangular bars of different heights or lengths. Good for displaying data collected over a period of time.
- **Pie chart** Represents proportions of a whole. Useful for displaying budgets, and results of opinion polls.
- **Scatter graph** Shows data points plotted in an X-Y coordinate system. Not as commonly used

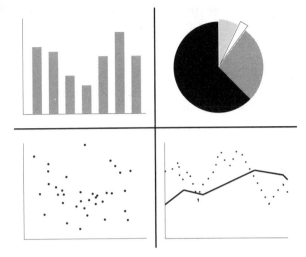

Figure 3 Some common types of charts.

as the other two, but useful for showing trends and groupings in a population.

- **Line graph** Shows data plotted on an X-Y graph, connected by lines to emphasize the direction of the latest trend.

It is customary to dress up charts and graphs with FRAMES, CLIP ART, DISPLAY TYPE, and lots of color (when available). One effective way to add interest is to add PERSPECTIVE to the chart. Rendering the bars, or RISERS, as three-dimensional rectangles lends a bar graph a sense of solidity. Some charting software can even use the third axis for plotting information. Another trick is to use a PICTOGRAM as a unit of a bar graph. This is sometimes misleading, as it is very hard to have .75 of a single unit (e.g., a person). Be careful that the import of the chart or graph is not obscured by overly cute pictures.

Check

CHECK

1. a caron (v-shaped accent, as in š). *See* ACCENTS.
2. a common dingbat character.

Check box

CHECK BOX a small box in a DIALOG BOX that the user can turn "on" or "off" with the mouse. When "on" it displays an "X" or check mark in the square; when "off," the square is blank.

Unlike OPTION BUTTONS, check buttons do not affect each other. Any check box can be "on" or "off" independently of the others. The new settings do not take effect until you exit the dialog box by clicking "OK." *See* WINDOW for illustration.

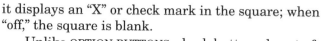

Chevrons

CHEVRONS an angular style of quotation marks «like this». Also called GUILLEMETS. *See* FRENCH.

CHICAGO a name used from 1992 to 1994 for a version of Microsoft Windows that was planned as a replacement for Windows 3.1. In late 1994 this still-unreleased product was renamed Windows 95.

CHICAGO MANUAL OF STYLE an invaluable guide to writing; the standard reference and arbitrator of questions of usage, punctuation, and typography as defined by the University of Chicago Press.

Cinnamon bun

CINNAMON BUN a nickname for the @ symbol, which stands for "at." *See* AT SIGN.

Circumflex

CIRCUMFLEX a hat-shaped accent mark, as in ê. *See* ACCENTS.

C/LC caps and lower case. Usually written "c/lc" and sometimes "u/lc" (upper and lower case).

CLICK to press the mouse button very briefly (usually the leftmost button if there is more than one). This is how you make choices in a windowed environment. *Contrast* DOUBLE-CLICK *and* PRESS.

CLIENT

1. a person who receives services from another person.

2. an application program that receives data from another application program. *See* OBJECT LINKING AND EMBEDDING.

CLIP ART artwork that can be freely reproduced. Creative use of clip art can change a boring desktop publishing project into a lively, eye-catching piece. Available in a bewildering variety of subject matter, clip art collections can be purchased on DISK or CD-ROM. The quality varies quite a bit, also. Some companies take greater care in DIGITIZING their artwork and it gives a cleaner, sharper look.

If you want to, you can alter clip art in the appropriate editor to customize it for your job. You use a PAINT PROGRAM to edit BITMAPPED clip art; a DRAW PROGRAM to edit VECTOR GRAPHICS. (You can import bitmaps into a drawing program, but it is generally not possible to edit them there.)

If the piece of artwork you want to use is from a printed clip art book, you can either SCAN it in or leave a large enough white space to paste it in the old-fashioned way.

See also DISK, CD-ROM, DIGITIZE, PAINT PROGRAM, DRAW PROGRAM, SCANNER, VECTOR GRAPHICS, BITMAP.

CLIPBOARD on the Macintosh and in Microsoft Windows, a holding area to which information can be copied in order to transfer it from one application program to another. For instance, the Clipboard can be used to transfer text from a word processor into a drawing program.

Be aware that the contents of the Clipboard vanish when the computer is turned off. Also, only one item at a time can be on the Clipboard; the next CUT or COPY command will replace the old item with a new one.

CLIPPING (Macintosh System 7.5) a fragment of text or graphic image that can be moved from one application to another simply by dragging the item with the mouse (see DRAG AND DROP). The clipping may even remain on the Desktop until needed. This provides another way (other than the Clipboard) for transferring information from one program to another. Not all applications can support Drag and Drop at present; this will probably change as programmers catch up with the recent System 7.5 upgrade.

CLONE TOOL a tool available in paint and photopaint programs that allows you to duplicate areas. To use the clone tool, click on the center of the area you wish to copy. Move the cursor to where you want the new area to be. Press and hold down the mouse button (the leftmost button if there is more than one) while you paint in the image. The clone tool can be

Clone tool

used to create a crowd out of a small group of people, cover a gap left by deleting a CUTOUT, or to put a third eye on someone's forehead. It is not necessary to define the outline of an area or object when using the clone tool; it works from the center out as far as needed. *See also* RUBBER STAMP.

The clone icon shown is from Corel PhotoPaint.

CLOSE

1. (Windows) to exit a program and clear it from the computer's memory. This is different from MIN-IMIZE in that a program reduced to an icon is still running and waiting for input from you, but a closed program has been put away. Most importantly, a minimized program is still being held in the computer's memory. If you close a minimized program, you will regain the memory it is taking up.

2. (Macintosh) to reduce a window to an icon *without* quitting the application software. The "Close" button is at the far left of the title bar. Click once to close the open window. This sense of *close* is analogous to MINIMIZE in Windows. To clear the program from memory, choose QUIT from the File menu.

This illustrates one of the most basic areas of confusion between Macintosh and Windows terminology. Be careful when talking to your cross-platform friends or you'll both end up confused!

CLOSING PUNCTUATION the second of a pair of some punctuation marks (i.e. parentheses, curly braces, brackets, quotation marks). When proofreading, make sure you have a closing mark for each opening mark.

Cloverleaf

CLOVERLEAF nickname for the Macintosh Command key.

CMYK abbreviation for the four standard printing inks: **c**yan, **m**agenta, **y**ellow, and blac**k**. When combined, these four colors can reproduce a full-color image. If you ask your computer to make color separations for a PROCESS COLOR job, four COLOR SEPARATIONS will be generated, one for each of the standard inks. See also SPOT COLOR.

(You may be wondering why K is used to stand for black instead of B. It's to avoid confusion with *cyan,* which is a vivid shade of blue and could also lay claim to B.)

COACH a WordPerfect 6.0 help feature that displays tips and other helpful information upon request. For example, a coach will appear to help you understand formatting your document. The coach will remain on-screen while you finish setting the necessary items (unlike the *help* screen which disappears). Coaches can be very useful for novices. Similar program features are called CUE CARDS, WIZARDS, or BALLOON HELP.

COATED STOCK paper that has a thin coating of kaolin (clay) to make it shiny and smooth. Coated stocks are more expensive that noncoated papers, but they reproduce photographs and full-color illustrations better.

COLD TYPE type produced photographically or digitally. *Contrast with* HOT TYPE, which are fonts formed from metal.

COLLATE to place printed pages in order, such as pages to be bound into a book. Some photocopiers have the ability to collate multipage documents automatically.

COLLATING SEQUENCE the alphabetical order of all characters on a computer (including digits, punctuation marks and other special characters). The collating sequence is important because it is sometimes necessary to sort (alphabetize) data that includes characters other than letters.

COLOPHON
　　1. a brief description of the production techniques, equipment, and other technical data related to the production of a document. A colophon will typically be found at the end of the piece. It will tell you what typefaces were used, what sort of computers and software were utilized, and useful information about special printing techniques (such as the use of metallic inks or varnish). For an example, see the last page of this book.
　　2. a publisher's special symbol or logo and name, often appearing on the title page.

COLOR a phenomenon of perception caused by the partial ability of our eyes to recognize different wavelengths of light. Color adds impact and interest to any design. Think of what grabs your attention as you sort through your daily mail—you tend to notice the colorful pieces first. As a desktop publisher, you want to utilize anything that will help communicate your message. Color can be one of your most powerful tools.

Despite that, many find the prospect of working with color intimidating. It is a complex subject, and so is unsuited for quick treatment. (I'm going to try anyway.) If you need more information, do make use of your local library or bookstore; there are several basic primers on color available.

The first thing you need to be aware of is that what appears on your computer monitor is *not* what will appear printed in ink on paper. There are many colors that you can see that cannot be represented accurately by mixing inks; the set of colors that can be accurately displayed on a monitor is even smaller. Even if you have gone to great pains to CALIBRATE your system, you should not expect glowing phosphors on a computer screen to give an accurate representation of what is to be printed on paper. It is essential that you check color proofs carefully.

Most graphics programs give you several options of how you want to describe colors. The major methods are CMYK, HSB and SPOT COLOR.

CMYK stands for **c**yan, **m**agenta, **y**ellow and blac**k**, which are the four inks used to print PROCESS COLOR. This is what you need to use if you are including color photographs or complex multicolored artwork in your publication.

HSB stands for **h**ue, **s**aturation and **b**rightness. Hue is what artists call color; whether the color in question is blue or orange—that is its *hue*. Saturation refers to how *pure* the hue is. If you add a contrasting color (let's say we add some red to a pure green) you *decrease* its saturation. Brightness refers to how light or dark the hue is (whether we add white or black). HSB is the preferred method of describing colors for someone who paints; the process is very similar to mixing pigments. Be aware that this is an internal description, just between you and your software. When you ask for color separations, the software will generate CMYK plates for the printer.

Spot color is for when you do not wish to use full four-color printing. You specify which color to use, and you can use as many as your printing budget will allow. With the use of tints and overprinting, just two different colors can give a wide range of color combinations. Spot color can be very economical; you can have the impact of color for the cost of two press runs. And it's very easy to accomplish. Just specify which objects are to be printed in which color and your computer can make the separations for you.

With spot color the question is, "*Which* color?" You may find yourself in the position of taking your ready-to-print publication to the printer and asking for blue ink. The printer will inquire which one you want as he throws an entire book of ink samples at you. There will be *pages and pages* of different blues. Do you want a funky Florida blue-green or a excruciatingly proper navy blue? How dark does this blue need to be? Are you going to print black on top of it? It could make a big difference. Again, remember that what was on the screen may be close, but it won't be exact.

Even harder is choosing two colors to go together. Life is full of examples of clashing colors. How do you choose the right ones? Here is where you make a big decision: Do you see yourself as an artist or do you like to leave the artist stuff to the artists? If you feel creative and confident in your judgement, you should educate yourself about the COLOR WHEEL and, remembering to use printed ink samples instead of what you see on the monitor, choose what seems to you to be a good combination.

What if you are a color klutz? Don't despair—there are books devoted to simply displaying pleasing color combinations. You might make use of one of those. Or dig into your SWIPE FILE. Perhaps you have collected an example of a color combination that you like and that you can ask the printer to match.

And then there is the question of colored paper. That can be a reasonable way to inject some interest into a boring, black-on-white design. Be careful when printing color onto colored paper; the results can sometimes be unpredictable.

See also COLOR WHEEL.

COLOR FOIL a product that allows metallic color to be added to individual printouts. It works by fusing itself to the laser toner during a second pass through the printer. Although relatively expensive and too time-consuming to apply to a large number of printouts, color foil is an ideal way to add spot color to a certificate.

COLOR/GRAY MAP a photopaint filter that allows adjustment of a picture's color balance. In gray scale mode, it can be used to adjust the exposure of an imperfect black and white photo.

COLOR KEY a method of photographically proofing color printing jobs. Because pulling a color key is as labor-intensive and time-consuming as preparing the printing plates, it is more common today to proof color separations with a color printer (either LASER, THERMAL WAX, or DYE-SUBLIMATION.)

Color replacer

COLOR REPLACER a tool available in paint and photopaint programs that replaces the primary color with the secondary color as you drag the tool across the image. The size and shape of the color replacer can be adjusted like any of the brush tools. The color replacer icon shown is from Corel PhotoPaint.

COLOR SEPARATIONS camera-ready artwork that has been broken down into individual printouts, one for each color that is to be printed. All the elements that should print in black will be on one sheet, and all the elements that should print in red will be on another, and so forth. Each printout will have registration marks so that the colors can be aligned properly (REGISTERED). *See* PROCESS COLOR *and* SPOT COLOR.

COLOR WHEEL a circular diagram of the color spectrum. The color wheel, because of its round shape, is good for explaining some basic color concepts. *See Figure 4.*

The *primary colors* are red, yellow and blue. Mix

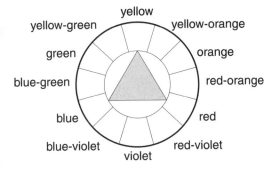

Figure 4   Color Wheel

any two primaries and you will get a secondary color (orange, green, and purple).

Complementary colors are directly across the wheel from each other. (Red-green, orange-blue, yellow-purple.) When you use complements together, the juxtaposition of the two will seem to vibrate. Complements will dull each other if you mix them.

Warm and cool colors: red, yellow, and orange are considered "warm"; blue, green, and purple are considered "cool." Notice that this breaks the color wheel in half.

Triads are groups of three colors. Inscribe an equilateral triangle on the color wheel and notice where the vertices of the triangle fall. These three colors will be a pleasing color combination. An example would be yellow-orange, red-violet, and blue-green.

COLUMN

1. a block of text or numbers; a subdivision of a page.

2. a regularly appearing contribution to a magazine or newspaper.

COLUMN MOVE a text editing operation that allows you to shift a column of material to a new position in one step. *See* WORD PROCESSING.

COMBINE a drawing program command that merges two separate PATHS into one so that the whole thing can become one object. This is similar to GROUPING objects, but there is an important distinction. A group of objects can be treated as a single object, but the individual elements retain their separate attributes. A combined object *is* a single object; it has only *one* outline and only *one* fill. Interestingly, a combined object can have holes in it that you can see through. *See* MASK.

COMMAND BUTTON in a dialog box, a command button is a small box that executes a command when clicked on with the mouse.

⌘

Command symbol

COMMAND KEY on the Macintosh, the key marked with a cloverleaflike symbol. It is used like a shift key to change the meanings of the other keys or to perform special functions. For example, you can print a picture of the current screen by holding down Command and Shift and pressing 4. If you press 3 instead, a picture of the screen will be saved as a MacPaint document. Menus often show key commands you can use instead of clicking with the mouse. (*See* SHORTCUT).

COMMUNICATION the primary goal of the graphic arts. All of a desktop publisher's efforts should work toward the clear expression of ideas. Font changes, color, layout, and visual images are as valuable as the content of message; skillful use of these tools will result in an effective publication.

COMP a COMPREHENSIVE layout.

COMPOSITION the act of constructing a page layout from individual elements.

COMPREHENSIVE (comp) a detailed layout, showing the exact location and size of all the design elements.

Before computers, graphic designers usually went through many distinct stages when designing a publication or advertisement. First came THUMB-NAILS (small drawings of the design), then ROUGHS (a quick sketch of the proposed layout at full size). Then a COMP would be produced for client approval. A comp would be hand-drawn in full color, with the large type rendered by hand and the body copy GREEKED in.

With desktop publishing at our disposal, there is not much difference between a comp and the final

CAMERA-READY ARTWORK. The advantages are obvious: speed, corrections easily made, and precision. The drawback is, believe it or not, the speed. When you can produce a comp in 10 minutes rather than 24 hours, you *may* not spend enough time evaluating the design and trying to improve it. The answer is to use the technology to your advantage. Allow yourself enough time to pin the printout on the wall and actually *look* at it. Be critical. Try different typefaces. Don't settle for the first thing that you come up with.

COMPUTER a machine capable of executing instructions on data. The distinguishing feature of a computer is its ability to store its own instructions. This ability makes it possible for a computer to perform many operations without the need for a person to type in new instructions each time.

Modern computers are made of high-speed electronic components that enable the computer to perform millions of operations each second.

COMPUTER SECURITY precautions necessary to protect your equipment and data. The advent of personal computers has made it easy for important records or confidential data to be lost, sabotaged, or misused. Computers need protection from the following kinds of hazards:

- **Machine failure.** Make backups of important files frequently. Every disk drive in the world *will* one day fail, losing all data.

- **Physical hazards.** Protect the computer from fire, flood, and similar hazards, and store backups at a remote location. Remember, too, that the machine can be stolen.

- **Operator error.** It is easy to delete information accidentally. This hazard can be minimized with software that retains original files while alternate copies are being made.

- **Computer tampering.** Can someone come in and alter your records without your knowing it? Bear in mind that large numbers of people know how to use popular software packages. If necessary, use software that keeps records of changes *recording who made them when* and requires

49

validation (such as a password) to make large changes.

- **Dial-up "break-ins."** This is a hazard only with computers that are physically connected to telephone lines and are programmed to answer incoming calls. Use software that requires users to type passwords and limits their access to the computer system. Be aware of the possibility of break-ins through networks of computers.

- **Easily guessed passwords.** The simplest approach to securing a computer is to require users to type passwords at the beginning of a work session. However, some people are sure to choose passwords that are too easy to guess, such as the names of their spouses or children.

- **Excessive security measures.** Excessive measures to build automated security into a computer can easily make the computer so hard to use that productivity is crippled. In the final analysis, all computer security depends on human trustworthiness. Concentrate on securing the people, not the machine. That is, ensure that employees are trustworthy and that strangers have no access to the machine, then give authorized users all the access they need to do their job effectively.

CONCEPT the idea, either visual or verbal, that is the main point of an advertisement. The concept is the thing that stimulates the intellect, entertains, and delights. An advertisement with a concept is much more effective than a purely informational advertisement.

CONDENSED narrow; a *condensed* typeface has letterforms with reduced width. It looks "skinny." Condensed typefaces are good for labels and captions because you can set a lot of copy in a short LINEWIDTH. *See Figure 5* for an example.

You need to consider how condensed a font is when designing your layout. A very condensed font will need a *shorter* linewidth. Remember that an extremely condensed typeface will be hard to read as continuous text.

The lazy dog slept.
Regular proportions

The lazy dog slept.
Condensed proportions

Figure 5 Condensed type

The opposite of condensed is EXTENDED.

CONFIG.SYS in DOS, a file that contains information about the machine configuration, including device drivers, the type of keyboard (if not the standard U.S. model), and the amount of memory to be set aside for disk buffers.

CONFIG.SYS is read only when the machine boots up. Ordinarily, the computer user doesn't have to worry about it. But when installing new software, it is wise to make a copy of your CONFIG.SYS and AUTOEXEC.BAT files to another directory. Some ill-mannered installation programs *have* been know to trash the configuration file. If anything goes wrong, you'll be able to restore the old file while troubleshooting the problem. *See* AUTOEXEC.BAT.

CONFIGURE to set up a computer or program to be used in a particular way. Many commercial software packages have to be *configured*, or installed; this involves setting them up for a particular machine (including video card and printer) and for a particular user's preferences.

CONSTRAIN a method of restriction or limitation. For example, when drawing a circle with a circle tool, you must hold down the control key to constrain the rounded shape to a circle. If you let go of the constraining key too soon, you may get a fat oval rather than a perfect circle.

The constrain command is also used with the rectangle drawing tool (constrains to a square) and the line drawing tool (constrains to preset angles).

Bodoni
Bookman
Type contrast

High/low contrast

Control Box

CONTINUOUS TONE composed of smooth transitions from one color or brightness to another. Photographs, original drawings and paintings are continuous tone artwork. Commercial printing methods cannot reproduce these works without converting them into a grid of dots of different colors. *See* HALFTONE.

CONTRAST

1. in typography, the difference, if any, between the thick and thin strokes of a letter. If there is no contrast, the font is said to be MONOLINE.

Typefaces like Bodoni have high contrast. Text set in Bodoni has a sparkle as you scan the lines of type with your eyes. This is delightful for a headline, but provokes headaches for book readers. A better choice for a text font would be a typeface with lower contrast, such as Bookman.

2. the range of light and dark tones in CONTINUOUS TONE artwork. A *high contrast* image is mostly black and white, with little or no intermediate gray. A *low contrast* image has little difference between the darkest darks and the lightest lights.

Photopaint programs have a filter or control for adjusting the brightness and contrast of images. These are usually slide controls, but sometimes you are allowed to edit a HISTOGRAM of the image. Spreading the endpoints of the histogram will increase the contrast — pulling them together decreases the contrast. *See illustration at* HISTOGRAM.

Scanning software lets you adjust the contrast and brightness of an image as it is being scanned into the computer. This let you compensate for a poorly exposed or printed photograph. *See* SCANNER.

CONTROL BOX (Windows, OS/2) a small box at the left of the title bar of a window. Clicking the Control Box pops up a menu for controlling the size of the window. Double-clicking on the Control Box closes the window and the application running in it.

CONTROL KEY a key on computer keyboards that is used like a shift key; that is, you hold it down while pressing another key or clicking the mouse. (To type Ctrl-D, hold down Control and type D.)

The Control key gives the other key a new meaning that depends on the software being used. Many command shortcuts are accessed with Ctrl key combinations. In some drawing programs, Control is used to CONSTRAIN the action of the mouse.

CONTROL MENU (Windows, OS/2) a menu that appears when the user clicks on the CONTROL BOX (the box at the left of the title bar). The Control Menu for each window will allow you to maximize, minimize, restore, resize, or close the application. *See* WINDOW.

Control Menu

In OS/2, the Control Menu also offers access to configuration dialog boxes and information about the application.

CONTROL PANEL a program that gives you the ability to adjust certain features of your computer environment like the desktop color, mouse tracking, and the rate of cursor blinking. These are easily customized and give a rather high degree of personalization to your working environment. Look for the Control Panel under the Apple menu on the Mac or in the Main Program Group in Windows.

CONTROL POINTS see NODES.

CONVERSION PROGRAM a program that is capable of changing a file from one format to another. For example, if I had a graphic image in Encapsulated PostScript (.EPS) format, but my page layout program required .TIFF (Tagged Image File Format), I would need to use a conversion program. Please note that simply changing the file extension will *not* change the type of file. Most software packages can do a limited set of conversions to a set of standard file types. *See* EXPORT; IMPORT.

COPY

1. to transfer an item from one place to another, leaving the original unchanged (*contrast* MOVE).

2. textual matter. "Please proofread my copy before I send it to the printer."

COPY CAMERA a machine that photographically transfers an image from an original to a film negative or directly to a printing plate. Copy cameras can also be used to make PHOTOSTATS or VELOXES. *See* CAMERA-READY COPY.

COPYFITTING adjusting the attributes of type so that the text fits in a desired space. Copyfitting is a fine art *and* a science. Desktop publishing software has taken a lot of the difficult computations out of copyfitting and, by the magic of WYSIWYG (what you see is what you get), made it an interactive experiment. You can make changes and watch the type rewrap on screen; if it's still not to your liking, you can adjust it some more.

What to do with too little copy: If the copy is running short, your object is to increase the space it occupies. You *can* increase the point size, but if you are using a multi-column format, you will want to keep the type the same size. First try increasing the line spacing. Just an additional 1 point of LEADING will make 36 lines of 12 point type take up $6\frac{1}{2}$ inches instead of 6. Sometimes this is all that you will need.

Making the column a little narrower also will stretch the copy. Turn the hyphenation off or decrease the size of the HOT ZONE. By doing this, you will force the computer to go to a new line instead of breaking a word. Be careful: the column may be unpleasantly ragged or, if the column is JUSTIFIED, there may be RIVERS of white space down the interior of the column.

You can also add graphics or PULL QUOTES to fill space; these will also make the page more inviting to readers by adding visual interest to the text block.

What to do with too much copy: This, unfortunately, will be the more common problem. If your problem is very minor, say one word wrapping over to page two, you can often gain the desired space by simply tightening the TRACKING (letterspacing). Check the linespacing. Your page layout program may be automatically giving you 2 points of leading; you can decrease this to 0 points (SET TIGHT). This can literally mean inches of room to work in.

If your copy is *still* running long, consider reducing the size of the type or increasing the line length. Be careful not to hamper the legibility of the text.

If all else fails, edit the copy. You would be surprised at how much space can be gained by deleting all the occurrences of "however," "also," and "therefore." You'll actually be doing your reader a favor by pruning some of the excess verbosity. If the authors object to your gentle editing, ask *them* to do it themselves. After all, there *is* a space limit.

COPYRIGHT (the *right* to *copy*) a legal restriction on the copying of books, magazines, recordings, computer programs, and other materials, in order to protect the original author's right to ownership of, and compensations for reproduction of, an original work. Most computer programs are protected not only by copyright but also by a software license. *See* SOFTWARE LICENSE; FREE SOFTWARE. In the U.S., a work is protected by copyright if it contains a notice of the form

Copyright 1996 John Doe

or

© 1996 John Doe

in one or more prominent places.

U.S. copyright law allows limited copying of books and magazines for private study or classroom use. However, this does not apply to computer programs, which can only be copied with the permission of the copyright owner, or in order to make backup copies that will not be used as long as the original copy is intact.

Copyright protects expressions of ideas, not the ideas themselves. Copyrights do not cover algorithms, mathematical methods, techniques, or the design of machines (which, however, can be patented). Derivative works can infringe on copyrights; for example, if the source photograph for an illustration is recognizable, permission is needed to use it.

COUNTER the interior opening in such letters as *A, O, q,* and *g.*

q

Counter

COUPON LINE a dashed line. If you are puzzled about how to make a dashed line for a coupon, try looking in the stroke (or pen) attributes dialog box. There you will find a menu of different dotted and dashed lines.

· · · · · · · · · · · · · · · ·

— — — — — — -

· · — · · · — · · ·

Coupon lines

Handgloves

Courier

Cove serif

COURIER a typewriterlike typeface. Unlike most other typefaces, Courier has a FIXED PITCH, that is, all the characters are the same width. Courier is often the default font for laser printers. It does have its uses, especially if it suits your sense of humor to use your laser printer to emulate a typewriter.

COVE SERIF a serif that is attached to the main stroke of the letter by a triangular or curved support. Also called BRACKETED SERIFS.

CRASH

1. an application program failure (usually due to programming mistakes). Sometimes the operating system (System 7 and OS/2 in particular) will allow you to close the application program and then continue, but often it is necessary to REBOOT the computer. All recent changes to the document or drawing you were working on will be lost. (It's a good idea to save your work often.)

2. a severe hardware malfunction (most usually a hard disk *crash*, where the drive head actually loses its cushion of air and plows into the *platter* of the hard drive). In theory, a hard disk crash *could* happen at any time! This emphasizes the need to maintain complete and current backups of your files. *See* BACKUP; HARD DISK MANAGEMENT.

CREDIT LINE a caption acknowledging a person's work or assistance. The credit line is usually set below the contributed article or artwork. A BYLINE is a special type of credit line that appears just below the headline of a story.

CRITIQUE to review a proof or finished publication in order to discover if there is any way to make it better. When your own work is being critiqued, there is often a sense that you are under personal attack; *this is not true!* Your friends, clients, and colleagues are trying to help refine your work. Listen closely to the comments offered. They will give you a valuable insight into how an impartial reader views the piece.

If there is no other person available to help critique your work, do it yourself. Pin the laser printout up on the wall and look at it. Is the most important element the one that you notice first? Is the layout balanced? Is there a logical flow to the design? Is it neat? Do objects that are supposed to line up really line up?

Now, hold the printout at reading distance. Imagine yourself to be a member of the intended audience. Does everything make sense to you? Is everything clear? How could this piece be improved?

You may wish to have several critiquing sessions depending on the severity of the deadline pressure. If at all possible, put the printout away for a short time, and allow yourself a break from the project. Fresh eyes can spot errors better.

CROP to delete unwanted or unnecessary elements from a piece of artwork. Intelligent cropping can greatly improve the impact of a photograph.

CROP MARKS hairline-thin lines that indicate where the printed piece is to be trimmed.

Crop marks

Crosshairs

CROSSHAIRS a targeting cursor. Occasionally your mouse cursor will change from its normal appearance to the crosshairs. *See picture.* They are like the crosshairs in a rifle scope and are designed to help you pinpoint an exact location on screen.

CROSS HEAD a heading that extends over more than one column of type.

CROSS-PLATFORM available for both the Macintosh and IBM families of computers.

C/SC caps and small capitals. This is sometimes written "C + SC."

CTRL *see* CONTROL KEY.

CTRL–ALT–DEL a keystroke combination that RE-BOOTS IBM PC compatibles running DOS. You must hold down the Ctrl and Alt keys, and simultaneously press the Del key. This famous "three finger salute" is sometimes your only recourse when a program hangs up and refuses to accept any input from the keyboard or mouse. You should be aware that you will lose any changes made since you last saved your file.

Windows and OS/2 handle hung application programs a bit more graciously, allowing you to exit to the operating system instead of rebooting the system from scratch. Again, data will be lost unless you have just completed saving your file.

If you should ever find yourself working on a Macintosh, and your program hangs, hold down Command, Option and press Escape. This will take you back to the Finder. *See* FORCE QUIT.

CUA **C**ommon **U**ser **A**ccess, a set of guidelines promoted by IBM for standardizing the way that computer programs communicate with the people using them. This will make it easier for people to learn to use new pieces of software.

CUA includes standards for the design of menus and the use of keystrokes. All software manufacturers are encouraged to follow CUA guidelines. *See also* GUI, SAA, WIMP.

CUBIC SPLINE a curve that connects a set of points smoothly by solving a system of cubic equations. Unlike a Bézier spline, a cubic spline is defined only by the points that the curve must pass through; it has no control points that are not on the curve. For picture, *see* SPLINE.

Cubic splines are the natural shapes of bent objects that are secured at particular points and are free to bend in between. The spline goes through each point smoothly, without sharp bends.

Each segment of the spline (from one point to the next) is modeled by a third-degree (cubic) polynomial of the form $y = ax^3 + bx^2 + cx + d$ where a, b, c, and d depend on the endpoints of the segment and the slope that the segment should have at each end.

If (x_1, y_1) and (x_2, y_2) are the endpoints and y_1' and y_2' are the slopes, then a, b, c, and d can be found by solving the four-equation system:

$$
\begin{aligned}
y_1 &= ax_1{}^3 + bx_1{}^2 + cx_1 + d \\
y_2 &= ax_2{}^3 + bx_2{}^2 + cx_2 + d \\
y_1' &= 3ax_1{}^2 + 2bx_1 + c \\
y_2' &= 3ax_2{}^2 + 2bx_2 + c
\end{aligned}
$$

More commonly, the slopes are not known, but the slope at the end of each segment is set equal to the slope at the beginning of the next segment. The slopes and coefficients are then found by solving a system of simultaneous linear equations (linear, because x, x^2, and x^3 are known and can be treated as constants).

CUE CARDS a help feature that displays tips and other helpful information automatically. For example, a cue card that accompanies a DIALOG BOX can help you understand the purpose of all the possible settings. Cue cards can be very useful for novices; more advanced users can turn them off. Similar program features are called COACHES, WIZARDS, or BALLOON HELP.

CURSIVE typeface designs that resemble handwriting. Sometimes called SCRIPTS.

Handgloves

Cursive

CURSOR the symbol on a computer screen that shows where the next character you type will appear. Cursors often appear as blinking dashes, rectangles, or I-bars; some programs change the appearance of the cursor to remind you which tool you are using. Most keyboards have cursor movement (arrow) keys that allow you to move the cursor vertically or horizontally around the screen. This ability is essential for text-editing. You can also use the MOUSE or other pointing device such as a trackball or graphics tablet to move the cursor. *See* MOUSE, POINTER.

CUSP NODE a type of NODE that marks a sudden change in the direction of the line. Contrast with SMOOTH NODE. *For picture, see* NODE.

CUT

    1. to remove objects or text from the file you are editing and to place it into a holding area. *See also* COPY and PASTE.

    2. to trim printed paper to the finished size.

CUTOFF RULE a horizontal rule that marks the end of an article.

CUTOUT a portion of a bitmapped image. A cutout can be moved, copied, or have a multitude of filters and transformations applied to it. SELECTION TOOLS (Box Selection, Lasso, Magic Wand, Scissors) are used to define cutouts.

Clockwise

CW clockwise.

АБВГДЕЖ
абвгдежзик

Cyrillic

CYRILLIC an alphabet used to set type in Russian and neighboring languages. Named after St. Cyril, who went to spread Christianity to the Slavs in 863 A.D.

A Cyrillic alphabet has more characters than a Roman alphabet, and the fonts are proportionally larger. It is sometimes challenging to set Cyrillic type on a computer keyboard designed for English. Some word processors are up to the task, but you may need special software to make everything work.

D

DAGGER (†) a symbol used to mark footnotes. *See also* FOOTNOTE.

Dagger

DASH a punctuation mark similar to a hyphen, but longer. On a typewriter, people used to type two hyphens to indicate a dash. When setting type, you need to use the special characters supplied with your type font. Each font should have two dashes: an EM DASH (—) and an EN DASH (–). The em dash (sometimes called a "long dash") is the same width as the height of the typeface (and thus is proportional to the size of the font). You use the em dash to separate sentence clauses—indicating a pause in the train of thought. An en dash (short dash) is just half the length of the em dash and is used as as abbreviation for the word "to," e.g. 1982–94.

    The terms *em* and *en* are very old; they date back to the the earliest days of printing with movable type. An *em-quad* (*em* for short) is a square block of wood, equal in dimension to the size of the font. A capital letter M was usually the same width, hence, "em-quad." An en-quad was one half the width of the em-quad. There were also 3-to-the em and 4-to-the-em blocks. These spacers were used to adjust wordspacing for justified type.

DASHED LINE *see* COUPON LINES.

DDE (**D**ynamic **D**ata **E**xchange), in Microsoft Windows and OS/2, a mechanism by which some programs can exchange data with each other while they are running. For example, through DDE, a cell in a spreadsheet can be connected to data that is being continuously updated by some other program. In this case the spreadsheet is the DDE client (the information requester) and the other program is the DDE server. A DDE connection between programs is called a *hot link* if the shared data can be updated continuously by the server, or a *cold link* if the data is updated only when the client requests it. *See* OBJECT LINKING AND EMBEDDING.

DEFAULT an assumption that a computer makes unless it is given specific instructions to the contrary. In a windowed environment, the default choice is HIGH-LIGHTED. Many application programs try to provide you with a reasonable set of default combinations for margins, page orientation, typeface, etc. You can change any of the defaults to suit your needs.

DEFAULT DIRECTORY in many operating systems (DOS, OS/2, Windows), the default directory is where the computer looks for files or writes files if no directory is specified. You need to be careful to *specify* which directory you want a file saved in; it is far too easy to accept the default directory and then have to search the entire hard disk for a file.

DEFAULT DRIVE (DOS, OS/2) the disk drive where the computer looks for files or writes files if no drive is specified.

DEGAUSS to demagnetize. Color monitors need to be degaussed when they show areas of weak or incorrect color. Some monitors degauss themselves every time they are turned on. If you wish to repeat the degauss cycle on such a monitor, wait 5 seconds each time you turn it on or off before flipping the switch again; otherwise, the power supply may be damaged.

DEL the DELETE key.

DELETE to remove an unwanted item (character, word, art, file). *See* RECOVERING ERASED FILES for help on restoring deleted files. *See also* PROOFREADER'S MARKS.

DEMIBOLD a typeface weight in between NORMAL and BOLD. *See* WEIGHT.

DENSITOMETER an electronic instrument that measures the relative darkness of an image (on paper or film). Photographers often use densitometers to help them determine the correct exposure when printing their pictures.

The electronics in a scanner can be used like a densitometer and can adjust the values of an image to cover a wider contrast range.

Descender

DESCENDER the part of a letterform that extends below the baseline.

DESELECT to tell the computer you do not want to work with a particular object. There are minor differences in how different software does this, but usually clicking on the background or another object will deselect the current object. If you want to select multiple objects, you can hold down shift while clicking on the desired object. This allows you to select as many items as you want. To deselect just one item of a group, use shift-click again (in other words, selection toggles).

Hint: If you wish to select all but one or two objects in a drawing, the fastest way is to "Select All" (either by using the edit menu option or by MARQUEE SELECT), and then deselect the unwanted objects.

DESIGN AXES the range of characteristics which will be computed in a MULTIPLE MASTER FONT. For example, one design axis might be the font's weight; the range of possibilities set by the designer might be to go from light to extra-bold. The computer can compute any intermediate weight. *See* MULTIPLE MASTER FONTS.

DESK ACCESSORY a small, useful program that is meant to be always at hand while you are working at your computer. Examples include the clock, calculator, Character Map (KeyCaps for Mac users), and the control panel. All Macintosh programs provide access to the Desk Accessories under the Apple menu. Windows desk accessories are found in the Accessories program group.

DESKEW to straighten; to undo the effects of a SKEW command.

DESKTOP your whole computer screen, representing your workspace. You manipulate objects (ICONS) with the mouse in much the same way that you work with a stapler or calculator on your physical desktop.

DESKTOP PUBLISHING the use of personal computers to design and print professional-quality typeset documents. *See* TYPEFACE. A desktop publishing program such as Pagemaker or Quark Express is much more versatile than a word processor; in addition to typing documents, the user can specify the layout in great detail, use multiple input files, have comprehensive typographic control, insert pictures, and preview the appearance of the printed document on the screen.

Since 1990, the distinction between word processing and desktop publishing has become blurred. Most word processors can produce elegantly typeset documents. The difference is that desktop publishing programs put more emphasis on graphic design and facilities for handling longer works.

A new facet of desktop publishing is ELECTRONIC PUBLISHING; producing documents that are meant to be viewed on screen, not printed out. These electronic documents are distributed by computer networks (*see* WORLD WIDE WEB) or CD-ROMs. An electronic document may have sound, music, illustrations, animations, video clips, or HYPERTEXT links (special buttons or keywords which jump the reader to a new text or picture). So, soon it will not be enough to be a master of typography, grammar, illustration, graphic design, and computer technology, but we will all be needing a course in film editing and musical scoring!

DESTINATION place to which information is copied. If I copy a file from my hard disk to drive A:, A is the destination drive. *See also* TARGET; SOURCE.

DIALOG BOX a window that appears when the program needs to collect information from the user. When the user has filled in the necessary information, and clicks "OK," the dialog box disappears. *Figure 6* shows a composite dialog box. If you would like more information about any feature of a dialog box, see that entry in this dictionary.

DICTIONARY a reference book that defines words and gives their correct spelling. General purpose dictionaries also give the correct pronunciation and the etimology of the word. Some dictionaries provide equivalent words or phrases in two different languages; other, more specialized dictionaries, seek to define terms relevant to a particular field.

The dictionary for a spell checker is simply a list of correctly spelled words. The spell checker works by literally looking up every word in your document. When the program finds a word that is not in the

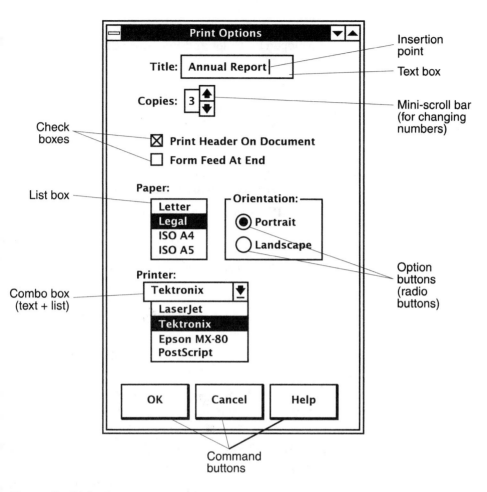

Figure 6 Dialog box.

list of correctly spelled words, it shows the presumed misspelled word to you, usually with a list of suggested alternates. Do not add new words to the spell checker's dictionary unless you are certain of their spelling. A dictionary of misspelled words is not worth much.

DIDONE a classification of roman typefaces characterized by abrupt changes in contrast. The stress of the letterforms is vertical and the serifs have no brackets.

Handglφves

Didone

65

Also called MODERN. These typefaces were originally developed by Didot and Bodoni in the late 1700s.

DIDOT the first MODERN typeface, designed by Firmin Didot in 1784.

DIE a metal stamp used to press a design into paper or foil. Dies are also used to cut out irregular shapes from paper. Dies are quite expensive to have made. The die can be produced from camera-ready art that you supply. Use EMBOSSED or DIE-CUT designs only when there is an adequate budget for the project.

ë

Dieresis

DIERESIS accent mark consisting of two dots; *see* ACCENTS.

DIFFUSE a photopaint filter that randomly scatters colors. The effect is rather impressionistic if you set the degree of diffusion relatively high. You might want to experiment case by case to see if the diffuse or BLUR filter gives the desired appearance.

DIFFUSION a type of halftone screen in which the dots are randomly scattered; this helps to avoid MOIRE patterns when scanning printed halftone pictures.

DIGITAL PRESS a printing press that can print directly from a computer file, bypassing the stages of CAMERA-READY COPY and PREPRESS PRODUCTION.

DIGITIZE to convert into a form recognizable by a computer. To digitize an image (photograph or drawing) means to use a SCANNER to turn the image into a BITMAP. *See* SCANNER.

×

Dimension sign

DIMENSION SIGN *see* MULTIPLICATION CROSS.

DIMMED not available for selection. If a menu option appears in light gray rather than black type, it cannot be chosen. For example, if you wish to align two objects, the align command will be dimmed until you have two or more objects selected. If you click on a dimmed command, nothing happens.

Dingbats

DINGBATS a collection of commonly used symbols and graphical elements. Also called a PI FONT or SYMBOL FONT.

DIN PAPER SIZES *see* PAPER SIZES (ISO).

DIRECTORY the computer's list of files on a disk. On the Macintosh, directories are called FOLDERS. Each disk has at least one directory (the main, or root directory), and an operating system has a way of displaying a list of names of the files on the disk. A directory can contain other directories (SUBDIRECTORIES).

Subdirectories are listed in the directory where they are contained as if they were a special kind of file. If you are working with a diskette, you may not need to create subdirectories, since the number of files on the disk is relatively small. However, the number of files on a hard disk rapidly becomes so large that you will have difficulty finding particular files if you have not created subdirectories. It is wise to have a subdirectory for each major software package that you run. Create additional subdirectories under the major subdirectory to organize the various projects you are undertaking. *See* HIERARCHICAL FILE SYSTEM.

DISCRETIONARY HYPHEN a hyphen which is used only when the word falls near the end of a line; sometimes called a SOFT HYPHEN. By specifying where you want the word to be broken, you override the word-processor's automatic hyphenation. *Contrast* REQUIRED HYPHEN, HARD HYPHEN.

DISK a round, flat device for storing computer data. There are three main kinds: DISKETTES, HARD DISKS, and OPTICAL DISKS (of which CD-ROMs are the most common kind).

Diskettes are made of flexible plastic coated with iron oxide. Information is recorded on them by magnetizing the iron oxide coating in specific places. The diskette will be erased if it comes near a magnet or a source of a magnetic field, such as an electric motor.

The iron oxide on the disk consists of microscopically small needles, each of which acts like a tiny bar magnet. Information is stored by magnetizing these needles. The read-write head, which skims the surface of the disk, can either generate a magnetic field to magnetize the needles, or detect the magnetic field of needles that are already magnetized. The binary digits 0 and 1 are represented by changes in the direction of magnetization.

Data on disks is stored in many concentric circles, each of which is called a *track*. Each track is divided into *sectors,* which are the smallest units that the computer can read into memory in a single step. On a double-sided or multilayer disk pack, the set of tracks in corresponding positions on different layers is known as a *cylinder.*

The *directory* of a disk is a special area in which the computer records the names and locations of all the files on the disk. In most operating systems, the user can create many directories on a single disk.

Data stored on a disk cannot be read as quickly as data stored in the main memory of the computer, but disk storage has a larger capacity and is not erased when the computer is turned off. Storing data on magnetic tape is even cheaper than using disks, but is impractical to use on a daily basis because it takes so long for the computer to retrieve the data. However, tape is an excellent medium for BACKUPS.

Computers cannot read each other's diskettes unless the computers are designed to be compatible. This sometimes gets to be a problem when sharing data with someone else. Macintoshes can read and write to preformatted IBM diskettes through the Apple File Exchange program.

A disk has to be *formatted* before it can be used. Formatting is the process of marking out the tracks and sectors magnetically and creating the main directory. Diskettes for PC-compatible computers are often sold preformatted.

Table 3 lists the kinds of diskettes usually used by PC-compatible computers. The $3\frac{1}{2}$-inch diskettes used by the Macintosh are physically the same as these but are formatted differently by the computer.

Hard disks are like diskettes except that the iron oxide is coated on stiff aluminum disks, there are normally several layers in a single disk pack, and the whole device is normally mounted permanently in the computer. Most hard disks have capacities ranging from 100 to 1000 megabytes (equal to hundreds of diskettes).

Optical disks store information by etching a transparent plastic medium with a laser beam. An

Table 3 Types of diskettes used on PC-compatible computers.

Size	Density	Sides	Capacity
$5\frac{1}{4}''$	DD	Single	180K
$5\frac{1}{4}''$	DD	Double	360K
$5\frac{1}{4}''$	HD	Double	1.2M
$3\frac{1}{2}''$	DD	Double	720K
$3\frac{1}{2}''$	HD	Double	1.44M
$3\frac{1}{2}''$	ED	Double	2.88M

The most common size is $3\frac{1}{2}''$ HD.

optical disk stores about ten times as much information as a magnetic disk of the same size, but it cannot be erased. (Some kinds can be overwritten to erase old data, so that new data can be written in a different location on the disk.) Optical disks are used mainly for large data files that are often read but seldom changed. *See* CD-ROM.

DISK DRIVE a device that enables a computer to read and write data on disks.

DISKETTE a removable flexible magnetic disk on which computer programs and data can be stored. The main sizes are $3\frac{1}{2}$-inches and $5\frac{1}{4}$-inches. *See Table 3* for the capacity of different diskettes. The $5\frac{1}{4}$-inch diskettes are sometimes called "floppies" because the entire diskette, including the cover, is flexible. The smaller $3\frac{1}{2}$-inch diskettes have a more rigid plastic shell and are more robust. *See* DISK.

DISPLAY

    1. type larger than 14 points is referred to as *display type*.

    2. typeface designs meant to to attract attention. Every quirky, offbeat, or unusual typeface design gets lumped into this category. The main caveat is: *remember to use display fonts sparingly*. They are not suitable for paragraphs of text.

Display type

DISPLAY INITIAL a decorative letter used as the first letter of a paragraph. The display initial should be set in a different font and set much larger than the body copy. *Figure 7* shows three types of display initials: HUNG INITIAL, DROPPED INITIAL (also called INSET INITIAL), and RAISED INITIAL.

DISTRIBUTE a drawing program command that places objects evenly over a defined area.

DITHERING in computer graphics, the representation of an intermediate color by mixing dots of two other colors. This is very similar in concept to Seurat's pointillism and halftone printing. Limitations of your hardware make it impossible to print or display all possible colors. Sometimes your computer has to fake it by using dithering. (This is why some colors have discernible patterns in them when displayed on your monitor.)

Your software usually takes care of dithering automatically. About the only time you have to concern yourself with it is when you are going to EXPORT your drawing to another program (i.e. exporting a vector graphic as a bitmap). You will get a more faithful representation of color if you specify the colors to be dithered. Dithering should *not* be used if you are going to scale the image; sharpness will be lost.

DL *see* ENVELOPE SIZES.

DNS a proofreader's mark for **d**o **n**ot **s**et.

DOCUMENT a file containing a text to be printed (e.g., a letter, article, or book chapter) or a drawing.

DOCUMENTATION written descriptions of computer programs. Documentation falls into several categories:

1. *On-line documentation,* i.e., information that is displayed as the program runs or that can be called up with a help command. The user should be able to control the amount of information displayed (more for beginners, and less as the user's experience increases). Also, help commands should be sensitive to the context in which they are invoked; for instance, clicking on "help" within an editor should call up information about the editor, not the whole operating system.

Figure 7 Display initials.

2. *Reference cards* containing easily forgotten details for quick reference. A reference card assumes that the user is already familiar with the general principles of the program. Reference cards printed on paper are becoming obsolete, but the same kind of documentation is often made available online.

3. *Reference manuals,* setting out complete instructions for the program in a systematic way. Related information should be grouped together, and a good index should be provided.

4. *Tutorials,* serving as introductions for new users. Unlike a reference manual, a tutorial gives the information in the order in which the user will want to learn it; items are grouped by importance rather than by function or logical category.

DOCUMENT MODE the normal way of typing documents in a word processor. The word processor includes codes that indicate hyphenation, page breaks, and so forth, thereby producing a special word processing file. Documents saved this way must be edited with the same or similar word processor. *Contrast* TEXT FILE. *See also* IMPORT.

DOS (**D**isk **O**perating **S**ystem) a name used by many computer manufacturers for various operating systems, including the disk operating system for the Apple II (Apple DOS); MS-DOS, developed by Microsoft for 16-bit microcomputers; PC-DOS, a version of MS-DOS sold by IBM; and Novell DOS (formerly DR-DOS), a replacement for MS-DOS sold by Novell. These days "DOS" means MS- or PC-DOS to most people.

After the introduction of Windows 3.0 in 1990, it became common to refer to an IBM PC program as "for DOS" if it did not require Windows.

DOT LEADERS a dotted line that leads the eye from one side of the page to another. Usually simply called LEADERS. You most often see leaders in a Table of Contents or a price list.

DOT PITCH the spacing of the dots of red, green, and blue phosphor on the screen of a color monitor.

These dots do not correspond to pixels; instead, the dot pitch of a screen imposes a blur on any image regardless of its electronic resolution. For example, on a 15-inch screen with 0.28-mm dot pitch, a 1024×768-pixel image is no sharper than an 800×600 image, although it may look slightly smoother.

The smaller the dot pitch, the sharper the image; 0.28 mm is generally considered satisfactory, and anything higher than 0.35 mm is too blurry for serious work. Monochrome (black-and-white) screens do not have dots, and their dot pitch is effectively 0, making them sharper than even the best color screens.

DOTS PER INCH *see* DPI.

á

Double acute

DOUBLE ACUTE an accent mark used in Hungarian; *see* ACCENTS.

DOUBLE-CLICK to depress the button of a mouse twice very rapidly (if the mouse has more than one button, use the leftmost one). This is usually the shortcut to open or launch the selected file. If you find it difficult to double-click quickly enough, you can adjust the mouse's double-click speed. You'll find the mouse adjustments in the Control Panel (Macintosh and Microsoft Windows).

‡

Double dagger

DOUBLE DAGGER (‡) a symbol used to mark footnotes. Use the double dagger only if the single dagger marked the previous footnote.

ë

Double dot

DOUBLE DOT an accent mark, as in *ë,*, that has two functions. As a DIERESIS it shows that two adjacent vowels form separate syllables; thus Latin *praeësse,* French *Noël,* Spanish *lingüista,* and even English *coöperate, preëminent* (although *cooperate* and *pre-eminent* or *pre-eminent* are the preferred spellings).

As an UMLAUT the double dot marks a German vowel that has undergone fronting (*ä, ö, ü*). In transcribed Russian, *ë* denotes an *e* that is pronounced *ya*, as in *Gorbachëv.*

DOWNLOAD to transmit a file or program from a central computer to a smaller computer or a computer at a remote site.

DOWNTIME the time that your computer system is unavailable for work due to hardware failures or necessary maintenance and backups.

DPI dots per inch. The first generation of laser printers had a resolution of 300 dots per inch; 600 and 1200 DPI laser printers are now available. *See* RESOLUTION for further details.

DRAFT QUALITY a printout in low resolution, unsuitable for CAMERA-READY COPY, but perfectly adequate for proofing the copy and checking the placement and alignment of graphics.

DRAG to move an object by using a mouse. To do this, move the mouse pointer to the object, then hold down a mouse button (usually the leftmost button if there is more than one), and move the mouse. The selected object will move with the mouse pointer, as if the pointer were *dragging* the object. When you are finished, drop the object by releasing the button.

DRAG AND DROP

1. a method of opening an application program quickly. Simply pick up an file icon and drag it to the icon of an application program that can open the file.

2. the ability to move text or graphics by dragging it to a new location with the mouse.

In the newest version of the Macintosh operating system (System 7.5), objects may be selected and then dragged onto the desktop or into another program. *See* CLIPPINGS.

DRAW PROGRAM one type of program for drawing pictures on a personal computer. Unlike a paint program, a draw program treats the picture as a collection of objects, each of which can be moved around and altered without affecting any of the other objects. Because of this OBJECT-ORIENTED approach to graphics, drawings are printed as sharply as the printer can print. The sharpness of the picture is not limited by the resolution of the screen. Also, stored drawings are much smaller than their bitmapped counterparts. On the other hand, draw programs cannot edit individual pixels.

Draw programs are preferred for drawing diagrams, while paint programs are sometimes superior for pictorial work. Each drawing needs to be planned in advance, and the proper tool used to produce it.

Some popular draw programs include MacDraw and Adobe Illustrator (Macintosh); CorelDraw and Micrografx Designer (Windows); Freehand and Canvas (available for both platforms).

DRILLING making holes in the margins of pages so that they can be bound or inserted into a ring binder.

DROP-DOWN MENU a menu that appears when a particular item in a menu bar is selected. Also called a pop-up menu. For picture, *see* WINDOW. *See also* MENU BAR, PULL-DOWN MENU.

DROP FOLIO a page number at the bottom of the page.

DROP OUT a halftoned image in which the highlight areas are pure white, with no halftone dots in them. *See* HALFTONE.

DROPPED INITIAL a display initial that aligns its top with the CAP HEIGHT of the first line of the paragraph. Also called a *drop cap*. *See diagram at* DISPLAY INITIAL.

DUMMY a physical mockup of a printed piece used to work out the BINDERY details and page IMPOSITIONS.

I recommend that you always make a dummy to show to the printer how you want your printed piece to appear. Show where you want all folds and perforations. Even if you are only producing a newsletter printed front and back on a single sheet of paper, take laser-printed proofs and tape them together to show how you want it printed. (HEAD-TO-HEAD or HEAD-TO-TAIL?) To make sure that the dummy is not mistaken for the CAMERA-READY ART, write "FPO" (FOR POSITION ONLY) across it.

Some software is intelligent enough to do page impositions. If not, you can make a dummy out of blank paper to figure out which pages should be printed together. *See* IMPOSITION for more details.

DUOTONE a photograph printed with a color overprinting the black halftone. The effects are very variable; it helps to be able to preview duotones on screen to make sure that you have a reasonable balance between the black and the second color.

DYE SUBLIMATION PRINTER a type of color printer that gives excellent color proofs. Dye-sub printouts appear to be continuous tone images like photographs. Actually they, too, are composed of tiny dots (like laser or thermal-wax printouts), but the dots of dye have spread together. The intense colors, glossy finish, and lack of apparent halftone dots make these printouts especially suitable for presentations to clients. Dye-sub printers are expensive machines and are out of the reach of most individuals, but many service bureaus have them.

Editor's alteration

Ear

Edge detect

E

EA *see* EDITOR'S ALTERATION; PROOFREADER'S MARKS.

EAR the small stroke on the right side of the letter g.

EDGE DETECT a photopaint filter that outlines the edges of objects.

EDGE PADDING the amount of extra color around the edge of an area necessary to properly color an irregularly shaped object. For example, when you use a RADIAL FILL on an object, you may find the resulting effect too subtle. There is too much of the central color and not enough of the contrasting outer color. This is because of the way the FILL command works. The computer is actually filling the entire BOUNDING BOX, but the object is not showing enough of the fill. You need to increase the *edge padding* (which is usually expressed in percentages). You may need to experiment to get the desired effect. *See* FILL; RADIAL FILL.

EDGE STAPLED an inexpensive method of binding a short booklet. The staples are passed through the left margin of all pages. This will prevent the booklet from being opened flat, and requires an extra wide middle gutter. *See* BINDING for other options.

EDIT to examine a file and make changes in it, usually with the aid of an editor. (See EDITOR.)

EDITION BINDING hardcover binding. *See* BINDING.

EDITOR

1. a computer program that enables the user to view the contents of a file and add material or make other changes. There are two main types of file editors: graphics and text. *Graphics editors* include PAINT PROGRAMS (for editing bitmaps) and DRAW PROGRAMS (for editing OBJECT-ORIENTED GRAPHICS.) *Text editors* are used to edit text.

2. the *person* who does the work of editing. An editor is responsible for seeing that that all the text is spelled correctly, properly punctuated, grammatical, and organized in a logical fashion. A good editor is interested in consistency and pays attention to details.

It is sometimes remarkably difficult to edit your

own writing. You lack the objectivity to spot a muddled paragraph or catch the occasional HOMONYM error. Be aware of this. No matter how tight the deadline, make sure that another person has PROOFED the CAMERA-READY COPY before it goes to press.

Lastly, you need to assume some responsibility for the *content* of the text you edit. Are all your facts straight? Are you being objective? Are you willing to take the responsibility for all that flaming rhetoric? If not, you need to tone it down, or make the necessary corrections.

EDITOR'S ALTERATION a copy change suggested by the editor. Abbreviated *EA* in the margin of the manuscript.

EGYPTIAN a slab-serif typeface. Also called SQUARE SERIF. In an Egyptian typeface, the serifs are thick and very prominent; usually there is no bracketing to the main stroke of the letter, but there may be a small cove softening the intersection. If the serifs are thin hairlines, the typeface would be more correctly identified as DIDONE or MODERN.

Handgloves
Egyptian

ELECTRONIC DOCUMENT a document intended to be read as it is displayed on a monitor. Since it is freed from the constraints of printing, an electronic document can make use of HYPERTEXT, full screen resolution, and full color. Some MULTI-MEDIA presentations also make use of animation, sound, and music. Because of their large storage requirements, such electronic documents are usually distributed on CD-ROMS. *See* AUTHORING SOFTWARE.

ELECTRONIC PUBLISHING

1. the creation, manufacturing, and distribution of paperless documents. Examples of "electronic documents" are CD-ROM encyclopedias and the HOME PAGES on the WORLD WIDE WEB. Each of these new formats brings new challenges and technical problems, but all need the skill of someone who knows how to work with type and how to produce a pleasing combination of graphics and text.

2. the use of *dedicated* (devoted to one purpose), computer-controlled equipment in the publishing and printing industries. Desktop publishing may be considered part of this trend, but electronic publishing encompasses the use of specialized equipment not readily available to the mass market (powerful workstation class computers and DIGITAL PRESSES, for example). Electronic publishing is superseding traditional methods of PREPRESS production.

ELEVATOR BAR a SCROLL BAR; a part of a window frame that provides a convenient way of moving vertically or horizontally through a document or drawing that is too big to display all at once. The position of the *elevator box* (THUMB) gives you a graphical representation of where you are in the document. If the elevator box is near the top of the bar, you are near the top of the document, and likewise for bottom, left, and right. You can DRAG the thumb with the mouse for fast scrolling or you can CLICK on the arrows at the ends of the bar to scroll line by line. Unlike real elevators, elevator bars can be either vertical or horizontal.

ELITE a typewriter that types 12 characters to the inch. *See* PICA for contrast.

• • •
Ellipsis

ELLIPSIS the three periods (...) that indicate an omission of text. There is less than normal spacing between the periods in an ellipsis. Most fonts provide a single character for the ellipsis; use that instead of just typing three periods.

EMBEDDED OBJECT an object included in your file that was created in another software package, and that still maintains a LINK to the other software. If the object is changed in the original software, it will be updated in the second file. This is called OBJECT LINKING AND EMBEDDING (OLE).

Although it sounds complicated, the use of embedded objects may be a smart move for the desktop publisher. It allows you the freedom to create a publication out of many separate parts and frees you from worrying if the latest update of a drawing or chart is the one in the master file.

EMBOSS to create a raised, sculptural image in paper by pressing a metal die into the paper from the back side. Embossing a cover or letterhead gives an air of luxury and understated elegance. It's expensive to create a custom die; you may want to consider paper pre-embossed with a standard design for small jobs.

It is also possible to fake embossing. For picture, *see* BLIND EMBOSSING. Some photopaint programs come with a FILTER to transform any image into an embossed appearance.

See also BLIND EMBOSSING; FOIL EMBOSSING.

EM DASH a long dash (—). *See* DASH.

EMENDATION a correction or alteration intended to improve a work.

EMPHASIS, METHODS OF ways of highlighting words. *Italics,* **bold**, *bold-italics*, enlarging, underlining, ALL CAPS, SMALL CAPS, **switching typefaces** or printing in color (unfortunately, not available here) are all useful ways to show a change in tone of voice or spotlight a term's importance.

When setting type, one does not normally use underlining. Underlining is a typewriter representation of italics. When italics are available to you, use them instead.

The **best** advice I can give to you is this: *choose* just *one* method of *emphasis* and **stick with it** *throughout* your document. And, of course, don't overdo it. Otherwise, your page is likely to look like a battlefield.

See also ITALICS, UNDERLINING, BOLDFACE, SMALL CAPS.

ENABLER a Macintosh system update file that can customize the System 7 operating system for a new model of Macintosh.

ENCAPSULATED POSTSCRIPT (EPS) a FILE FORMAT that is widely supported by different computers, printers, and software. Most desktop publishing software supports the importation of Encapsulated PostScript files, thus providing a common denominator for exchanging files. *See also* POSTSCRIPT.

END the key on your keyboard that takes your cursor to the end of the current line. Some word processors use Ctrl–End as a keyboard shortcut to take you to the end of the document.

Engraved typeface

EN DASH a short dash (–). *See* DASH.

ENDPAPERS the sturdy paper lining used to connect bound pages to a hard cover.

ENGRAVED a typeface that has incised white lines in the thick strokes. This mimics the look of copperplate engraving and imparts an air of elegance.

ENTER KEY the key on your computer keyboard that you press to:

- force the end of a line in a word-processing environment, or
- to tell the computer that you are ready for it to take action on the command you've just given.

In a windowed environment, pressing enter is the same as clicking on the highlighted button with the mouse.

ENTITY an alternative term for OBJECT used by some CAD software.

ENVELOPE

1. the familiar envelopes that we mail letters in. *See Table 4* for sizes.

Envelopes are available in a variety of papers and colors and can be printed on by offset printing at your neighborhood print shop. Remember to leave $\frac{1}{4}$ inch (6 mm) on one end for GRIPPER ALLOWANCE when you set up your CAMERA-READY COPY. If you want to have printing BLEED off the edge, you'll have to contact a printer who specializes in custom envelopes, for the paper stock will have to be printed first and then manufactured into envelopes.

Some laser printers can also print directly on envelopes. You must check your manual to find out if your printer can successfully feed envelopes and how to line them up. *See* GRIPPER ALLOWANCE, CAMERA-READY COPY, BLEED EDGE, PAPER SIZES.

2. In a draw program, the envelope is the imaginary outline of an object. You can edit the envelope, turning it from a rectangle into a curved shape (*See picture*). Your computer then recomputes the contents of the envelope, making possible some rather spectacular effects. *See* DRAW PROGRAM.

Envelope

Table 4   Envelopes for mailing letters: the most common sizes

U.S. sizes:

No. $6\frac{3}{4}$	$3\frac{5}{8} \times 6\frac{1}{2}$ in	For $8\frac{1}{2} \times 11$ folded in sixths
No. 9	$3\frac{7}{8} \times 8\frac{7}{8}$ in	
No. 10	$4\frac{1}{8} \times 9\frac{1}{2}$ in	For $8\frac{1}{2} \times 11$ folded in thirds
Open–end	$6\frac{1}{2} \times 9\frac{1}{2}$ in	For $8\frac{1}{2} \times 11$ folded in half
Open–end	9×12 in	For $8\frac{1}{2} \times 11$ paper, flat

ISO (European) sizes:

C4	229×324 mm	For A4 paper, flat
C5	162×229 mm	For A4 folded in half
C6	114×162 mm	For A4 folded in quarters
DL	110×220 mm	For A4 folded in thirds

ENVIRONMENT   the display and human interface provided by software. On a computer, an environment defines what you can do with the computer. For instance, the operating system, a word processor, and a spreadsheet provide (at least) three different environments that respond to different commands. If you type a word processing command while you are in the operating system environment, or vice versa, the command will not be understood. The human computer user has to mentally change gears when changing environments.

EPS   *see* ENCAPSULATED POSTSCRIPT.

EQUALIZE   a photopaint filter that allows you to manipulate the light and dark values of a photograph. By changing the values displayed in a histogram, you can correct muddy photos, increase contrast, and create some unusual artistic effects. Sometimes this adjustment is called "Brightness and Contrast."

ERASER   a paint and photopaint program tool that does to a bitmap what its real-life counterpart does to marks on paper. The eraser is used by holding down the mouse button (the leftmost if there is more than one) and dragging the eraser tool. You can adjust the size and shape of your eraser to suit your needs. Some programs will even adjust how well the eraser works;

Eraser

81

it can erase thoroughly or just lighten the color. *See* NATURAL MEDIA PAINT PROGRAM.

The eraser icon shown is from Corel PhotoPaint.

ERGONOMICS the science of designing machines and working environments to suit human needs (from the Greek words meaning "the study of work"). An ergonomically designed machine is one whose design is based on the scientific study of human requirements such as vision, posture, and health risks. After all, let's not forget that the most important part of a desktop publishing system is the human being who is operating the computer.

Ergonomics goes beyond considering your comfort. Smart workers know that they need to work efficiently. When you work efficiently, you can get more done. Here are some things you can do:

- **Desk.** Your computer desk should be deep enough to comfortably accommodate all of your equipment. If the system unit keeps threatening to dump the keyboard in your lap, you may not have enough room. Investigate putting the system unit on the floor or to the side of the monitor. There are special stands that can turn the box on end.

    Check the height of your desk. Is it too tall for you to type comfortably? You may want to attach a keyboard drawer. That will lower the keyboard to a more comfortable level as well as give you a storage place for the keyboard.

- **Chair.** Your chair is most vital to the health and well-being of your back. You should choose a chair that has adjustments for height and good lumbar support. Try to find a chair that lets you adjust the tilt of the seat. Take frequent stretching breaks. It also helps to periodically make minor changes to the seat tilt or angle of the chair back during a long work session.

- **Monitor.** The monitor is one of the big ticket items when you purchase your computer system. Ergonomically speaking, you do not want to skimp here. A cheap monitor with lots of flicker can literally give you a headache. (*See* MONITOR for a more thorough discussion of how to choose a monitor.) Make sure you are comfortable with the height and tilt of the screen. You may need a swivel monitor stand, especially if you are taller than most people. You may need a special pair of glasses for working at the computer. *See* EYE-GLASSES FOR COMPUTER USERS.

If you work where there's more than one computer system running, make sure that you are *not* positioned directly to the side or back of a fellow worker's monitor. The research on the dangers of electromagnetic emissions show that the greatest risk is to the *side* and *back* of the monitor, extending 3 to 4 feet away. Most researchers feel that you are safe enough in front of the monitor.

- **Mouse and keyboard.** The big risk is *carpal tunnel syndrome,* a condition that creates a buzzing feeling or numbness in your hands. Prevention is the key. You should keep your wrists straight when typing; don't allow them to bend. Some people enjoy a cushioned wrist rest for their keyboard. If using the mouse gives you any discomfort, try using another pointing device such as a TRACKBALL.

- **Lighting.** To prevent glare on the screen, do not place your computer opposite a window. Overhead lighting should be soft (not as bright as it would be for reading). There are add-on anti-glare screens for monitors.

- **Posture.** Good posture *is* important. Try to imagine that an invisible string is pulling your head up and back in line with your spine. Be relaxed rather than stiff. Sit with your feet in front of you; if they won't reach, your chair is too high. (Office supply stores sell some nice footrests.) Take frequent stretching breaks.

ESCAPE KEY the key (labeled Esc) on a computer keyboard that has a special meaning depending on what software is being used. Its traditional meaning is, "get me out of here and back to where you were before" (as in Lotus 1-2-3). Some software (QEdit) uses Escape to pop up a command menu.

Handgloves

Evenly weighted

EUROPEAN PAPER SIZES *see* PAPER SIZES (ISO).

EVENLY WEIGHTED having all the strokes of a letterform of the same thickness. Helvetica is a good example of an evenly weighted typeface. *See also* STRESS.

EXE (DOS, Windows, and OS/2) a file that contains a machine readable code program and has a filename ending in .EXE (for *executable*). Most application programs are distributed as EXE files. To run such a program, double click on the icon or the filename in the File Manager (Windows, OS/2). In DOS, just type the program name, without the EXE extension.

EXECUTIVE SIZE a size of paper sometimes used for stationery in the United States, $7\frac{1}{4} \times 10\frac{1}{2}$ inches.

EXPERT SET a font that includes a full set of accented vowels, ligatures, small caps, and other special characters (such as an extended group of CASE FRACTIONS). It is assumed that someone using such a font will have the know-how and the software to be able to set the special characters. Not every typeface has a matching expert set; you may have to take this into consideration when selecting a typeface for a particular job or purchasing fonts.

EXPORT to save a file in a format other than the application program's native format. Many word processing and graphics programs have the ability to export to several different formats.

Because the export process is a type of file conversion (instead of a simple copy operation) there is the possibility of a loss of image quality.

EXTENDED a typeface that is proportionately wide. Extended typefaces are useful when setting a headline that is a bit short for the column width. Also, an extended font can be set in a wider column.

Handgloves

Extended width

EXTENDED CHARACTER SET any set of characters beyond the normal ASCII set — in other words, the characters that can't be typed directly from the keyboard. The extended character set tends to vary from font to font; use a utility like KeyCaps (Macintosh) or Character Map (Windows) to locate and select

Table 5 File name extensions in DOS, Windows, and OS/2

.AI	Adobe Illustrator subset of .EPS
.BAK	Backup copy of a file that has been edited
.BMP	Bitmap (Windows or OS/2 graphics)
.CDR	Vector graphics (Corel Draw)
.CMD	File of commands (in OS/2)
.COM	Command file (smaller version of .EXE)
.DOC	Document file (ASCII or Microsoft Word)
.DLL	Dynamic link library
.EPS	Vector graphics, encapsulated PostScript format
.EXE	Executable file (machine-language program)
.GIF	Bitmap graphics file (CompuServe format)
.HLP	Help file
.ICO	Icon (Windows or OS/2)
.INI	Initialization file (configuration settings)
.MID	MIDI digitized music file
.PCX	Bitmap graphics file (Zsoft format)
.PIF	Program Information File
.PS	PostScript printable file
.SYS	Component of the operating system
.TEX	TeX or LaTeX document file
.TIF	Bitmap graphics file (TIFF format)
.TMP	Temporary file
.TXT	ASCII text file
.WAV	Sound wave file
.WKQ	Quattro spreadsheet (worksheet) file
.WMF	Windows MetaFile
.WKS	Lotus 123 worksheet file (also WK2, WK3, etc.)
.WRI	Document file (Windows Write)
.XLS	Excel worksheet file
.ZIP	File compressed with PKZIP

the desired character. Or, you may type these special characters by holding down Option and typing the correct code (Macintosh). Windows users must hold down Alt and type a four-digit code on the numeric keypad. *See* ANSI CHARACTER SET for a chart.

EXTENSION

1. (Macintosh) a program that adds to the power and ability of the operating system. Extensions are loaded at boot-up time. Examples of common extensions are *AppleShare* and *QuickTime*. Other extensions customize the operating system for a particular printer.

2. (PC) a three-letter suffix of a file name that often indicates the nature of the file in some operating systems. When typing the file name, a period is used to separate the name from the extension. For example, in the file name MYDOC.TEX, TEX is the file extension. (This is an ASCII file to be used as T_EX input.) *See Table 5* for a listing of some common file extensions.

Note that merely changing the file extension does *not* change the type of file! It would be wonderful if you could change WordPerfect files to bitmaps by changing the name of the file to end in .BMP, but that's not how it works. You have to have conversion programs that *can* change the data in the file. In other words, you can lie to your computer, but doing so won't change the truth.

Extrude

EXTRUDE a special effect provided by drawing programs that creates a three-dimensional shadow. It looks as if the type (actually any object) has been extruded from a cookie gun.

Eye

EYE the enclosed area of the letter e.

Eyedropper

EYEDROPPER a tool available in PAINT and PHOTO-PAINT programs that allows you to match a color in the existing picture, and cause it to become the active color. All you have to do is to click the eyedropper on the area of color you desire and *that* becomes the selected color. You may sample for your primary, secondary, and background colors.

If at first this tool seems senseless, consider what would happen if you were working on a digitized 24-BIT color photograph. There are literally millions of colors available in this format—how are you going to find the right one to extend that background shade over that telephone line? Or how are you going to remember which of those colors you were using yesterday? The eyedropper will let you pick up the right color to use.

The icon shown is from Corel PhotoPaint.

EYEGLASSES FOR COMPUTER USERS eyeglasses for viewing a computer screen. Most eyeglasses are designed for vision at a great distance or for reading at about 18 inches. Neither of these is suitable for looking at a computer screen two or three feet away. In addition, the slight fuzziness of screen images causes some people's eyes to strain themselves trying to get it into sharper focus. As a result, many eyeglass wearers think the computer has harmed their vision, although in fact there is no evidence that computer work (or any other kind of close work) harms the eyes.

Computer screens emit tiny amounts of ultraviolet (UV) light and special glasses are available that block this. However, there is much more UV in ordinary sunlight than in the image on a computer screen, so UV-blocking glasses are probably more beneficial outdoors than in the office.

F

FACSIMILE *see* FAX.

FAT (**F**ile **A**llocation **T**able) the part of the disk that contains information about the sizes and locations of the files. It is like a map to the contents of the disk. If the FAT becomes corrupted, it is necessary to reformat the disk.

FAT BITS a mode in MacPaint that allows you to edit individual PIXELS. The pixels are shown greatly magnified (thus *fat*) on the screen. *See* ZOOM.

FAX a machine that transmits copies (*facsimiles*) of paper documents over telephone lines by converting the appearance of the document into an electronic signal. The output looks much like a photocopy. Software is available to give your computer the ability to send and receive faxes. This will allow you to work with clients across town or across country and to get nearly instantaneous feedback on the current project.

FEATURE a neat trick or ability of a program that is designed to get a little more of your hard-earned money by enticing you to order a new program or upgrade your old one. Some cynics claim that a "feature" is a figment of the software company's support staff — it's merely a bug the programmers haven't fixed yet. (That would technically be a *mis*feature.)

There are many people who fear that, in their desire to outdo one another, the software companies are piling feature upon feature onto their existing programs until the application programs are unwieldy, unworkable messes. (Does anyone really use all the features of WordPerfect 6?)

What can you do? When purchasing software, find a product that suits your needs closely. Are you comfortable with the working screen? Is it clean-looking and well laid-out? Are the menus grouped logically? Does the cursor keep up with you as you type? Does it take a reasonable amount of disk space? That sounds like a good program. However, if you feel confused with all the on-screen clutter, the cursor lags behind your typing and it's anybody's guess which menu the margin settings are under . . . that's another matter.

FILE FORMAT

When the inevitable upgrade offers come in the mail, scrutinize them carefully. Yes, you want the bugs to be fixed, but if you don't want or need new features, there's no reason to purchase the new version of the program. You can have *too many* features.

FILE a block of information stored on disk, tape, or similar media. A file may contain a program, a document, an image, or a collection of data (such as a mailing list or a set of accounting information).

FILE FORMAT a way of arranging information in a file. Almost every computer program has one or more file formats of its own (called NATIVE formats); for example, WordPerfect documents are not in the same format as Microsoft Word documents, and similar programs from different manufacturers cannot necessarily process each other's files. There are three reasons why file formats are diverse:

1. Different programs handle different kinds of data (text versus pictures versus spreadsheets, for example).

2. Different programmers simply pick different ways of doing the same thing. Sometimes, inventing a new format is a point of pride, or is necessary to avoid infringing someone else's copyright or patent.

3. Even when the end result is the same, the way different programs achieve it may be very different. For example, a Windows Paintbrush picture is a *bitmap* (a large grid of dots) but a Corel Draw picture consists of *vector graphics* (instructions to draw lines or shapes in particular positions). The two kinds of pictures are very different from the computer's point of view.

Many programs have the ability to *import* (bring in) files that are not in their own format. But the format of the imported file may not be very well suited to the way the program works, resulting in a loss of quality or partial loss of information (disappearance of italics or footnotes, loss of graphics resolution, inability to edit the imported material, or the like). It is also possible to *export* files to a format other than the usual one, but again, loss of information may occur. *See also* ENCAPSULATED POSTSCIPT.

89

FILL

Fill

FILL   the color of an object. You can imagine what spilling a bucket of paint into a closed shape would do; that's what happens when you ask the computer to fill an object. We take a verbal shortcut and call the color a fill.

In a drawing program, an object that is not completely closed (sometimes it's hard to tell) will not fill. In a paint program, trying to fill an open object can be disastrous. The entire picture will be flooded. Always be ready to UNDO any mistakes.

The usual icon for the fill tool is a spilling bucket of paint or a paint roller. There are many types of fills available; *see also* FOUNTAIN FILLS, LINEAR FILLS, RADIAL FILLS, CONICAL FILLS.

The fill icons shown are from Corel Draw 3 and Corel PhotoPaint.

Filled tools

FILLED TOOLS   tools that create objects filled with a selected color. This type of drawing command is found in BITMAP editing programs (paint and photopaint). Usually several filled tools are provided: rectangle (box), rectangle with rounded corners, circle/ellipse, and polygon. The filled polygon is drawn freehand with the mouse and is allowed to have a very irregular outline.

The icons shown are from Corel PhotoPaint.

FILTER   a transformation that can be applied to a bitmap or portion of a bitmap to alter its appearance. Filters take advantage of the computer's computational power; some of the programming necessary to find the edges of objects in bitmaps is quite sophisticated. A good test of a system's speed is to time how long it takes to apply a filter to a digitized photograph.

Here is a list of filters usually available in photopaint programs—if you'd like more information on a specific effect, see that entry.

BRIGHTNESS	EQUALIZE
CONTRAST	MOTION BLUR
ADD NOISE	PIXELATE
BLUR	REMOVE SPOTS
DIFFUSE	COLOR/GRAY MAP
EDGE DETECT	SHARPEN
EMBOSS	

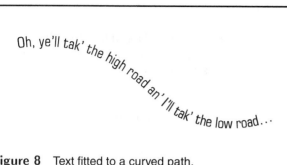

Figure 8   Text fitted to a curved path.

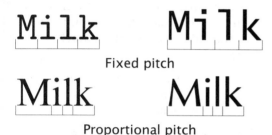

Fixed pitch

Proportional pitch

Figure 9   Fixed and proportional pitch fonts

FIND AND CHANGE   *see* SEARCH AND REPLACE.

FINDER   part of the operating system of the Apple Macintosh. It allows users to copy and manipulate files by moving icons on the DESKTOP. Disk drives are also treated as a special type of file; they can be "opened" and examined like any other file or folder on the desktop.

FIT TEXT TO PATH   a draw program command that warps the baseline of a line of text so that it follows the shape of a specified line (PATH). *See Figure 8* for example.

FIXED DISK   *see* HARD DISK.

FIXED PITCH   type in which all letters are the same width (e.g., *I* the same width as *M*). Most typewriters and nonwindowed computer environments use a fixed-pitch type. If you want to simulate a typewritten page or mimic the output of DOS (for computer documentation), you should use a fixed-pitch typeface such as Courier or American Typewriter. *See Figure 9* to contrast fixed and proportional pitch fonts.

F KEYS *see* FUNCTION KEYS.

FLAG the logotype of a periodical. *See* MASTHEAD, definition 1.

FLARED END SANS SERIF a typeface without serifs whose strokes swell at the ends. Sometimes this flaring is very subtle; at other times the flare is so pronounced that people argue over whether it has turned into a serif. The flared ends help to stabilize the letter designs. Optima, designed by Hermann Zapf, falls into this category.

Fleurons

FLEURON a typographical ornament. Fleurons may be used to mark the beginnings of paragraphs or for purely decorative purposes.

Flip Horizontal

Flip Vertical

Flip

FLIP HORIZONTAL a command that creates a mirror image of the original object. The image still appears right-side up, but left and right are reversed.

FLIP VERTICAL a command that turns an image upside down. The left-right orientation remains the same, just like a reflection in still water. This is *not* equivalent to rotating the object or defined area 180 degrees. (Try it and see.)

FLOATING ILLUSTRATION a picture, graph, table, or other image that should appear near a particular position, but need not be at a particular point in the text. This will allow your page makeup program to adjust the illustration's position as the type rewraps during editing. A nonprinting control code (called an ANCHOR) is inserted in the text to mark the preferred position. The figures in this book are floating illustrations.

FLOPPY DISK *see* DISKETTE.

FLOW to continue text from one page, column, or text box to the next. It helps to visualize the words pouring into the column like a liquid; when the column (or page) is full, the words *flow* into the next column. *See also* RUN AROUND, WRAP.

Figure 10   A fly-out menu.

FLUSH LEFT aligned to start each line at the
horizontal position, making a neat left edge.
Flush Left, ragged right means that the length of
the lines are allowed to vary. The right edge looks
like a torn piece of paper—in other words, *ragged*.
Legibility studies have shown that people can read
most quickly when text is set flush left because their
eyes have a set beginning point to come back to
at the end of each line. This paragraph is set
flush left, ragged right.

Type set flush left *and* right is also called JUSTI-
FIED type.

FLUSH RIGHT aligned to make each line of type
end at the same horizontal position.
The beginnings of the lines are irregular,
but the right margin is smooth. This paragraph
is set flush right, ragged left.
Avoid setting long texts flush right because readers find it tiring; their eyes have to search for the line
beginnings at each new line. Flush right is good for
headlines, charts, and tables.

FLY-OUT MENU a secondary menu that appears to
the side when you select an item of the primary menu
or TOOLBOX. The fly-out menu will give you several
options. For example, CorelDraw's zoom tool has a
fly-out that lets you select plus or minus zoom, 1:1
ratio, zoom to see all objects or full page view. *See
Figure 10*. Fly-out menus are good for keeping main
menus and toolboxes concise and uncluttered.

FOLD a bindery operation that folds a printed page. There are many different ways that brochures can be folded. Sometimes all of the folds are parallel to each other, but it is also possible to make the second fold at right angles to the first. To ensure that the final piece is folded the way you want it to be, make a DUMMY to show the printer. Also indicate with dashed lines on the margins of the camera-ready copy where the folds should be. *See* TRI-FOLD BROCHURE.

FOLDER

1. a directory on the Macintosh. Folders can contain programs, data files, and other folders. To open a folder, double-click on its icon. *See* HIERARCHICAL FILE SYSTEM.

2. groups of software icons on the Desktop on OS/2.

3. a machine that folds paper.

FOLIO

1. the page number. In newspapers and magazines, the folio often includes the date and the name of the publication as well. The folio can be at the top, bottom, or even the side of a page.

2. a sheet of paper, folded once, giving you four pages. A simple newsletter is usually a single folio.

3. a large book, over 12 inches high. Libraries have to maintain special sections for these oversize books.

FONT a complete collection of characters (including upper and lower case letters, numerals, punctuation, ligatures, reference marks, etc.), in a consistent style and size. *See Figure 11*. Most desktop publishing programs and word processors let you use more than one font in a single document. When you switch to italics or to bold or to a larger size, you are changing the *font* even though you may still be in the same TYPE FAMILY.

Some fonts are specifically designed to be printed at a particular size. For instance, if you have 8-point Dutch Roman and 12-point Dutch Roman on your laser printer font cartridge, you cannot use intermediate sizes such as 9-point. If the largest font you

ABCDEFGHIJKLMNOPQRSTUVWXYZ
abcdefghijklmnopqrstuvwxyz
!"#$%&'()*+,-./0123456789:;<=>?
@[\]^_`~,ƒ„…†‡^‰Š‹Œ''""•——˜™š›œŸ¡¢£¤¥¦§
¨ª«¬-®¯°±²³´µ¶·¸¹º»¼½¾¿
ÀÁÂÃÄÅÆÇÈÉÊËÌÍÎÏÐÑ
ÒÓÔÕÖ×ØÙÚÛÜÝÞß
àáâãäåæçèéêëìíîïðñòóôõö÷øùúûüýþÿ

Figure 11   A complete font for Windows.

have is 72-points, then you will not be able to set 96-point type. SCALABLE FONTS allow us to get around these limitations. (It's also muddying the definition of a font. In a scalable font, one set of character definitions will allow you to set type in any practical size. One font—many sizes. *See* SCALABLE FONT.)

FONT CARTRIDGE   a plug-in device for a laser printer or certain other printers that contains additional fonts recorded on ROM chips.

FOOLSCAP   a traditional British paper size, 8×13 inches, now being superseded by ISO A4. *See* PAPER SIZES (ISO).

FOOT   the bottom of the page. Opposite: HEAD.

FOOTNOTE   a short comment placed at the bottom (FOOT) of a page that provides a citation or insightful comment to the text.* Some word processors will not handle footnotes properly, placing them at the end of the chapter or article rather than at the foot of the page where they belong. When setting type for ACADEMIC STANDARDS be sure that your software can handle the required format for footnotes.

Footnotes should be numbered consecutively throughout an entire book, or beginning again for each chapter or page. Sometimes footnotes are not

*This is a footnote. Notice that the asterisk in the footnote matches the asterisk in the text. The typeface used for the footnote is smaller than the font used for the body copy. A horizontal rule or space should be used to separate the footnote from the text.

numbered, but are referenced by a traditional set of symbols. They should be used in this order: ASTERISK (*), DAGGER (†), DOUBLE DAGGER (‡), SECTION SIGN (§), and PILCROW (¶).

FOOTPRINT the amount of space a piece of equipment takes up on a desk. A smaller footprint is desirable because it leaves more space for other items on your desk.

FORCE QUIT (Macintosh) to wrest control away from a HUNG application program. Holding down Command, Option, and pressing Escape should return you to the Finder. Unfortunately, all work done since the last "Save" command will be lost. *See* HANG; CRASH.

The analogous Windows command is holding down Control, Alt and pressing Del. *See* CTRL-ALT-DEL.

FOREGROUND the parts of a picture that appear closest to the viewer. When creating an illustration, you should create the background first, then add objects in the far distance, then the middle ground, and, lastly, layer the foreground objects on top.

FOREIGN LANGUAGES languages other than English. Typesetting of any foreign language requires knowledge of the language *and* its typesetting conventions, many of which will not be known to a native speaker not trained in typography. Detailed information about a number of languages is given in the *Chicago Manual of Style;* for a comprehensive handbook, see G. F. Von Ostermann's *Manual of Foreign Languages,* available at most libraries. *See also* ACCENTS, CAPITALIZATION, FRENCH, GERMAN, SPANISH.

FOREWORD an introduction to a book. A foreword is usually written by someone other than the author. *See* PREFACE for contrast.

FORMAL a style of layout dictated by precise rules of classical typography. All type is centered and line breaks are carefully adjusted to give a pleasing shape to the text.

FOR POSITION ONLY a low-resolution image used to mark the place where artwork will be STRIPPED IN later. Always write "FPO" in black ink on the low-resolution image so it will not be mistaken for the final artwork.

FOUNTAIN FILL a fill that is composed of two colors. In between the two colors is a smooth blending. You are able to rotate the angle of the fill (linear) or have the blend radiate from a central point (radial). *See also* RADIAL FILL; CONICAL FILL.

Fountain fill

FOUNTAIN STRIPES stripes or banding visible in a fountain fill. This is often a side effect of the DITHERING used to display the different colors on your monitor. Also called *banding*.

FOUR UP to print four items on a single sheet of paper. This is an efficient way of reproducing small items such as tickets or business cards. *See* GANG UP.

FPO *see* FOR POSITION ONLY.

FRACTAL a shape that contains an infinite amount of fine detail. No matter how much you enlarge the shape, more detail will become visible. Fractals are very common in nature; examples are jagged edges of paper, coastlines, shapes of rocks, etc.

Four up

The use of fractal mathematics makes it possible to get some very sophisticated results in paint programs. The smear of the chalk, the blur of the watercolors, partial erasures, the translucence of the airbrush are all computed on the fly with fractals.

FRACTION a number representing a portion of a whole unit. Fractions often pose challenges for typesetters; there are many different ways to set them, some more elegant than others.

- **Case fractions** are one ASCII character. They are two small numbers separated by a slash or horizontal rule. These are supplied by the font designer; unfortunately you are usually limited to a handful of the most common fractions.

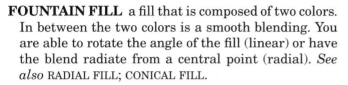

Case fraction

- **Piece fractions** look the same as case fractions but are actually constructed of three characters: the small numerator and denominator separated by a slash or horizontal bar. You can use piece fractions to supplement the font's collection of

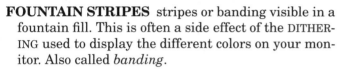

Piece fraction

case fractions. Some word processors have tools and macros that speed the building of piece fractions. For example, TEX can construct fractions with any numbers. Other word processors cannot do piece fractions and the typesetter must settle for *adaptable fractions*. Piece fractions are also called SPLIT FRACTIONS.

$$1/2$$
Adaptable fraction

- **Adaptable fractions** are set by separating two full-sized numbers by a slash. Less elegant than the other two methods, but considered acceptable if piece fractions are not available. Also called BUILT FRACTIONS.

FRAGMENTATION   a state in which many files on a hard disk are broken into little chunks and stored in physically different areas of the disk platter. This can dramatically slow down access time and create long waits while files are being read or written.

A disk becomes fragmented when many files are created and erased on it over a long period of time. Files are recorded continuously on an empty disk, but as files of various sizes get erased, empty spots develop which gradually become filled in with parts of newly-recorded files.

A disk can be defragmented by copying all the files to another disk. Programs exist that will defragment a disk "in place" by carefully rearranging the files without copying to another disk.

FRAME   an invisible box that can contain text or graphics; the building block of most page layout programs. The page is considered a frame. As the layout is constructed, frames are layered one on top of another. Some contain text, others will hold graphics. Text frames can be dynamically linked so that the words will flow to the second frame when the first one is full. RUN AROUNDS are created by placing a graphic frame across a portion of the text frame. *See* PAGE LAYOUT SOFTWARE.

FRAME GRABBER   an accessory board that takes an image from a video camera, VCR, or other video input and DIGITIZES it, creating a bitmap image. A video image consists of *frames* (successive pictures) transmitted at the rate of 60 per second, and the frame grabber must *grab* and digitize one of these.

FRENCH the language of France, Québec, and parts of Africa. French typography differs from that of English in numerous ways.

Besides the regular alphabet, French uses the characters:

À à Â â Ç ç É é È è Ê ê Ë ë Î î Ï ï Ô ô Œ œ Ù ù Û û

However, most typesetters omit some or all of the accents on capital letters; some use only *É* and no other accented capitals. It is acceptable to typeset Œ and *œ* as *OE, Oe,* or *oe* as appropriate.

Instead of English quotation marks, French uses *guillemets* «like this».

However, conversations in novels generally use dashes to indicate changes of speaker, thus:

— Are you coming? he asked.
— Yes, right away.
— Excellent! replied the inspector. We shall be glad to see you!

FUNCTION KEYS (F keys) keys labeled F1 through F12 on the IBM PC and PS/2 keyboards (F1 through F10 on earlier models). Their function depends on the software being used. For example, WordPerfect uses F1 to cancel the last command given.

G

GANG UP to print more than one item on a single sheet of paper. After printing, the finished work is then cut apart. Ganging up is most efficient when printing small items such as business cards or tickets. If you have ten tickets to a page, you are said to be printing the tickets *ten up*.

Handgloves

Garalde

GARALDE typefaces in which the axis of stress is to the left; the serifs are bracketed and the bar of the lower case *e* is horizontal. The stroke contrast is greater than that of the HUMANIST TYPEFACES. Garamond is a good example of a garalde face. Sometimes this classification is called OLD STYLE.

GB *see* GIGABYTE.

Handgloves

Geometric

GEOMETRIC a category of sans-serif typefaces designed on the basis of simple geometric shapes. Usually, geometric typefaces have no contrast in stroke width and have a single-story *a*. Eurostyle is a good example.

GERMAN the language of Germany and Austria. In addition to the regular alphabet, German uses the following characters:

Ä ä Ö ö Ü ü ß

Note that *ß* is a ligature for *ss* and is not the same as Greek beta (*β*). In fact, it is completely acceptable to set *ss* in place of it.

If *Ä Ö Ü* are not available, they can be set as *AE, OE, UE* (in all caps) or *Ae, Oe, Ue* (at the beginning of capitalized words) respectively. In short German quotations in English context, it is acceptable to set *ä ö ü* as *ae oe ue*. Do not make changes in the opposite direction; *Goethe,* for example, is never written *Göthe.*

German quotation marks look „like this" — quite different from their English counterparts. Guillemets are sometimes used (*see* FRENCH), but they often point in the opposite direction than in French, »like this«.

In hyphenation, *ck* changes to *kk* when split; thus *Neckar, Nek-kar.*

All nouns are capitalized, as are the polite pronouns *Sie, Ihr, Ihnen* 'you' (but not the otherwise identical-looking pronouns that mean 'her,' 'they,' and 'their').

See also FOREIGN LANGUAGES; ACCENTS.

GHOST a dotted outline of an icon that moves with the mouse pointer while the icon is being moved.

Ghost

GIF **G**raphics **I**nterchange **F**ormat; a format developed by CompuServe for storing bitmap images on disk. (*See* BITMAP.) GIF images can have up to 64,000 pixels and 256 colors. For comparison, *see* TIFF; PCX.

The pronunciation of "GIF" varies from region to region. Some pronounce it like "gift" without the *t* at the end; others claim it is a soft *g* as in "giraffe."

GIGABYTE (GB) approximately one billion bytes (2^{30} = 1,073,741,824 to be precise). It would take 715 HD diskettes (and an excruciatingly long time) to back up a 1 gigabyte hard disk.

GLOSS POINTS areas that look like shiny reflections. In a typeface such as Carino, gloss points are used to give a three-dimensional effect.

Gloss points

GLYPH any printable character.

GLYPHIC a typeface that appears to have been chiseled rather than drawn.

Handgloves

Glyphic

GOTHIC

1. sans-serif type in which all the strokes have the same thickness.

2. BLACK LETTER typefaces.

Handgloves

Gothic (1)

Handgloves

Gothic (2)

GPF a **G**eneral **P**rotection **F**ault; caused when a piece of software tries to use a portion of the computer's memory that was reserved for another use by Windows. As with other types of software crashes, GPF's lose all work done since the last "Save." Windows does *usually* manage to show an alert box fingering the guilty software. Numerous GPFs are a sign of a serious programming problem — you should re-evaluate the software involved.

GRADIENT PAINT ROLLER a tool available in some paint and photopaint programs that fills an area with a two-toned color scheme. This is analogous to a FOUNTAIN FILL in a DRAW PROGRAM.

Gradient Paint Roller

The icon shown is from Corel PhotoPaint.

GRAIN the direction of the fibers that make up a piece of paper. It is often important to note the grain of the paper, particularly when the finished job is to be folded. Paper will fold more crisply *with* the grain rather than across it. Laser printers tend to jam less with LONG GRAIN paper (paper in which the fibers run parallel to the long side of the paper).

GRAPH a graphical display of information, designed to make it easier for the reader to interpret and understand numerical data. *See* CHART.

GRAPHICAL USER INTERFACE (GUI) a way of communicating with the computer by manipulating icons (pictures) and windows with a mouse. It seems to be a superior method for training novice computer users. The menus help prevent annoying typing errors, and most commands have keyboard shortcuts for more advanced users. *See* MACINTOSH; WINDOWS; WIMP.

One of the benefits of so many software developers adopting GUIs is *standardization*. A computer user who is familiar with the Macintosh style interface can quickly adapt to Microsoft Windows and *vice versa*. In a way, this is analogous to automobile design: you can depend on the accelerator being to the right of the brake pedal, but the headlight switch can be almost anywhere on the dashboard. At any rate, you can drive the car.

GRAPHICS the use of computer output devices, such as laser printers and imagesetters, to produce pictures.

There are two basic ways to tell a computer how to draw a picture. In VECTOR GRAPHICS, the computer is told to put an imaginary pen in a particular position and then draw a line to another specific point. This mimics a plotter, and is the way that drawing programs (such as MacDraw, Adobe Illustrator, and CorelDraw) work. The drawing is held in the computer's memory as a series of formulas and attributes. The vector graphic can be enlarged without showing jagged edges. The amount of detail is limited only by the chosen output device. If you print to a laser printer, the RESOLUTION is probably 300-DPI; a service bureau can give you a 2400-DPI printout from their imagesetter.

The alternative is RASTER GRAPHICS, in which the screen is divided into a rectangular array of points (called PIXELS from "picture cells"), and the computer is told what color each dot should be. These BITMAPS can consume gigantic amounts of memory and disk storage space. However, raster graphics make it possible to edit photographs and produce drawings that resemble NATURAL MEDIA. You should create raster graphics at the size they are to be used. If you reduce them, you will lose detail. If you enlarge them, the pixels will become very prominent and diagonal lines will have a jagged "stair step" effect. *See* RESOLUTION.

GRAPHICS TABLET an alternative pointing device. A graphics tablet consists of a pressure-sensitive pad on which you draw with a special STYLUS. This is much more natural than a mouse for using draw or paint programs.

GRAVE ACCENT the accent mark in è. *See* ACCENTS.

è

Grave accent

GRAVURE a method of printing by etching the image into a metal plate, making a series of pits to hold the ink. After being inked, the image is transferred by pressing the absorbent paper against the plate. *Contrast* LETTERPRESS; OFFSET LITHOGRAPHY.

Arrange	
Align	Ctrl + A
To Front	Shift + PgUp
To Back	Shift + PgDn
Forward One	PgUp
Back One	PgDn
Reverse Order	

Grayed

GRAYED not available for selection. If a menu option appears in light gray rather than black type, it cannot be chosen. For example, if you wish to align two objects, the align command will be grayed (or DIMMED) until you have two or more objects selected. If you click on a grayed command, nothing happens.

GRAYSCALE

1. a series of boxes filled with a range of black tints from pure white to 100 percent black. A grayscale is used to test a printer, monitor, scanner or printing press.

2. (scanner terminology) the range of grays in an image as measured by the scanner.

3. a description of any image that contains shades of gray as well as black and white.

Greeked text

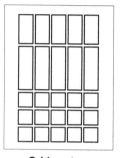

Grid system

Handgloves

Grotesque

GREEKING the use of random letters (Lorem ipsum dolor . . .) or marks to show the overall appearance of a printed page without showing the actual text. It's useful to use greeked text in a presentation comp when the text has not yet been drafted. With computers, greeking is used when the page is displayed too small for the text to be legible on screen. Some software lets you set the level below which text will be greeked.

GRID a feature of various draw programs and paint programs that allows lines and objects to be drawn only in certain positions. Objects in a draw program seem to have a magnetic attraction to the grid (this is called *"snapping to"* the grid). Although it's excellent for aligning type and making precise diagrams, you will sometimes have to turn the grid off to make fine adjustments.

GRID SYSTEM a way of standardizing the layout of many related pages, such as the pages of a multipage document. The designer first draws a grid that will define the possible positions of columns, horizontal divisions, and pictures. Not all the possibilities of the grid are used on any single page, but the grid ensures that column positions do not vary haphazardly and makes all the pages look related. *See* MASTER PAGE, STYLE SHEET.

GRIPPER ALLOWANCE a small margin (usually $\frac{1}{4}$ inch) that cannot be printed on because that is where tiny teeth (called *grippers*) catch the paper and pull it through the press.

GROTESK *see* GROTESQUE.

GROTESQUE a type of sans-serif typeface based on 19th-century designs. Grotesque types are characterized by having a squared look to the curves of the round letters. There is some contrast between the thick and thin strokes and the ends of the curved strokes are horizontal. Examples of this category would be Grotesque (designed 1832) and Headline. *See also* NEO-GROTESQUE.

GROUP (Draw program) to cause the computer to treat a number of objects as a single object. The indi-

104

vidual objects of a group retain their own attributes (see COMBINE for contrast). Most importantly, a group can be sized, stretched and moved as if it were one object. If you have several objects that form a complex element in a drawing, it is a good idea to *group* the objects to allow them to retain their relative position. It is surprisingly easy to make a mistake with the mouse and dislocate something. The grouped object can be UNGROUPED if needed.

GUI *see* GRAPHICAL USER INTERFACE.

GUIDELINES nonprinting lines that aid in aligning text and other objects in a draw program or page layout program. Some programs allow you to turn on a SNAP-TO-GUIDELINES feature that causes the guidelines and objects to have a magnetic attraction for each other.

GUILLEMETS "duck feet" style quotation marks «like this»; also called CHEVRONS. *See* FRENCH.

Guillemets

GUTTER the blank space between columns of type or pages. Some methods of binding will require larger middle gutters because the book cannot be opened fully. *See* BINDING.

GX FONT (Macintosh) a scalable font format that provides a very large character set — a single font can contain the standard alphanumeric characters, a full EXPERT SET (small caps, oldstyle figures, accented characters, ligatures), alternate characters, and swashes. A GX font can hold up to 16,000 characters. These new fonts will be programmable — the computer will be able give you more extensive typographic control, or to mix in alternate characters, or find an appropriate place to use a SWASH. GX fonts can presently only be used on Macintoshes running System 7.1 (or higher) and the QuickDraw GX extension. *See* SYSTEM 7.5.

H

Hairline

HAIRLINE a very thin line, usually about .003 of an inch, the thinnest line that a 300 DPI laser printer can print.

HAIR SPACE a very thin space, equal in width to a hairline (.003 of an inch).

HALF TITLE the very first right-hand page of a book. A half title page contains the title only; the full title page comes on the next right-hand page.

Halftone

HALFTONE the reproduction of a CONTINUOUS TONE image by converting it into a series of very small dots. In the margin is an enlargement of a halftone image. You can see that the dots vary in size. At a normal reading distance this gives the impression of shades of gray. All photographs must be printed as halftones. If artwork contains shades of gray or colors, it, too, will need to be halftoned before being printed. *See also* PROCESS COLOR; COLOR SEPARATIONS. *Contrast* LINE DRAWING.

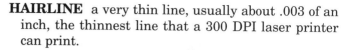

Handgloves
HANDGLOVEſ
Handgloves

Type samples

HANDGLOVES a word that is often used to set a small sample of type because the letters in it give a good representation of how the type designer handled the more challenging letters. You have, at a glance, a feel for the X-HEIGHT of the typeface, whether there are SERIFS or not, a reference for how EXTENDED or CONDENSED it is, how high the ASCENDERS go, how low the DESCENDERS go, whether the strokes are STRESSED or all of the same thickness, and the weight of the font. You'll know whether the LOWER-CASE *a* and *g* are ONE or TWO-STORIED, and if the *e* has a horizontal or slanted cross-stroke. The *o* and *s* are good examples of rounded letters and the *v* shows how diagonal strokes are handled.

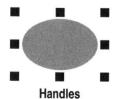

Handles

HANDLES the little black boxes at the corners and midpoints of BOUNDING BOXES. Handles give you a place to "grab" onto an object with the mouse and manipulate it. They only appear when an object is selected. Dragging a corner handle (any one of the four) will SCALE the object. Dragging a midpoint handle will stretch or shrink the object in one dimension.

HAND TOOL a tool available in some graphical environments that allows you to move the picture around the screen. If there is a Hand Tool provided, there will usually not be SCROLL BARS at the side and bottom of the viewing window.

Hand tool

The Hand icon shown is from Corel PhotoPaint.

HANG to cause a computer to come to a dead halt, so that it refuses to show any sign of activity or accept input from the keyboard, mouse or any other input device. The culprit is a software bug; unfortunately, all the poor computer user can do is to reboot the machine, thus losing all changes since the file was saved. Also called a *freeze*.

HANGING INDENT *See* HANGING TAB.

HANGING PUNCTUATION the practice of allowing small punctuation marks (commas, periods, quotes) to extend beyond the normal column margins. Optically, this gives a straighter edge to the column—the punctuation marks do not carry enough weight to fill the space.

HANGING TAB a new paragraph indicated by letting the first word extend to the left past the normal margin into the GUTTER. The opposite of INDENTION. Also called OUTDENT. The terms in this dictionary are set as hanging tabs.

Happy Mac

HAPPY MAC the icon of a smiling Macintosh that greets when you turn on your Macintosh and everything is well. *Contrast* SAD MAC.

HARD COPY a printout on paper of the computer's output (as opposed to the ephemeral and abstract copy that exists in the computer's memory or on disk).

HARD DISK a magnetic data storage medium using rigid aluminum disks coated with iron oxide. The read-write head travels across the disk on a thin cushion of air without actually touching the disk.

Hard disks have much greater storage capacity than do diskettes. Originally, 10 MEGABYTES was a common size for personal computer hard disks. More recently, 1 GIGABYTE disks have become available. Hard disks are sometimes called FIXED DISKS because they cannot be easily removed from the computer. *See* DISK, DISKETTE; HARD-DISK MANAGEMENT.

HARD DISK MANAGEMENT the practice of using a hard disk effectively. Here are some tips:

- Learn how to back up your hard disk, and do it frequently. *Every hard disk in use today will break down within just a few years!*

- Divide the disk into subdirectories (*see* DIRECTORY) and put related files in each subdirectory (e.g., all word processing files in one directory and all spreadsheet files in another). Use a further level of subdirectories where appropriate, that is, to separate letters from reports within the word processing directory.

- Delete files that you no longer need. Make a directory called JUNK or TEMP in which to put files that will not be needed very long, so that they will not clutter up other directories.

- Run a defragmentation program every few months. This will speed up disk access time. *See* FRAGMENTATION.

- (DOS, Windows) Use the PATH command in your AUTOEXEC.BAT file so that your commonly used commands will work no matter what directory you are in.

- (DOS) Use the command prompt `$P$G` so that the command prompt will tell you what directory you are in (e.g. `C:\MYDIR>` rather than just `C>`). Again, this command can be in your AUTOEXEC.BAT file.

- (DOS) Run CHKDSK or its equivalent to check for lost clusters (portions of files that have become separated from the main file and do not have a correct directory entry).

- (Mac) Periodically rebuild the Desktop by holding down Command and Option at bootup. This should speed up system performance.

Hard edge

HARD EDGE an edge that is smooth and sharp, with no blending or blurring of the boundary. Opposite: SOFT EDGE.

HARD HYPHEN *see* REQUIRED HYPHEN.

HARD PAGE a forced page break. In WordPerfect and Windows Write, the way to type a hard page is to hold down Control while pressing the Enter key.

HARDWARE the physical elements of a computer, such as the monitor, cables, motherboard, and mouse. *Contrast* SOFTWARE.

HAT the CIRCUMFLEX character (^).

^

Hat

HD *see* HIGH DENSITY.

HEAD

　　1. the part of a disk drive that reads and writes information magnetically. A double-sided disk drive or multilayered hard disk has a head for each side of each layer. (*See* DISK.)

　　2. the top of a page or printed piece (such as a newsletter).

　　3. short for a HEADLINE.

HEADLINE a title set in type larger and bolder than the body copy. Although headlines are usually set at the top (HEAD) of the page, some advertisements place headlines in totally unexpected places for the pure shock value.

　　Headlines may be set in a different type family than the body copy. Consider using a more decorative or unusual font to catch the reader's attention. Because the headline is usually short and set in a large size, very complicated letterforms can be used without compromising readability.

HEAD-TO-HEAD paper printed on two sides with the top the same on both sides.

HEAD-TO-TAIL paper printed on two sides with the back side upside down relative to the front. Use head-to-tail when you want or expect the reader to flip the paper over instead of turning it like a page.

HEAVY bold.

HELP an on-screen facility offered by most application programs. Help is usually accessed from the MENU BAR. For example, if you have forgotten how a particular command works, you can click on "Help" and get instant information. Many programs try to guess

Handgloves
Helvetica

guess what you are going to ask for. This is called CONTEXT-SENSITIVE HELP. Some help files are so well organized that they threaten to supplant the manual. *See* HYPERTEXT.

HELVETICA a sans-serif typeface designed by M. Miedinger (circa 1957). Helvetica is one of the most popular and widely distributed typefaces and can be recognized by its even stroke widths, two-storied lower case *a* (with a curved tail), the lower-case *g* resembling the *q*, and the oblique tail on the capital *Q*. It is available in a variety of widths and strokes.

HIERARCHICAL FILE SYSTEM organization of files into levels or layers. Items have a hierarchical arrangement if an item can be thought of as "below," or "belonging to," another item that is at a higher level. At the very top level of the hierarchy is an item (called the *root*) that is not below any other items.

Hierarchical items can be thought of as an inverted tree, with the root at the top and other items branching out below. For example, the executive branch of the U.S. government can be thought of as a hierarchy with the president at the top, cabinet secretaries one level down, and various bureau and office directors and their staffs below the secretaries.

The files on your computer's hard disk have a HIERARCHICAL structure. The main directory (or folder) contains other directories (or folders) which may in turn contain others. *See* DIRECTORY.

HIEROGLYPH a type of writing practiced by the ancient Egyptians using pictures to represent words and sounds. Some of these hieroglyphs were adapted by the Phoenicians and evolved into our alphabet.

HIGH DENSITY (HD) a diskette that records considerably more data per inch than the earlier double-density (DD) format. (A high density $3\frac{1}{2}$-inch diskette can hold 1.4 Mb versus 720 Kb for DD; in the $5\frac{1}{4}$-inch size, HD holds 1.2 Mb, DD holds 360 Kb.) If your computer has an older DD disk drive, it will not be able to read or write HD diskettes. An HD drive can read and write to both types of diskettes. When buying diskettes, make sure you purchase the correct type for your disk drive.

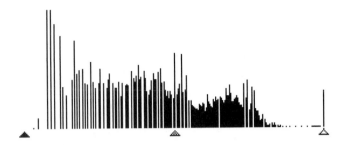

Figure 12   A histogram

Preformatted diskettes are available for both Macintosh and IBM-compatible computers.

HIGHLIGHT
  1. in a GUI environment, how the computer shows you which objects are currently selected or which items are the default choices. Different things have different methods of showing they are highlighted. Text or menu commands appear in reverse type. BUTTONS are a little different. It is sometimes difficult to see the method of highlighting used on buttons, but you should look for a thicker border. OPTION BUTTONS have black dots inside the selected choices.
  2. an area that is lighter than the rest of an object or image. Highlights help to round objects and indicate the source of lighting. Use the BLEND command to create highlights that merge smoothly into the background (draw program). When scanning an image, you may have to mark for the computer which area you wish to be the brightest so that the contrast of the photograph or artwork can be adjusted. *See also* SHADOW.

HINTING additional information encoded into a digital font to help the computer software correctly display and print the letters at different sizes and resolutions.

HISTOGRAM a bar graph in which the bars represent how many times something occurs. Histograms are often used in photopaint programs and scanner software to allow direct manipulation of the image characteristics. Each bar represents the total number of pixels of a particular shade of gray. By sliding the endpoints closer together, you decrease the image contrast; sliding the endpoints apart increases contrast. *See also* CHART; BRIGHTNESS; CONTRAST.

Hollow tools

HOLLOW TOOLS commands that create hollow objects in a BITMAP editing program (paint and photopaint). Usually several hollow tools are provided: rectangle (box), rectangle with rounded corners, circle/elipse, and polygon. The polygon is drawn freehand with the mouse and may have a very irregular outline. *Contrast* FILL TOOLS.

The icons shown are from Corel PhotoPaint.

HOME PAGE a screenful of information made available to the public through the Internet via HTTP (**H**yper**t**ext **T**ransfer **P**rotocol). The home page for a person or institution is the page that users are expected to read first in order to access other pages. Home pages are text files written in HTML. *See* WORLD WIDE WEB; HTML; ELECTRONIC PUBLISHING.

HOMOPHONE one of two (or more) words which sound alike but have very different meanings and spellings. Examples would be to/too/two, and their/there/they're. Be alert for these words when proofreading. A spell checker will *not* catch a misused homophone. *See* SPELLING.

HORIZONTAL side to side; across.

HOT SPOT the exact spot of a pointer (or any mouse cursor) that needs to touch an object to select it. The very tip of the arrow is the hot spot for the pointer.

HOT TYPE type cast in metal and set by hand or machine. *Contrast* COLD TYPE.

HOT ZONE the area at the end of a line of type which triggers the computer to hyphenate words. If a word extends into the hot zone, it will be hyphenated to make it fit on the line. *See* HYPHENATION.

HOURGLASS ICON a Windows icon that means

"Wait." It is analogous to the watch icon in the Macintosh environment. Your computer is too busy to accept any input from the keyboard or mouse and will beep if you try to interrupt its computations.

Hourglass

HSB **H**ue, **S**aturation, **B**rightness; a standard method of describing color. Hue is what artists call color; whether the color in question is blue or orange—that is its *hue*. Saturation refers to how *pure* the hue is. If you add a contrasting color (let's say we add some red to a pure green), you *decrease* its saturation. Brightness refers to how light or dark the hue is (whether we add white or black). HSB is the preferred method of describing colors for someone who paints; the process is very similar to mixing pigments. Be aware that this is an internal description, just between you and your software. When you ask for color separations, the software will generate CMYK plates for the printer.

HTML (**H**ypertext **M**arkup **L**anguage) a set of codes that can be inserted into text files to indicate special typefaces, inserted images, and links to other hypertext documents.

The main use of HTML is to publish information on the Internet. (*See* WORLD WIDE WEB). Here is a simple example of an HTML document:

```
<TITLE>The University of Georgia</TITLE>
<P>
<IMG SRC="ugaseal.gif">
<H1>U.Ga.</H1>
<P>
The University of Georgia is located in
Athens, Georgia, 75 miles east of Atlanta.
It was founded in 1785 and is the oldest
state university.
```

Here <TITLE> and </TITLE> mark the beginning and end of the title, and <P> marks paragraph breaks. <IMG SRC=*filename*> embeds an image in the document; many image formats are supported, but GIF is the most popular. Codes for special typefaces include the following:

<H1> ... </H1>	Heading, size 1 (largest)
<H6> ... </H6>	Heading, size 6 (smallest)
<B> ... </B>	Boldface

`<I> ... </I>`	Italics
`<U> ... </U>`	Boldface
`<T> ... </T>`	Typewriter type (`like this`)

A link to another document looks like this:

```
<A HREF="xxxxx.html">Click here.</A>
```

That means "Jump to file XXXXX.HTML (another HTML document) if the user clicks on the words 'Click here.'" A URL can appear in place of the file name. Additional codes support menus and neatly displayed lists. Comments (to be ignored by the HTML system) look like this:

```
<! This is a comment >
```

Even with no special codes in it, a text file is still a valid HTML document.

HTTP (**H**ypertext **T**ransfer **P**rotocol) a standard method of publishing information as hypertext in HTML format on the Internet. *See* HYPERTEXT; HTML; INTERNET; WORLD WIDE WEB.

HUE color. *See* HSB.

HUMANIST

Handgloves

Humnanist (1)

1. typefaces closely derived from 15th century handwriting; Centaur is a good example. The cross stroke of the *e* is slanted, stress is to the left, and the contrast between the thick and thin strokes is low. Also, the lower case ascenders are finished with an oblique serif. This classification is sometimes called VENETIAN.

Handgloves

Humanist (2)

2. a subcategory of sans-serif typefaces. These are sans-serif typefaces whose proportions are based on the traditional Roman capitals (as inscribed on the Trajan column) rather than mechanical models (as were the Grotesques). Optima and Gill Sans are considered humanist designs.

HUNG INITIAL a display initial placed outside the left margin of the body type. *See* DISPLAY INITIAL for illustration.

HUNG PUNCTUATION small punctuation marks placed outside of the normal column margins in order to present a visually straighter boundary.

HYPERTEXT a kind of document (called a *hyperdoc-ument*) that presents information that can be connected together in many different ways, instead of ordered sequentially as is done in a book. A hypertext document will present a computer screen with information (text, graphics, color, or sound). The user will have different options as to what related screen to go to next; typically options are selected by a mouse. Encyclopedic information is especially suitable for hypertext. Each entry would represent a screen of information; each cross reference would be a button that you could select if you wished to move immediately to that entry.

The help file that gives information about how to use a piece of software is also suitable for hypertext. The computer user does not need to read the help file information in order; instead, the user needs to choose whatever information is helpful at the moment.

There is a danger that the user might become lost in the middle of the hyperdocument. A good hyperdocument should include some navigational aids to allow the user to see an overview or index of the document. It is helpful if the computer maintains a record of the path that was followed, both so the user can go backwards and so the path can be retraced. Often a hyperdocument follows a particular sequence automatically if the user does not want to make the choices.

Hypertext documents can be difficult to create because of the need to establish all of the connections. Hypercard for the Macintosh is one hypertext-authoring software that has become popular.

A large hyperdocument (an encyclopedia for example) requires large amounts of storage, such as provided by a CD-ROM.

HYPHENATION the practice of breaking words in between syllables at the end of a line. This allows more text to be fit in the given space and makes the ends of the lines more even. Correct hyphenations follow one simple rule: *make both pieces pronounceable, and neither one excessively short.* In English, this can be elaborated as follows:

- If a word is a compound of shorter words, break it into meaningful parts; thus *headache* should be split as *head-ache,* not *hea-dache.*
- As far as possible, split between consonants, as long as the resulting pieces can be pronounced correctly; thus *bet-ter, par-lor.* But do not break up clusters such as *th, sh, ch.*
- If there is only one consonant between two vowels, it should usually go with the second vowel; thus *de-re-lict,* not *der-el-ict.*

There is often more than one acceptable way to break up a word, and dictionaries often disagree with each other.

Most desktop publishing software can automatically hyphenate text. The computer tries to put as many words as possible on one line. When it enters the last half inch of the line (the HOT ZONE), it calculates whether the next word will fit; if not, the word is looked up in the hyphenation dictionary, or hyphenated according to phonetic rules.

Fully justified type will always look better when hyphenated; otherwise LOOSE LINES (lines with big gaps between the words) become a problem. If you are setting type flush left, ragged right, be aware that the size of the hot zone will affect how ragged the right margin is. It's considered bad typesetting to have three or more lines in a row end in hyphens. Try increasing the hot zone and see if this corrects the problem. You may need to manually override the computer to get the effect that you want.

Proofread carefully for unfortunate line breaks. The traditional example is the word "therapist" — don't let the computer hyphenate it as "the-rapist." Learn how to mark REQUIRED HYPHENS so that hyphenated names and phone numbers won't be broken across lines. *See also* REQUIRED HYPHEN, DISCRETIONARY HYPHEN.

I

I-BAR symbol showing the mouse cursor in a text editing environment. The height of the I-bar will give an indication of the size type currently selected.

I-bar

IBM International Business Machines, one of the world's largest manufacturers of computers.

IBM PC the IBM Personal Computer (PC), introduced in 1981, the first of a family of very popular microcomputers, including not only IBM products but also "clones" (imitations) made by other companies. The original IBM PC used very little proprietary technology, and it was easy to build compatible machines without violating patents.

   IBM has maintained a high level of "upward compatibility" within the PC, PS/1 and PS/2 line. This means that later-model machines in this line will run virtually all software written for earlier models.

ICON a picture on a computer screen that represents a particular object, command file, or group of files. For example, on a Macintosh computer, the picture of a trash can stands for "delete." Use the mouse to move a file to the trash can and it will be deleted. You have the option of changing your mind and taking a file out of the trash until you "empty the trash." *See* RECOVERING ERASED FILES.

IDENTIFYING TYPEFACES the art of recognizing and recalling the name of a particular font from typeset examples.

   When you are new at working with typefaces, the sheer number and variety are numbing. Soon, the various typefaces will become old friends and you'll learn to recognize them. Just become familiar with the fonts on your own system. Print out a catalog (there are utility programs for this), so you will have a reference at hand.

   Make a game of identifying the typefaces you see around you. This will sharpen your eye and clue you in on the latest trends. The decorated fonts are particularly easy to spot. They are being used for their distinctiveness.

But how, you may ask, do I identify a regular type-face? It is a matter of noticing details, some of them very minute. It's helpful to have a type catalog from a major type company on hand in your studio/office. Is the typeface in question SANS SERIF? or does it have SERIFS? Is it ROMAN or ITALIC? Is it a SCRIPT? The serifs, if there are any, are tremendously important. Do they come to a point, are they rounded or square? How do the serifs attach to the main stroke?

Next, you will want to note whether the lower-case a is *one storied* or two (ɑ or a). Is the lower-case g drawn like your handwriting or with the closed loop (ɡ or g)?

Now consider the proportions of the typeface. Is it CONDENSED or EXPANDED or of normal proportions? Check the x-height. Is there a contrast in the thickness of the strokes? How pronounced is the contrast? How bold does the typeface appear?

If there *is* a contrast in the width of the strokes, is the STRESS vertical or slanted approximately 30 degrees to the right? Is the stress slanted to the left?

This whole procedure of identifying a typeface can be either done informally or you may choose to follow the PANOSE system. PANOSE uses numerical codes to describe characteristics of typefaces to aid in their identification and classification. *See* PANOSE SYSTEM for further details.

If all else fails, check the COLOPHON. Many publishers are thoughtfully providing details of production, including the fonts used, at the end of the publication.

IDEOGRAM, IDEOGRAPH a form of writing in which the symbols represent ideas rather than sounds.

Also, symbols such as &, $, numerals, and computer icons are ideograms.

IGNORE part of DOS's infamous "Abort, Retry, Ignore, Fail?" error message. If you can fix the immediate problem (by putting a disk in the drive, for example), then choose "Retry." Otherwise, press or click on "Abort." Choosing "Ignore" is asking for trouble.

IMAGESETTER a high-quality output device. Imagesetters can deliver up to 2400 DPI (dots per inch) instead of the 300 or 600 DPI of ordinary laser printers.

IMAGE TYPE the selection of the type of image being scanned. The usual choices are DRAWING (LINE ART), BLACK AND WHITE, or COLOR. It may sometimes suit your purposes to treat one type of image as another; for example, I may want to scan a color photograph as a black and white image. A photograph scanned as a drawing will be very contrasty, but will be suitable for tracing and importing into a draw program.

IMPORT to open a file not in the software's regular format. Many word processors and graphics programs have import filters to allow conversion of files from one format to another. *See* EXPORT.

IMPOSITION arrangement of the pages of a book so that when the printed pages are folded, bound, and trimmed, they will appear in the correct numerical order.

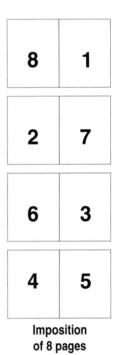

Imposition
of 8 pages

To demonstrate how this works, take two pieces of paper and fold them in half. You now have a DUMMY of an eight-page newsletter. Write the page numbers on the pages. Now take it apart and look at how the page numbers relate to one another. The inner spread, pages 4 and 5, appear normally. You could easily run a design across both pages, utilizing the normal GUTTER. Turn that page over. You will find page 6 is on the left-hand page and page 3 is on the right!

It is extremely important to make sure that the page imposition is worked out correctly; the more pages in the newsletter or booklet, the more complicated it becomes. Some page layout software is capable of working out the imposition plan for you. Obviously, if your laser printer can only print one page at a time, you will need to match up the correct pages yourself. Always make a dummy, and enlist the aid of your friendly neighborhood printer to make sure everything comes out as planned.

INCREMENTAL BACKUP a regular backup that copies only the files that have not already been backed up. *See* BACKUP COPY.

INDENT to leave a space (usually 1 em) at the beginning of the first line of a paragraph. Indented margins are also used to set off long quotations.

INDEX

1. an alphabetical listing of key words and concepts found in a book and the pages on which these terms may be found. Many page layout and word processing programs have the ability to automatically generate indexes from properly tagged terms. Note that the process is not wholly automatic; the human still has to specify which words should be indexed.

2. a pictograph of a pointing hand. Sometimes called a *fist*.

Index

NON-PROFIT ORG.
U.S. Postage
PAID
Permit No. 000
Athens, GA

Indicia

INDICIA the boxed information that takes the place of a postage stamp when printed on a postcard or envelope. The local postmaster must grant a special permit to the organization to use indicia on their mailings.

INFERIOR CHARACTERS small letters and numbers set on or below the baseline likethis. Used mainly in mathematical typesetting.

INFORMAL an asymmetrical layout. *Contrast* FORMAL.

INFORMATION SUPERHIGHWAY a network of electronic and digital communication equipment that is quietly revolutionizing businesses and our private lives. It is unlikely that we will look at communication in quite the same way as we did before. Not only is information being disseminated faster than ever, but world-wide electronic communication is creating a unique community—one that does not have a physical location, but rather exists in what is called *cyberspace*. Some portions of cyberspace are rather lawless right now; an ill-considered message may bring an avalanche of angry messages (called *flames*) upon your e-mail account. However, some standards of ethics and personal behavior are being worked out (hopefully before government feels compelled to force regulations upon the electronic community).

The *look* of the Information Superhighway is now becoming important to many people. The trend is going away from text-only screens to elaborate displays utilizing color, multiple typefaces, and graphics. (*See* WORLD WIDE WEB; MOSAIC). There is a need for individuals who have an eye for design and who are able to create a good-looking screen of information.

There are some differences in designing for displaying information on a monitor rather than printing on paper. The height-to-width ratio of a screen is not as great as a normal size piece of paper; the format is so close to being square that sometimes layouts look scrunched in the middle. Yet you must be careful not to go too close to the image borders because some monitors overscan and lose the outer rows of pixels. There is not much standardization of hardware; color schemes should remain rather basic. Resolution of type and images is not as sharp as printed pieces, so you'll have to design accordingly. Don't set the type too small or rely on small details in a graphic.

Other related concerns are the design of HYPERTEXT and MULTIMEDIA documents that are commonly distributed on CD-ROM.

See ELECTRONIC PUBLISHING; HYPERTEXT; INTERNET; PORTABLE DIGITAL DOCUMENT; MULTIMEDIA; WORLD WIDE WEB.

INITIAL the first letter of a paragraph, set larger and often in a different typeface for a decorative effect.

Initial

INK JET PRINTER a printer that forms characters by firing tiny dots of ink at the paper. Advantages include speed, high resolution, and quietness. An ink jet printer is often an economical alternative to a laser printer. The Hewlett-Packard DeskJet is a popular monochrome printer and the PaintJet is a color ink jet printer.

INLINE

1. a type design that seems to have a white line inscribed inside the strokes of the letterforms. Sometimes, the only difference between INLINE and ENGRAVED is how the type designer named the typeface.

Inline

2. similar to an OUTLINE, but the line is drawn *inside* the contour of the letterform.

INSERTION POINT in a full screen editor or drawing program, the place where characters will appear if you start typing. The insertion point is usually indicated with a cursor or a thin vertical bar.

INSET INITIAL an initial letter set within the margins of the normal text. The opposite would be a HUNG INITIAL. *See* DISPLAY INITIAL for illustration.

INTERCHARACTER SPACING the spacing *in between* characters. Also called LETTERSPACING. In a quality font, one that is well designed and properly HINTED, you should not have to concern yourself with adjusting intercharacter spacing. However, DISPLAY type (over 14 points) may need to be KERNED to look right. *See* LETTERSPACING; KERNING; TRACKING.

INTERNAL FONT a font that is permanently encoded in the hardware of the printer. For contrast, see SOFT FONTS and FONT CARTRIDGES.

INTERNATIONAL BUSINESS MACHINES *see* IBM.

INTERNET a cooperative message-forwarding system linking computer networks all over the world. Users of the Internet can exchange electronic mail, participate in electronic discussion forums (newsgroups), send files from any computer to any other via FTP, retrieve information via Gopher or HTTP, and even use each other's computers directly via remote connection if they have appropriate passwords. *See* HTTP; WORLD WIDE WEB.

The cost of running the Internet is paid largely by the sites that receive messages, and the sites that pass them along, not by the sites that send messages out. This has important legal and ethical implications. *Advertising on the Internet is almost always unwelcome,* as is any self-serving misuse of electronic communications, because the sender of the material is not paying the cost of distributing it.

Interrobang

INTERROBANG a combination question mark and exclamation point. This is perhaps the newest of our punctuation marks; it was proposed in the 1960s and has not quite caught on. If you want to use an interrobang, and your font does not have one, it is quite easy to make your own in your draw program or font manipulation software. Or just type "!?"

INTERWORD SPACING the spacing *in between words*. Also called WORDSPACING.

INVERT to change all colors to their photographic negative. In a black and white image, this would change white to black and black to white.

Invert

INVOICE a business form for billing clients. A well-designed invoice will have adequate space to list detailed charges for merchandise and services. The same "look" should carry over from company letterheads, business cards, and other company paperwork.

ISO PAPER SIZES *see* PAPER SIZES (ISO).

ITALICS letters slanted to the right and designed with a more calligraphic feel than their roman counterparts. *This sentence is set in italics.* Italics are used for emphasis, for setting the titles of books, and for foreign words.

Most type families have an italic font designed to match the normal weight roman type.

IT'S the contraction for *it is*. It is common to find *its* and *it's* confused. There is an easy way to check if you are writing the right one. Simply read the sentence substituting the words "it is" for the word in question. If it reads correctly, then you need to use *it's* with the apostrophe. Example: "It is hot in here" will contract to "It's hot in here." On the other hand "It is windows were tinted" makes no sense. That sentence should read, "Its windows were tinted." (*No* apostrophe.) *See* SPELLING.

ITS the possessive form of the pronoun *it*. Note that, like *his* and *her*, *its* does not have an apostrophe between the t and the s. *Contrast* IT'S. *See* SPELLING.

J

JACKET the plastic outer part of a diskette. It contains a hole to give the disk drive access to the inner magnetically encoded disk. On a $3\frac{1}{2}$-inch diskette, this hole is covered by a metal slide. There is also a hole at the central hub to allow the disk drive to spin the disk. The disk should never be removed from the jacket.

JAPANESE WRITING *see* KANA.

JUMP to continue a story or article on a following page. At the bottom of the column on the first page of the story should be a *jump line* ("Please turn to **Streets**, Page 3" or "See **Streets**, Page 3") directing the reader where to find the rest of the story. When continued, the story should have a *jump head* matching the jump line from the previous page. In order to aid readers, you should add "Continued from Page 1" in the same size and style of type as the body copy. If your publication makes extensive use of jumps, make sure you have the page numbers visible on every page.

JUSTIFICATION the insertion of extra space between words in lines of type so that the left and right margins are even and smooth. *See* MICROSPACING. Most of the type in this book is justified.

Most word processors and desktop publishing programs can automatically do the computations necessary to justify type. You will occasionally need to overrule the computer's linebreaking decisions. Problems generally arise only when the column width is too narrow or too large a HOT ZONE has been specified. Then you will get RIVERS of white space running down the column (not too attractive). To cure this, make sure hyphenation is enabled, shrink the hot zone, go to a smaller type size, or increase the column width.

K

K an abbreviation for KILOBYTE, a unit of computer memory capacity equal to 1,024 characters. 1000 K equals one MEGABYTE.

KANA the Japanese phonetic writing system usually used when printing Japanese on computers. There are two styles, *hiragana* and *katakana*. Kana contrasts with *kanji*, the Chinese-derived symbols for whole words. Printed Japanese books use a mixture of kana and kanji.

KANJI *see* KANA.

KATAKANA *see* KANA.

We Tr FA Y.

We Tr FA Y.

Figure 13 Some letter combinations that benefit from kerning.

KERNING an adjustment in the amount of space between certain combinations of letters in proportional-pitch type. If the combination Tr is typeset with normal LETTERSPACING, the letters seem to be too widely spaced. Tr looks better if the top of the T is allowed to overhang the r slightly. *See Figure 13.* The goal is to achieve the same optical spacing between all letters. Sometimes, round letters such as O and C need to have space added between them.

Many full-featured word processors and page-layout programs have the ability to automatically kern type. Ideally, you should be able to hand-kern headlines. Type set in all caps is most likely to need a great deal of adjustment. You should not have to kern lower case text *if the typeface is properly designed.*

KEY buttons on a keyboard.

KEYBOARD the primary computer input device for alphanumeric data. There are many different types of keyboard layouts; for the most part the alphabet and numbers are consistently placed, but there is considerable variation in the placement of the auxiliary characters, editing keys, and function keys. (Switching keyboards can be quite traumatic.)

When buying a new computer, be sure to carefully evaluate the keyboard offered with the package. Some of the cheaper keyboards feel "dead." Practice typing on several different models to find one that feels good to you. It is usually possible to get a better keyboard for a few dollars more.

KEYBOARDING entering data through the keyboard; typing.

KEYBOARD SHORTCUT *see* SHORTCUT.

KICKER a short phrase, set in small type, that runs above the main headline. Also called a TEASER.

KILOBYTE a unit used to measure the size of a computer's memory or storage capacity. 1 kilobyte is equal to 1024 bytes (where a BYTE is the amount of memory needed to store one character). 1000 K or 1024 K equals 1 megabyte (usage varies).

L

LABEL

1. a caption or line of type that identifies or gives information about a chart, figure or illustration.

2. (DOS and OS/2) identifying names ("volume labels") recorded on disks. This is very helpful in managing your files.

3. die-cut, self-adhesive paper that can be used to make labels. When purchasing labels for your laser printer, be sure that the labels are *specifically* manufactured for laser printing. If the adhesive is not strong enough, the labels may peel off inside the printer and ruin the mechanism. It is possible to buy labels that have a preprinted color design on them.

LANDSCAPE orientation of paper turned so that it is wider than high, like a landscape painting. You have the choice of whether to work in landscape or PORTRAIT orientation (taller than wider).

LASER PRINTER a printer that uses a laser beam to generate an image, then transfers it to paper electronically. Laser printers use technology similar to that of a photocopier. They provide high-quality output for text and graphics. 600 DOTS PER INCH is becoming popular; high-end laser printers can achieve 1200 DPI. 600 DPI laser printer copy is adequate for offset printing in most cases. (*See* RESOLUTION.) Laser printers are also quieter and faster than the previous generation of printers (dot-matrix and daisy-wheel printers).

LASSO a SELECTION TOOL commonly found in PAINT PROGRAMS; you use it to define an area that you wish to work with. After selecting the lasso icon, you drag the mouse *freehand* around the desired area. Once the area is defined, you may scale, move, rotate, change color, apply filters, or perform any operation that is available. Because the lasso is a freehand tool, it is very dependent upon your skill as a mouse operator. Knowing how difficult it is to draw accurately with a mouse, you may want to see if your paint program has other selection tools (such as a MAGIC WAND) that would suit your needs better.

Lasso

The Lasso icon shown is from Corel PhotoPaint.

LATIN

1. the standard alphabet, A–Z, including the letters J, K, and W, which were not known to the Romans; as opposed to the Greek or Russian alphabets or other systems of writing.

2. the language of ancient Rome. Latin text requires no accents or special characters, but textbooks and dictionaries use the macron and breve to mark long and short vowels ($\bar{a}$ $\breve{a}$) and the dieresis to separate syllables (*praeësse*). Material to be read in church sometimes uses acute accents on stressed syllables. Hyphenation is much like that of English; capitalization and text layout tend to follow the practice of the country in which the text is printed. Dictionaries and textbooks distinguish *j* from *i,* but ordinary printed texts use only *i.* Some particularly fastidious editions of classical texts write *u* for *v* because the distinction between the two letters is postclassical.

LAUNCH to start a computer program. "Launch File Manager by double-clicking on its icon."

LAYOUT

1. (v.) to arrange elements of a publication, advertisement, or book.

2. (n.) the finished composition of an advertisement or publication.

LEADER a dotted line that leads the eye from one side of the page to another. You most often see leaders in a Table of Contents or a price list.

LEADING (pronounced "ledding") the insertion of extra space between lines of type. In old letterpress typesetting this was actually done by inserting strips of lead between the rows of type. Computer-based typesetting is a bit easier; spacing control is usually one of the pull-down menus. You can specify the amount of leading in POINTS or as a percentage of the type size. Type set with no leading is said to be "set solid."

For example, if we had a paragraph of 10 point type that ran 7 lines long, it would be 70 points deep.

If we needed this text to fit a depth of 84 points (approximately 14 PICAS) we could increase the leading by 2 points (or 20%). This text would be set "10/12" (10 on 12).

Proper leading can increase the legibility of paragraph text. A good rule of thumb is that your leading should be 20% of the type size. Very small type and type set in long LINE LENGTHS will need proportionally more leading.

LOREM IPSUM DOLOR
Negative leading

There may be cases where you would like to have negative leading, e.g., a headline set in all caps that you want to be very bold and tight. Since you don't have any DESCENDERS, you don't have to leave room for them. This is very easy to accomplish with your computer, but it would be difficult with metal type.

LEARNING CURVE a graph representing mastery of a skill plotted against the time spent on it. If the new program is drastically different from anything else you have used previously, you *may* have a difficult time learning all the new features. Work will be slow for a few days. This could be described as "having a steep learning curve."

LEGAL SIZE the size of paper used for legal documents in the United States, $8\frac{1}{2} \times 14$ inches. *Contrast* LETTER SIZE, EXECUTIVE SIZE. *See also* ENVELOPE SIZES; PAPER SIZES.

LEGEND explanatory caption accompanying a map, chart, or other graphic.

LEGIBILITY the properties that make type easy to read.

Many factors influence how we read. Some experts feel that we read most easily what we are accustomed to, and we become accustomed to what we read the most of. In other words, it may be a circular argument. At any rate, it is beyond dispute that some printed matter is more difficult to read than most. (Sometimes this is the fault of the author, but let's put *that* aside for now.)

Here are some things you'll want to keep in mind as you are designing your document:

4 8
5 9
6 10
7 11
12

Type size

Lorem ipsum
Lorem ipsum
Large vs. small x-height

Lorem ipsum dolor
Lorem ipsum dolor
Spacing

REVERSE

Bodoni
This type is too small

Reverses

- **Size** Body copy should be between 8 and 12 points. Laser-printed copy should rarely be set smaller that 10 points because of the coarser resolution.

- **Use typefaces with serifs.** Research shows that most people read more quickly with traditional roman fonts than with SANS SERIFS. Again, this *may* be a matter of what the population is used to, but some researchers feel that the serifs actually help guide the eye along the line of type.

- **Choose a font with a larger x-height.** For legibility, you might prefer Century Schoolbook over Goudy. The larger x-height makes the text set in Century Schoolbook seem to be bigger. It may also run longer. *See* COPYFITTING.

- **Line length.** Not too short, not too long. What's just right? About $2\frac{1}{2}$ alphabets (65 characters).

- **Spacing.** This is tricky. If the LETTERSPACING is too LOOSE, and the WORDSPACING is too TIGHT, you run the risk of the words literally running together. If the defaults are not to your liking, try adjusting the TRACKING to be about 10 percent tighter and leave the wordspacing alone. If the letters are touching, return to the default tracking and increase the wordspacing slightly. LINESPACING can be a way of compensating for longer line lengths. If the line length is 20 percent over the ideal length, increase the linespacing by a similar percentage. The challenge is to separate the lines visually, but not to make the block of type so airy that the reader feels he cannot continue to the next line.

- **Reverses.** For technical reasons, reversed type is extremely difficult to read, and should be limited to very short headlines and the occasional paragraph. You'll find that typefaces with hairline strokes like Bodoni do not reverse well. The thin strokes get lost in the inkspread. Likewise, the COUNTERS of the letters tend to fill in. Use a sans-serif font for maximum legibility. Go ahead and increase the point size. Run a test on the laser printer if you have any doubts about the legibility of a reverse.

- **Type on color.** You need a strong contrast for the words to stand out from a colored or gray background. Experience will be your best guide here. My personal rule of thumb is not to use a gray screen darker than 20 percent behind black type. The coarse resolution of the laser printer sometimes causes problems with the counters of 8-point type printed over gray. The answer is to use larger type. There are books available that show examples of type printed over screens of different colors in many different combinations. If you are using a lot of SPOT COLOR in your publications, you should have such a book on your reference shelf.

Overprinting

LENS a tool available in CorelDraw 5.0 that lets the user define an area and apply different effects to that area. This makes possible renderings of transparent objects, tints, and other unusual tricks previously available only in a paint program. *See* TRANSPARENT.

Lens effects greatly increase the size and complexity of the saved files; in effect you are changing an area of the VECTOR-BASED graphic into a bitmap.

LETTER QUALITY print equal in quality to that of that of the best carbon-ribbon typewriters. All laser printers are considered letter quality; so are some ink-jet and 24-pin dot matrix printers.

LETTER SIZE paper that is $8\frac{1}{2} \times 11$ inches. This is the size of paper used for business letters in the United States. Elsewhere, ISO size A4 is the nearest equivalent. *Contrast* LEGAL SIZE, EXECUTIVE SIZE. *See also* ENVELOPE SIZES; PAPER SIZES.

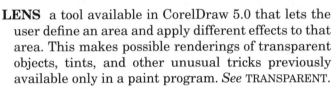

Letterspacing

LETTERSPACING the space between letters (characters). Many desktop publishers don't realize the amount of control they have over the letter spacing. Look for the letterspacing controls with other FRAME attribute commands (sometimes called TRACKING).

In small sizes, you'll want to leave the letter spacing loose for greater legibility. In display sizes, you may wish to tighten it up. You may even find that certain character combinations need adjusting by hand. *See* KERNING.

LIBRARY a collection of reference materials. Although you might make use of a public or university library, desktop publishing is such a rapidly developing field, you are going to find it necessary to maintain a small library in your office.

What should be in your library? Standard reference works like a dictionary, a thesaurus, and a manual of style come immediately to mind. (These could even be stored in digital form on the hard disk or on CD-ROM). You should also have DOCUMENTATION for all your computer equipment and software at hand. You will want to maintain a library of CLIP ART and a SWIPE FILE. You will also probably want to start collecting books of technical interest: books on design or production techniques, books on how to use your software more productively and creatively. There are also many magazines and journals that might be of interest; after all, you are not the world's only desktop publisher, you might as well tap into the experiences and knowledge of some of the others.

If you are a "font junkie," you probably have a variety of fonts from many different sources. You need a catalog of all *your* fonts. Yes, all of them—installed and uninstalled. You'll probably have to do this yourself. There are programs that will print a catalog for you, but go a step further. Do a quick classification (serif, sans serif, scripts, display fonts). Print a page of each class so that you can see at a glance all of your similar fonts. This will make your life a lot easier.

fi

Ligature

LIGATURES combination letterforms; two or three letters have been combined into a single character to improve spacing. Examples are "ffl." "fi," "ff." Not all fonts have a full set of ligatures designed for them. *See* EXPERT SET.

LIGHT type that is designed and drawn with very fine strokes; the opposite of BOLD.

LIGHT BOX; LIGHT TABLE a work surface with a system of lights underneath a frosted glass top. A light table is useful for viewing slides and negatives or for lining up color separations printed on 20 pound bond paper.

Handgloves

Lineale

LINEALE sans serif; a typeface without serifs.

LINEAR FILL a fill that ranges from one color at one side of an object to a second color directly opposite. You can specify the angle of the linear fill.

Linear fill

LINE CAP attributes associated with the end of drawn lines. You can choose blunt or rounded ends or even arrowheads.

LINE DRAWING an illustration that can be represented as a series of hard-edged black lines and black areas on a white background. Line drawings are easily converted to vector images by tracing them. Also called *line art*.

LINE GAUGE a metal ruler customized for the printing and typesetting industries. Not only will it have inches and picas on different scales, but there will be cutouts marked for measuring LINESPACING in points.

LINE LENGTH a major factor in text legibility. If your text lines are too long, the reader's eye has trouble coming back to the beginning of the next line. If the lines are too short, words and phrases are broken up.

The optimal line length for maximum legibility for any font can be easily measured. Using the same point size and letter spacing as you plan for the final job, type the alphabet $2\frac{1}{2}$ times (through m) on a single line, in lower case. Then measure the length of the result. Lines of this length have been shown to be the most comfortable for readers. Condensed typefaces will, of course, need to be set in shorter lines than expanded faces. Larger point sizes can tolerate a longer line. You'll want to keep this measurement in mind when planning the layout of lengthy texts. *See* LEGIBILITY.

LINESPACING the space between lines of type. Also called LEADING. Proper linespacing can increase the legibility of paragraph text. A good rule of thumb is that your linespacing should be 20% of the type size. Very small type and type set in long LINE LENGTHS will need proportionally more spacing. Very large type, like that used for headlines, needs less linespacing. *See* LEADING.

LINING FIGURES full-height numerals that align to the baseline like this: 1 2 3 4 5 6 7 8 9 0. *Contrast* LOWER CASE FIGURES; OLD STYLE FIGURES.

LINK

1. any kind of communication path between two computers.

2. under Microsoft Windows or OS/2, a DDE communication path between programs is called a *hot link* or a *cold link*. *See* DDE; OBJECT LINKING AND EMBEDDING.

3. to create a connection between text FRAMES so that text will automatically flow to the next frame in the chain. This allows the page layout program to automatically handle rewrapping the text from page to page as the text is edited.

LINOTYPE an obsolete method of setting type for letterpress printing. A linotype machine was a large, noisy, lead-spewing contraption that poured molten lead into molds of type. *See* HOT TYPE. It set one line of type at a time, hence its name, "line o' type." The operator ran the linotype from a typewriter-like keyboard. If a mistake was made, the entire line had to be reset. (Makes you appreciate your computer, doesn't it?) Linotype machines were popular with newspapers, which had short deadlines and needed a relatively cheap method of setting type. When you got through with the day's run, the lead type was unlocked from the print bed and melted down for the next day.

Linotype machines were supplanted by PHOTOTYPESETTING and OFFSET LITHOGRAPHY.

LIST BOX in a dialog box, an area in which the user can choose among a list of items, such as files, directories, typefaces, or the like. For picture, *see* DIALOG BOX, *Figure 6*.

LITHOGRAPHY a method of printing that takes advantage of the fact that oil and water do not mix. In fine art lithography, the artist draws directly on the lithographic stone with a greasy crayon. The stone is then wet down before being inked. Ink will take to the marks made with the crayon, but is repelled by the wet stone. A different stone will have to be prepared for each color used. The commercial form of lithography is called OFFSET LITHOGRAPHY, or simply OFFSET PRINTING.

LOAD to transfer information from an auxiliary storage device into a computer. When you open a file to work on it, you are loading the file into the computer's memory.

LOCATOR TOOL a tool that allows viewing of the same portion of a bitmap when multiple copies of the same image are loaded and on-screen at the same time. To use this tool, click on the center part of the active image and the copies will display the same area.

Locator tool

 The Locator icon shown is from Corel PhotoPaint.

LOCK (Macintosh) to mark a file or disk as "Do not change" by clicking on the "Locked" box in the "Get Info" window.

 A diskette may be physically locked by sliding the small plastic tab (on the back of the diskette) toward the edge. This uncovers a square hole that tells the disk drive that the diskette is "READ-ONLY." This is called WRITE PROTECTION.

 Any disk sent to a service bureau should be locked so that VIRUSES cannot be written on the disk.

LOGO short for LOGOTYPE.

LOGOTYPE a graphic device, with or without words, that is used to represent a company or its products. Some logotypes are simply the company name, set in a special typeface. Others are more elaborate, and include some sort of pictorial design element.

 When reproducing a logotype in your document, be sure to get a good rendition of it. Scanning a business card is usually *not* good enough. Ask for a digital file or a CAMERA-READY logotype to scan.

 Designing a logotype for a new business venture can be a rewarding challenge. Keep in mind that the new logo will have to be simple enough to reproduce well on business cards. Limit the number of colors used to hold down reproduction costs. A simple, well-conceived design will be more memorable than a complex one.

g

Loop

LONG GRAIN PAPER paper in which the fibers run parallel to the long side of the paper. *See* GRAIN.

LOOP the DESCENDER of the *g*, which is also called a TAIL.

LOOSE letterspacing that has been adjusted to increase the space between the letters. *See* LETTER-SPACING for illustration.

LOREM IPSUM DOLOR ... a nonsense text which is used to set samples of type. The point is, you are supposed to be appreciating the forms of the letters and appearance of the overall paragraph, not reading the copy.

The question remains, "Does it (Lorem ipsum dolor) really mean anything?" Despite looking like Latin, it is not. To someone who reads that ancient language, the passage looks like gibberish although occasional words can be read.

Other favorite passages for setting type samples are the writings of Ben Franklin, quotes from famous type designers, the Preamble of the American Constitution and, a new text, *Ladle Rat Rotten Hut*.

LOWER CASE the small letters. The term "lower case" goes back to the early days of letterpress printing. The metal type was kept in divided drawers called cases; the capital letters in the upper drawer, and the small letters in the lower.

LOWER CASE FIGURES numerals that have descenders and ascenders—like this: 1 2 3 4 5 6 7 8 9 0. These are also called OLD STYLE FIGURES.

LPI Lines Per Inch. a measure of the resolution of a halftone screen. Most newspaper screens are 85 LPI; good quality magazines use 150 LPI. 300 DPI screened output is roughly equivalent to a 50 LPI screen (draft quality). 600 DPI on a plain paper typesetter should be acceptable for most work; it can produce the equivalent of a 100 LPI halftone. When higher resolutions are needed, the file should be output to a 2400 DPI imagesetter.

M

MAC popular nickname for a Macintosh computer.

MACINTOSH a family of personal computers introduced by Apple in 1984; the first widely used computers with a graphical user interface, windowing, and a mouse. Users copy files and activate software by pointing to symbols (icons) on the screen rather than by typing commands. The screen is always in graphics mode: it is divided into windows and can display all the typefaces that the printer can print. The Macintosh user interface was derived from Xerox workstations; it has been imitated by a number of other operating systems, including Microsoft Windows and OS/2 Presentation Manager.

Most importantly, the mechanisms for using windows, icons, and mouse menus are provided by the operating system, which means they look virtually the same in all programs. Thus, anyone who knows how to use any Macintosh software package will also know how to perform similar operations in any other software package.

The original Macintosh used a 7.80-MHz Motorola 68000 microprocessor with 128K of RAM (see MICROPROCESSOR). This was not enough for the software to perform well, and later models used 68020 and 68030 processors with several megabytes of RAM. The latest Macintoshes use PowerPC CPUs, which can software-emulate the Motorola 68000 to run older software.

Macintoshes have always been on the forefront of practical computer graphics and related technology. QuickTime video and TrueType scalable fonts originated on the Macintosh. Macintosh hardware, although expensive, is simple to set up because of Apple's early commitment to widely recognized standards such as PostScript and SCSI. Things work easily or not at all; little experimenting is required.

The entire field of desktop publishing owes a great debt to the Macintosh. Although the technical groundwork was laid by research at Xerox, it was Apple's aggressive marketing of the Mac that brought the technology to the people.

See also MICROPROCESSOR; POWERPC; QUICKTIME; TRUETYPE; SCSI; POSTSCRIPT.

MACRO a keystroke that stands for a sequence of instructions.

Many programs allow you to define macros to stand for frequently typed words or sequences of commands. For example, I could define the F10 key to type a long, unwieldy company name every time I pressed it. Many macros are much more complicated; some people treat macros as a sort of programming language and have produced some absolutely astounding results.

ā

Macron

MACRON a phonetic symbol (ā) that is used to show that a vowel is pronounced with a long sound. *Contrast* BREVE; *see also* ACCENTS.

MAGAZINE a book-like publication produced on a regular schedule (commonly monthly) that contains a variety of articles and is usually supported by paid advertisements. Many of the national magazines have enthusiastically embraced desktop publishing technology and are now completely or mostly produced with Macintosh or PC platforms.

Magazines vary widely in size, column format, and design complexity. This means that whoever designs the magazine's layout has a great deal of flexibility and control over the final product. The typography alone can allow a reader to judge how trendy, how elegant, or how trustworthy a particular magazine is trying to be. A quick glance at any newsstand will show that an amazing variety of tone can be achieved.

Magic wand

MAGIC WAND an editing tool that selects an entire area of a particular color, regardless of its shape; magic wands are found in many photo editing programs (Adobe Photoshop, Aldus Photostyler, Corel PhotoPaint). You use the magic wand to select an area for editing. Its power lies in its ability to do a lot of tedious work for you. When you click on a pixel, the magic wand selects an area of that particular color, no matter how jagged the edges. You can then copy, delete, move, rotate, flip, shrink, stretch, or apply filters to this area as if it were a single object. *See also* SELECT, SELECTION TOOLS, BITMAP, PAINT PROGRAM.

The icon shown is from Corel PhotoPaint.

MAILER

1. an envelope or tube made of a sturdy, lightweight cardboard. Mailers are used to send diskettes, photographs, and artwork safely through the mail. If necessary, an extra piece of rigid cardboard can be used to back flat artwork. This should only add a few cents to the required postage. Remember to write or stamp "DO NOT BEND" on the front of the mailer below the address.

2. an advertising flyer. This type of mailer may be included with a cover letter or may be designed to be self-mailing by including a preprinted return address and space for postage and address label on one side.

MAJUSCULE capital letters.

MANUSCRIPT a handwritten, typewritten, or word processed text ready to be submitted for publication.

MARCHING ANTS slang for the moving dashed lines that indicate the borders of a selected object. Some programs allow you to hide the ants if they distract you.

MARGINS the white space at the top, bottom, and both sides of a page. The design decision about the width of the margins is very critical; small margins make a page look crowded; wide margins look elegant but may waste space. Make sure to leave an adequate margin for the GUTTER in a multipage project. And remember that neither your laser printer or the printing press will be able to print to the edge of the paper. If you wish the design to BLEED off the page, the paper will have to be trimmed to size after being printed.

MARK-UP to indicate formatting and typesetting instructions on a manuscript or proof.

MARQUEE SELECT a method of selecting more than one object at a time in a graphical user interface (GUI). It gets its name from the animated effect of the dashed line of the bounding box—it resembles a theater marquee.

To marquee select items, sight along the top and

the left edge of the group of items you wish to select. Position the mouse cursor there. While holding down the mouse button, pull diagonally down and to the right. When the marquee encloses all the items, release the mouse button. *See also* MOUSE, GUI, SELECT.

MASK, MASKING

1. (draw program) to create an object with a hole in it, so that the view of an underlying object is controlled.

Each object created in a drawing program is normally opaque. You can stack other shapes on top of an object, but if the lowest object is completely hidden, it's as if it doesn't exist. How can you create an object with a hole in it so that you can see through to the object on the bottom? By *combining* two outlines into one object, the central area will become open and you can see through. *See Figure 14.* This has many practical applications: you can mask off an unwanted part of a bitmap; you can create TRAP for printing SPOT COLOR; you can create type seemingly filled with a bitmap or complex drawing.

See COMBINE.

2. (natural media paint program) to mark an area of the drawing as protected from the drawing tools. The mask can be removed as the drawing progressing. This is analogous to the masking used in watercolor painting.

MASTER PAGE a template that defines the overall appearance of every page of the document. *See also* GRID SYSTEM.

MASTHEAD

1. the logotype of a periodical. A masthead usually runs across the top of the first page of the publication and contains the date and volume number of the publication. Also called a FLAG.

2. the listing containing information about the staff and operation of a publication. The masthead is usually placed on the inside front page or in an inconspicuous spot just past the Table of Contents.

MATCHING TYPEFACES the art of setting new type to resemble as closely as possible an existing sample.

Figure 14 Masking

At some point, you will probably find it necessary to match an existing type sample. This can be very difficult; you are battling inconsistent naming, differences in how well the font was digitized, and the resolution of the output device (usually a laser printer). There is also a bewildering number and variety of typefaces available commercially. The chances that you have the same selection of decorative typefaces on your computer as another person are rather slim. Even so, with a little practice you can usually come up with a reasonable match.

Try to identify the typeface you are trying to match. If you are lucky, it will be an "old friend" that you recognize. If not, I recommend using the PANOSE system to identify and match the sample.

If you do not have the PANOSE system or something similar to it, you should at least have a catalog of fonts available on your computer system. The first question is whether the sample is a ROMAN, ITALIC, SCRIPT or a DISPLAY font. If it is a roman or italic font, is it a SERIF or SANS-SERIF font? Looking at your catalog, find a typeface with similar CONTRAST, WEIGHT, and proportions. Do the serifs match? Check the X-HEIGHT. Look at the key letters a, g, Q, and S. By now, you should have a reasonable match.

Now to match the size. Using a TYPE GAUGE, measure your sample in points BASELINE to baseline. This measurement is the point size of the font plus any LEADING. Set two lines with normal leading on your

Maximize button

Mean line

computer and print it. If you are fortunate enough to have a light box, here's a chance to use it. Lay the new printout on top of the sample, aligning the baselines. Measure the difference (if any), and make the necessary adjustments. This light box test will also give you an opportunity to check the LETTERSPACING and WORD SPACING.

If you do not have a light box, simply hold the printouts up to the window or your desk lamp.

MAXIMIZE (Windows) to make a window take over the whole screen. To do this, click the mouse on the MAXIMIZE BUTTON (the box with the up arrow that is at the far right of the title bar). *See also* MINIMIZE; RESTORE. Maximize is also an option under the CONTROL MENU.

On a Macintosh, use the ZOOM box (at the far right side of the window's title bar) to enlarge a window.

MEAN LINE the imaginary line that marks the X-HEIGHT.

MEASURE line length, usually measured in PICAS.

MECHANICAL the CAMERA-READY COPY, complete with any color separations or special instructions attached.

MEGAPIXEL an image containing about one million pixels or more. For example, a 1024 × 1024 pixel image is often referred to as a megapixel. *See* BITMAP.

MEMORY the space within the computer where information is stored while being actively worked on. Most microcomputers have a small amount of read-only memory (ROM), containing the built-in programs that start the operation of the computer when it is turned on, and a large amount of random-access memory (RAM) for your programs and data. Except for ROM, memory goes blank when the computer is turned off; any data in it must be copied to disk or tape if they are to be saved.

How much memory do you need? It depends on the kind of software you need to run. Desktop publishing programs run better when they have 8 or more megabytes of RAM to operate in. Paint programs in particular are very demanding of hardware; large and full-color bitmaps require 16 megabytes or more of RAM.

MENU a list of choices that appears on the screen in response to your actions. Most windows have a MENU BAR just under the title bar. When you click on an item in the menu bar, its corresponding menu will appear. You select the command you want by clicking on it with the mouse. Commands with an ellipsis (. . .) after them will pop up a dialog box for you to give the computer further instructions before executing the command. If there are keyboard shortcuts for any command, they will often be listed to the right of the command.

Menus make a program user-friendly. It's very easy to learn and use software with a menu-driven command system. You don't need to memorize all the commands. By looking at the menus, you can see all the options.

The problem with menus is that it often takes a substantial amount of time and mousing to work through them. Experienced users use the keyboard shortcuts to speed up their work. Also, if you are not careful, it is possible to "get lost" in a series of nested menus. Many manuals provide a tree-shaped diagram of the menus; when learning a new program it's a good idea to have that chart at hand.

MENU BAR a horizontal menu at the top of the screen or window. Depending on the software, the items in the menu bar are chosen by clicking on them with a mouse, or by typing the first letter of each item, or possibly by typing the first letter while holding down Alt. Usually each item is a further menu. For picture, *see* WINDOW, *Figure 26.*

MERGE a special command that lets you create personalized documents. Here's how it works: You will need a file, quite possibly from a database program, that contains the *names* of all the people you wish to send letters to. You can then create a master letter with a word processor, leaving special codes in place of the name, address, etc. When you choose "Merge" from the file menu, an individualized document is

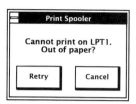

Message box

printed for each name on the list file.

Some draw programs also have merge commands. This would let a teacher make a certificate for each member of a class, for example.

MESSAGE BOX a small window that appears when your application program or operating system has an urgent message for you. A familiar example is the message box that pops up when your printer is not ready. Even when there is no action you can take, you must *still* click on the "OK" button for the box to disappear. (But most people definitely do not feel OK about "Fatal Errors" and other such catastrophes.)

METALLIC INKS special printing inks with fine metallic flakes suspended in the pigment. When dry, the metal particles rise to the surface, creating a shiny surface. As a design element, metallic inks are an unsurpassed attention-getter. They look rich and give an air of elegance to any printed piece.

Technically, metallic inks can be quite challenging. Some types of paper accept the ink better than others. It is easy for larger areas of metallic color to CHALK and flake off if the ink coverage isn't perfect. Lastly, when used in combination with PROCESS COLORS, it is impossible to get an accurate proof before the press run. It may be necessary to evaluate a PRESS PROOF before giving the OK for the remainder of the run. The best bet is to work with a printer who has had experience with metallic inks and is comfortable working with them.

When a shiny highlight is needed for an award or certificate, consider using COLOR FOILS that can be applied to individual printouts. This method is too expensive and time-consuming for multiple copies, but may be just the thing for one or two copies.

MICRO- prefix meaning one millionth. For example, one microsecond means one millionth of a second (0.000001 second).

MICROCOMPUTER a computer whose central processing unit (CPU) consists of a single integrated circuit known as the *microprocessor*. Ordinarily, a microcomputer is used by only one person at a time;

some people prefer the term PERSONAL COMPUTER. All home computers are microcomputers. *See* MICRO-PROCESSOR.

MICROPROCESSOR an integrated circuit containing the entire "brains" of the computer, all on one chip, so that only the memory and input-output devices need to be added.

MICROSOFT the world's leading software-producing company, headquartered in Redmond, Washington, and founded by William Gates and Paul Allen in 1975 when they wrote a version of BASIC for an early hobbyist microcomputer, the Altair. In the late 1970s the company grew as it sold versions of BASIC to other computer makers, but it was still fairly small when it was approached by IBM to design the operating system for the IBM PC (released in 1981). This operating system (known as PC-DOS, MS-DOS, or simply DOS) became a huge seller, since almost all PC and PC clones used it.

Since 1993, IBM and Microsoft have been developing new versions of DOS separately, and PC-DOS and MS-DOS are now separate, though virtually identical, products.

In the late 1980s Microsoft worked with IBM on the development of a new multitasking operating system, OS/2. However, in the 1990s Microsoft and IBM split over operating system strategy, with IBM pushing OS/2 and Microsoft focusing on Windows. The collaboration has ended, and OS/2 is now solely an IBM product.

In 1990 Microsoft introduced version 3.0 of Windows, a much improved version of an earlier product that provides a graphical user interface for computers in the IBM PC line. Windows 3.0 rapidly became a best seller, and many other software makers wrote programs to operate within the Windows environment. Windows 3.1 added minor improvements and greater reliability and became the standard operating system for PC-compatible machines. *See* WINDOWS.

MICROSPACING the insertion of extra space between words to make the lines JUSTIFIED. Microspaces are in units smaller than the size of normal blank spaces. *See* JUSTIFICATION.

MIDLINE the imaginary line that marks the position of the middle horizontal strokes of the *A*, *E*, and *H*. The precise positioning of the midline is at the discretion of the type designer. Usually, it is approximately at the optical center of the height of the capital letters, with the *A*'s midline set slightly lower. This is a *standard* midline. If the midline is constant, the *A* will look pinched at the top. Some typefaces have their midlines unusually high or low; this gives the designer a great deal of freedom of expression. *See Figure 15.*

MILLI- prefix meaning one thousandth. For example, a millimeter is one thousandth of a meter.

Minimize button

MINIMIZE to make a window as small as possible; usually this means it becomes an icon rather than a window. To do this, click the mouse on the minimize button (the small button with the down arrow at the right side of the title bar). This is a handy way to get one piece of software out of the way temporarily while you turn your attention to something else. You can then RESTORE the window when you want to resume working with it. A caution—the minimized program is still taking up memory and you'll find that graphics-intensive programs (such as paint programs) need all the memory you can give them. You will want to CLOSE all minimized programs before LAUNCHING a program that needs lots of memory. Some utilities can run minimized in the background (print spoolers, for example). *See also* MAXIMIZE; RESTORE.

MINI-SCROLL BARS small SCROLL BARS that appear with a list of choices inside of a dialog box. *See diagram at* DIALOG BOX.

MINUSCULE lower case (small) letters.

Mirror image

MIRROR to flip an object so that the resulting image is a mirror image of the original.

MITER to cut at an angle. A way of specifying how lines should intersect; *mitered* joints come to neat points (contrasting methods would be *rounded* or

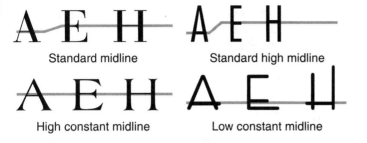

Figure 15   Midlines

beveled). Mitered joints are the normal way to make corners.

This may be easier to understand if you have ever done any woodworking, or used any presstape to make borders. You have to trim the overlapping tape at a 45 degree angle to make a neat corner. At a basic level, this is what your computer is doing as it creates the intersection of two lines. If it did not miter the corners, there would be an ugly gap at the intersection of two lines, or the endpoints of the lines would overlap because of the thickness of the stroke.

Mitered joint

Most drawing programs will let you set the *miter limit*; the threshold at which the computer bevels a sharp angle when two lines have a narrow angle of intersection. This prevents the pointed joint from extending way past the end of the line.

MIXED CASE   type set with normal capitalization, i.e., upper and lower case. *Contrast* ALL CAPS.

MNEMONIC   an association that helps you remember something. For example, the expression "Spring forward, fall back" is a mnemonic that helps you remember which way to adjust your clocks in the spring and the fall for Daylight Saving Time. Many keyboard shortcuts rely on mnemonics to help you remember them: Ctrl-X for e**x**it, Ctrl-S for **S**ave. *See* KEYBOARD SHORTCUTS; MENU.

MODEM   (short for **mo**dulator-**dem**odulator) a device that encodes data for transmission over a particular medium, such as telephone lines, coaxial cables, fiber

147

optics, or microwaves. Modems can be either external peripherals or they can be *internal*, mounted inside the computer's case.

A modem can be your window on the world; with the proper communication software, you can join in discussions about nearly anything on the commercial online services (CompuServe, America Online, Prodigy), or explore the INTERNET and the WORLD WIDE WEB (*see* ELECTRONIC PUBLISHING). Any of these services can be a valuable resource for you. Thousands of people worldwide read the posted messages every day. You may see the solution to a software or computer problem you are having. You can also ask for help yourself; many knowledgeable users are willing to offer suggestions. Some companies use the online services to distribute bug reports, bug patches, and device drivers. Many shareware programs, fonts, and clip art files are available for DOWNLOADING.

Modems can be used to send files to service bureaus. Make sure to compress the file (using PKZIP or Stuffit) before transmitting it. At 9600 baud, it takes an hour to transmit 3 megabytes. Be careful! Estimate how long it will take to transmit a file *before* you start an upload. Not only could you tie up your phone for an inordinately long time, you could incur some impressive long-distance phone charges. *See* UPLOAD.

A modem can also allow you to use your computer as a fax machine. You will need special software, but it's a great convenience not to have to make room for another piece of machinery on the desktop. When you wish to receive a fax, you start the fax software and allow the computer to automatically answer the phone and accept the fax. The fax document can be printed out or stored on disk.

Many people are reluctant to install a modem on their computer because they have heard of "hackers" who randomly dial phone numbers until they find a computer and then cause great mischief. Rest assured that no one can connect to your computer simply because you have a modem installed. The computer must be set up to answer incoming calls (*auto-answer mode*) and must be running a special communications program in "host mode" to be able to respond to transmitted commands. If you never set up your computer in this special way, no one can "break in." Even when you are waiting for a fax, your computer is not at risk. The computer will not respond to any data other than incoming fax codes.

MODERN
1. a roman typeface in which the STRESSES of the letterforms are vertical rather than slanted (OLD STYLE). Didot and Bodoni are good examples of this classification of typefaces.

2. In the PANOSE classification system, modern and OLD STYLE refer to overall proportions of the letters. Modern proportions are more uniform than old style; the *O* is oval rather than circular and the *E* is widened to be about the same width.

MOIRÉ an unintended and distracting pattern that occurs when two or more halftone screens are overprinted at the wrong angle. *See picture.*

MONITOR a device similar to a television set that accepts video signals from a computer and displays information on its screen; also known as a CRT or cathode ray tube device. The monitor itself does no computing at all.

The two most important considerations when buying a monitor are the *dot pitch* and the screen size. The dot pitch should be 0.28mm or less. Page layout programs benefit from being displayed on a larger screen; 17 inches will display more in the 1:1 zoom.

Next, consider the controls for color and size adjustment. Are they easy to reach? Is there a DEGAUSSING button? It may also help if there is color calibration software included with the monitor.

MONOCHROME MONITOR a computer monitor that can display only one color. Monochrome monitors generally are better than color monitors when working with text because they provide sharper resolution for characters. However, a color monitor is needed if you would like to use your computer to do color graphics.

Handgl◊ves
Modern

Moiré

MONOLINE having one thickness. Typefaces that have no discernible difference in stroke width are said to be monoline.

MONOSPACE a typeface design that gives each letterform the same width. *See* FIXED PITCH.

MORGUE a collection of reference materials. Your morgue might include clip-art, photo CDs, an encyclopedia, a dictionary, and a thesaurus. *See also* SWIPE FILE.

MOTION BLUR a photopaint filter that blurs the image along a specified axis to give the effect of motion.

Motion blur

MOUSE a computer input device that is used by rolling it around on your desk and pressing one or more buttons. The mouse lets you control a special CURSOR on screen. Graphical user interfaces such as Microsoft Windows and the Apple Macintosh operating system are built around the mouse. *See* WINDOWS; MACINTOSH; PAINT PROGRAM; DRAW PROGRAM; TRACKBALL; GRAPHICS PAD.

For more information on how to use a mouse, *see* CLICK; DRAG; DOUBLE-CLICK; POINT.

MULTIMEDIA the combination of sound and visual information. It opens up endless possibilities for presentations, computer-aided instruction, and electronic publications. (Just imagine a book coming to life complete with animation and music!) Multimedia is usually distributed on CD-ROM because of the tremendous amount of information to be stored. Multimedia presentations need to be run on special computer systems with sound cards and CD-ROM DRIVES installed.

MULTIPLE MASTER FONTS a font with two or more master designs, with the intermediate variations generated by the computer.

Imagine a situation in which you were called upon to create a family of typefaces. With multiple master technology, you could design the lightest and heaviest weights and then design the most condensed and expanded versions. These are called your DESIGN AXES. The desired combination of characteristics would be generated by the computer as needed. You could have extra-bold condensed or light expanded.

Multiple master fonts excel at creating companion display and text fonts. The OPTICAL SIZE axis can automatically adjust the stroke width, letter width and x-height to be correct at any point size.

MULTIPLICATION CROSS the character × centered on the CAP HEIGHT of the font, used to indicate the mathematical operation of multiplication. This same symbol is also called the DIMENSION SIGN and is used to write dimensions (i.e. 8 × 10, 4 × 4). Do not use the letter x for this purpose.

×

Multiplication cross

MULTIPLICATION DOT a small dot (·), somewhat larger than a period and centered on the CAP HEIGHT of the font, used to indicate the mathematical operation of multiplication. This symbol is the preferred decimal point in some European countries.

·

Multiplication dot

MULTIPLICATION SIGN *see* MULTIPLICATION CROSS; MULTIPLICATION DOT.

MULTITASKING the apparent execution of more than one program at the same time on the same computer. I say "apparent" because the computer can really do only one thing at a time. In reality, the computer rapidly switches its attention among the various programs. You don't usually notice any delays because the computer can switch so rapidly, hundreds of times per second. Multitasking makes it possible to print one document while editing another.

N

NATIVE designed for a specific hardware or software environment (rather than for compatiblity with something else).

NATIVE FILE FORMAT the file format proprietary to an application program; the format in which it normally saves documents or drawings. Most programs can, with the IMPORT command, convert similar file types to their own format. If you want to convert a native file to a more generic file type, use the SAVE AS... or EXPORT commands.

NATURAL MEDIA a kind of paint program that accurately simulates the effect of actual artists' materials. With a natural media program, you can specify the kind of paper or canvas you are working on. The tools available behave very much as their real-world counterparts would act—the chalk smears, the watercolors spread, and markers bleed. The main differences are that you have the ability to combine unlikely media (try to paint watercolors over chalk in real life), and you don't have to wait for anything to dry.

Natural media programs are very demanding of your hardware; they create huge files, and require lots of RAM, fast video boards, and fast CPUs.

NAVIGATION finding your way around a complex system of menus or help files. This can be a real challenge, but there are a few tricks to help you.

HYPERTEXT FILES (such as help files) usually have a command called "Back" that allows you to backtrack to the previous screens. This is similar to Tom Sawyer using a rope to find his way around caves. A frequent frustration is having a vague memory of a subject you read about yesterday, but no memory of where it was. Familiarize yourself with the "Search" capabilities of the help file; it can save you a lot of time. As always, a good index is worth its weight in gold. If the index is too general to be useful, I advocate a suitably grumpy letter to the software vendor. (If enough of us complain, something might be done.) In the meantime, you may want to make a few notes on an index card and slip it into the manual.

Learning how to navigate menus requires an adventurous spirit. Make yourself a map (if there's not one already in the manual), as any good explorer would do. Sometimes the logic of grouping certain commands together will not be apparent to you, and you'll have to learn some rather arbitrary distinctions. The best defense is to be familiar with your software. If you know that there *is* a command to do whirligigs, but can't remember whether it's under "File" or "Arrange," it's only a matter of a fraction of a second to look under both categories.

Menus can nest like the wooden Russian dolls. One will lead to another in a rather infuriating way. Just remember to take one thing at a time. After making your decisions at each level, click "OK." If you've gotten lost in the menus, you can back out at any time by choosing "Cancel." Note: If you cancel out the changes you made will *not* take place.

Be aware that menus can interconnect at lower levels. This means that there *can* be more than one way into the same DIALOG BOX.

NEAR-LETTER QUALITY a printing mode on a dot-matrix printer that produces a thickened form of the normal letterform by overprinting. Near-letter quality is acceptable for some business communications, but is not recommended for producing camera-ready copy.

NEGATIVE a photographically reversed image; black becomes white, white becomes black, and colors become their complements.

In desktop publishing, we usually call white letters on a black background a REVERSE. We think of a negative as the physical film that is the intermediate step between camera-ready copy and a printing plate. *See* PRINTING; DIGITAL PRESS.

NEO-GROTESK NEO-GROTESQUE.

NEO-GROTESQUE a category of sans-serif typefaces whose designs were derived from the 19th century grotesques. Neo-grotesque typefaces are second generation designs; in each case, a designer was trying to correct the deficiencies of an earlier design. The

Handgloves

Neo-grotesque

letterforms are more regular in design. The ends of the curved strokes are oblique rather than horizontal (that would be a *grotesque typeface*). Helvetica and Univers are considered neo-grotesque designs.

NETWORK a set of computers connected together allowing them to share files and devices such as printers and scanners.

NEWSLETTER a short and timely publication that is produced on a regular basis. A popular format for a newsletter is to print on both sides of 11 × 17 inch cover stock and then fold in half for a finished size of $8\frac{1}{2}$ × 11 inches. This gives four full-size pages; if more are needed, they can be added in groups of four.

NEWSPAPER COLUMNS a word-processor mode that specifies a newspaper-like format with text flowing from one column into the next.

NODE

1. an individual computer (or occasionally another type of machine) in a network.

2. (draw programs) a point on a line that helps define the shape of the line. A node usually has one or two control points; you can change the shape of the line by moving the node or moving the control points. It is a very elastic process that sometimes is reminiscent of pulling on a garden hose. Generally speaking, the further away from the node the control points are, the larger the curve will be. The angle of the control points is also important. *See Figure 16.* If the control points are in line with the node, the node is said to be *smooth*. If the control points form a sharp angle (with the node as the vertex of the angle), the line will come to a point at the node. This is a *cusp* node.

NONDOCUMENT MODE a type of word processing that produces plain-text (ASCII) files with no special codes for hyphenation, page breaks, fonts, or the like. You would want to do this if you are going to import the copy into another program (a page layout program, for example). Some word processors require you to save in a special way to get a text file. WordPerfect calls it "Text Out," and you have to specify which

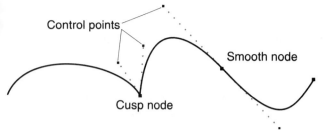

Figure 16 Smooth and cusp nodes

format you want. In many windowed word processors, you need the "Save as ..." option; make sure to change the file's format while you are in the dialog box.

NONREPRO BLUE a special tint of blue that is invisible to photographic film and thus can be used for marking guidelines and instructions on CAMERA-READY COPY.

NUDGE to move a selected object in small increments by using the arrow keys instead of the mouse.

O

OBJECT the basic building block of a drawing program. Sometimes called an ENTITY. *See* DRAW PROGRAM.

OBJECT LINKING AND EMBEDDING (OLE) (in Microsoft Windows 3.1 and later versions) a method of combining information that is processed by different application programs, such as inserting a drawing or a portion of a spreadsheet into a word processing document. The outer document is called the *client* and the document or application that supplies the embedded material is the *server.* OLE supersedes an older feature of Windows called *dynamic data exchange* (DDE).

OLE can be done either of two ways. An *embedded object* becomes part of the document that it is inserted into. For example, if you embed a drawing into a word processing document, the whole thing becomes one file, and to edit it, you use the word processor, which will calls up the drawing program when you double-click on the drawing to edit it. A *linked* object has a life of its own; it remains a separate file and can be edited separately. When you edit it, the information that is linked from it into other documents is automatically updated. Thus, you can use a word processor to create a report that has links to a spreadsheet, and when you update the information in the spreadsheet, the corresponding information in the report will be updated automatically. Embedding and linking correspond to "cold links" and "hot links" in Windows 3.0 DDE.

OBJECT-ORIENTED GRAPHICS *See* DRAW PROGRAM.

Handgloves

Oblique

OBLIQUE slanted. The italics provided with some typefaces are actually mechanically skewed roman fonts rather than true italics. Watch for these oblique fonts when choosing a typeface.

OCR *See* OPTICAL CHARACTER RECOGNITION.

OCTAVO the most popular size for printed books, originally made by folding an uncut sheet of paper in eighths (hence the name) and measuring about 5×8

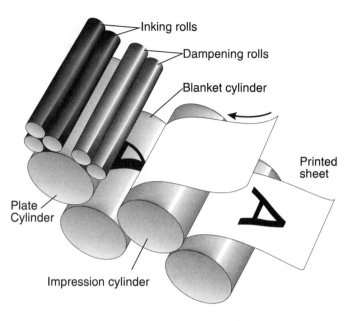

Inking rolls
Dampening rolls
Blanket cylinder
Printed sheet
Plate Cylinder
Impression cylinder

Figure 17 Offset Printing

to 6×10 inches, depending on the paper used and the whims of the designer.

OCTOTHORPE proper name for the cross-hatch symbol (#) on your keyboard. Most people use it to stand for the word "number" or "pound" (weights, not currency).

#
Octothorpe

OFFSET PRINTING the commercial form of lithography. Fast and inexpensive, offset printing is the backbone of printing industry. The basic principle is identical to fine arts lithography: grease and water do not mix. The printing PLATE (either metal or disposable) is photographically etched with special chemicals. The ink will cling to the positive image, but not to the negative area. In the press, the printed image is first laid on a BLANKET and then transferred to the paper (hence, offset). This is all accomplished at fantastically high speeds, thanks to the high degree of mechanization. *See Figure 17*.

OLD STYLE

1. a roman typeface one in which the STRESSES of the letterforms are slanted approximately 30 degrees. Contrast with MODERN, which means the typeface has a vertical stress. Garamond and Times Roman are good examples of old style typefaces. *See Figure 18.*

2. In the PANOSE classification system, MODERN and old style refer to overall proportions of the letters. Old style proportions are based on pure geometric shapes; the *S* is based on two stacked circles, the *E* is the same width (narrow), and the *O* is a perfect circle. Modern proportions are more constant, but there is still noticeable variation in the letter widths.

OLD STYLE FIGURES numerals with ascenders and descenders, the opposite of LINING FIGURES. They are sometimes called LOWER CASE FIGURES.

The following are old style figures:
1 2 3 4 5 6 7 8 9 0
These are LINING or MODERN FIGURES.
1 2 3 4 5 6 7 8 9 0

Why would you want to use old style figures? It is admittedly a very fine point of typography. Have you ever noticed how numbers in a body of text jump out at you? "The 1990 census estimated the current population to be 45,325." If you were to use old style figures in that situation, the numbers would appear to be of the same texture as the rest of the text. "The 1990 census estimated the current population to be 45,325." Adds a bit of elegance to the typesetting, doesn't it?

OLE *see* OBJECT LINKING AND EMBEDDING.

OPAQUE solid; unable to be seen through.

When selecting paper for your finished project, consider how opaque the paper is. If you are going to have heavy *ink coverage*, you will need a thicker paper to avoid SHOW THROUGH.

Printing inks can be made transparent or opaque by mixing the pigment with the appropriate base. *See* VARNISH.

In drawing programs, the objects you create are generally opaque. You can layer one on top of the other

Oranges Oranges

Old style   Modern

Figure 18   Old style versus modern typefaces

---

and hide things. Some programs (CorelDraw 5, for example), have LENSES that can render TRANSPARENT effects.

OPEN

1. to call a file or document from disk in order to work with it.

2. the first member of a paired set of punctuation marks (PARENTHESIS, BRACKETS, BRACES, QUOTES). It is important to remember to have a matching closing mark for every opening one.

3. a type design with an outline around the contours of the letterform and the insides left white.

OPEN WINDOW   in a GRAPHICAL USER INTERFACE (GUI), a framed area of the screen reserved for some purpose. An open window can contain other icons, or it may be running a separate program. You may have several windows open at once, although only one window can be the ACTIVE WINDOW.

OPERATING SYSTEM   a program that controls a computer and makes it possible for users to run application programs.

A completely unprogrammed computer is incapable of recognizing keystrokes on its keyboard or displaying messages on its screen. Most computers are therefore set up so that, when first turned on, they automatically begin running a small program supplied in read-only memory (ROM). *See* BOOT. This program in turn enables the computer to load its operating system from disk.

Under the control of the operating system, the computer recognizes and obeys commands given by the user. In addition, the operating system manages

HANDGLOVES
Open

the interaction between hardware and software to allow you to use the printer, see graphics on the monitor, etc. A computer running under one operating system cannot run programs designed to be run under another operating system, even on the same computer, unless the operating system can emulate another operating system (as OS/2 emulates DOS, for example).

OPTICAL CHARACTER RECOGNITION (OCR) a process for converting printed text to computer files, using a scanner. Technological advances have made it possible to scan printed material and to have your computer, running special software, process the digitized file and deliver to you a text file. OCR can save a lot of tedious typing. OCR works best with certain specially designed fonts, although recent technological advances have improved its reliability with any normal text font.

Some programs can even decipher handwriting (with a certain amount of error expected).

It is wise to carefully edit any scanned text, just in case the computer mistook one letter for another (it is very easy to confuse the letter *O* and the number *0*). Most substitutions will be caught by a spell checker, but watch the punctuation—most OCR systems have trouble telling a comma from a period.

OPTION a key on the Macintosh keyboard that acts as another kind of shift key, allowing special characters to be typed quickly. *See also* COMMAND.

ORNATE in typeface classification, a highly decorative typeface.

ORPHAN the last line of a paragraph is an orphan if it appears by itself as the first line of a page. Some word processors automatically adjust page breaks to avoid orphans. *See also* WIDOW.

OS/2 a multitasking, virtual memory operating system for 80386 and higher PC-compatible computers. (Versions for the PowerPC and other CPUs are under development.) OS/2 can run four kinds of software, and it automatically distinguishes between them:

- OS/2 text-mode software written for any version of OS/2;

- OS/2 Presentation Manager (graphical user interface) software;
- DOS software;
- Windows software, which is run by executing a copy of Windows under OS/2.

OS/2 has been marketed, with some justification, as "a better DOS than DOS and a better Windows than Windows." By using VIRTUAL MACHINES OS/2 gives each DOS program the equivalent of a complete computer to itself, with more memory than a real PC would offer. Windows programs run in windows under OS/2 Presentation Manager and can use OS/2's CLIPBOARD and other data exchange facilities. Perhaps most importantly of all, unlike Windows 3, OS/2 uses *preemptive multitasking* so that programs need not yield time to each other in order to run concurrently. It is almost impossible for a malfunctioning program to disable the whole computer.

OS/2 was originally developed by Microsoft in cooperation with IBM. Since version 2 it has been solely an IBM product, competing against newer versions of Windows. *See also* MULTITASKING; WINDOWS; WARP.

OUTDENT to mark the first line of a paragraph by letting it extend into the left margin; the opposite of INDENT. The entry terms in this dictionary are outdented.

OUTLINE

Handgloves

Outline

1. a typeface design in which a black line marks the contours of the letterforms, leaving the inside white.

2. (DRAW PROGRAM) the vector description of the shape of a character or other object. The attributes of every object's outline can be specified in great detail: color, thickness, end caps, and pen shape. You can even specify a dotted or dashed outline. The outline of the object is represented by a thin line in the WIREFRAME VIEW. *See also* STROKE.

3. (PAINT PROGRAM) a command that will create an outline around each shape in the image.

4. to create an overview of an article, report, or book by listing the major points in a hierarchical structure. When typesetting outlines, you may want to use a 3-pica ($\frac{1}{2}$-inch) indent instead of a 1-em indent.

OUTLINE FONT a font stored as the mathematical descriptions of the letters' outlines. Also called SCALABLE FONTS.

OUTPUT the information that the computer generates as a result of its calculations. Computer output may be printed on paper, photographic slides, displayed on a monitor, or stored on disk or tape.

OVERHEAD TRANSPARENCY a clear plastic sheet, about $8\frac{1}{2} \times 11$ inches, for use with an overhead projector. It is made with a special type of plastic that can be used in your laser printer. Make sure that you purchase the material designed for laser printers—the wrong type of plastic may melt and damage your printer.

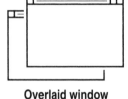

Overlaid window

OVERLAID WINDOW a window that is overlapping and hiding parts of other windows. To bring another window to the front, move the mouse pointer into it and click the button. This makes it the ACTIVE WINDOW. *Contrast* TILE; CASCADE.

You should be aware that windows *can* completely cover and hide other windows and icons. It's actually quite easy to lose something on your computer screen. Many panicky situations can be avoided if you MINIMIZE all of the open windows and search the DESKTOP. Windows provides a TASK LIST that also helps you find lost files or programs. Macintosh users can use the Application menu to find hidden windows.

OVERLAP to coincide with and/or cover. *See* OVERLAID WINDOWS.

Overlapping is the basis for several special effects in DRAW PROGRAMS. First, you use the ability to overlap objects to create TRAP for printing. Second, layering an object of the same color as the background gives you the ability to hide or cleverly conceal all or part of the lower object. Let's say I'm creating a map and wish to show a road crossing another by bridge. I don't want to simply show two crossed lines . . . that would look like an intersection. First, I make the line representing the lower line, then layer a small white

Figure 19   Using overlap in a drawing

square on top of it. Then draw the upper road over
the white square. *See Figure 19.*

P

PADDING a bindery operation that creates pads by gluing sheets of printed paper to a piece of cardboard.

PAGE FRAME an indication of the edges of the paper displayed by your computer's software. The area around the page frame is called the PASTEBOARD.

PAGE LAYOUT SOFTWARE software specially designed for creating CAMERA-READY COPY. Page layout programs, such as Pagemaker, Quark Express, and Corel Ventura Publisher, allow the desktop publisher to combine many separate files of different types into a specified design. These special designs, called TEMPLATES or STYLESHEETS, give a framework to put the individual elements into. Most programs come with a library of predefined stylesheets.

Page layout software also allows more control over typography than most word processors. *See* DESKTOP PUBLISHING; FRAME.

PAGE MAKEUP creating a page by the appropriate use of display type, text, and graphics. Many types of programs can do this work, but PAGE LAYOUT SOFTWARE has been custom-designed for the purpose.

PAINT PROGRAM one type of program for drawing pictures on a personal computer. The user draws with the mouse pointer (or a graphics tablet), and commands are provided for drawing circles, lines, rectangles, and other shapes, as well as for drawing freehand and choosing colors.

Paint programs treat the picture as a grid of pixels. *See* PIXEL; BITMAP. Shadings are easy to produce by manipulating the color of each individual pixel, but the pixel puts a fundamental limit on the sharpness of the picture. It is also hard to move an element of the picture if it is not where you want it. *Contrast* DRAW PROGRAM.

The new generation of PHOTOPAINT programs are able to work around some of these limitations. You can work on portions of a drawing separately and therefore the resolution is dependent on the output device, not your screen. The renderings can be startlingly realistic with such a program. A high-end photopaint program will have many different types of SELECTION TOOLS that overcome many of the drawbacks of working on a bitmap; for instance, the lasso will let you move a defined area.

PALETTE a set of colors chosen from a much larger set. For instance, the IBM VGA can display millions of colors, but only 256 at any one time. You have to choose which colors you want. Usually your program will give you a reasonable default palette, which you can customize and save.

PAMPHLET a small unbound printed piece. Pamphlets can be used as self-mailing pieces if one side is left blank for the address and stamp.

PAN *see* SCROLL.

PANEL CARD a $4\frac{1}{4}$-inch × $5\frac{1}{2}$-inch (109-mm × 149-mm) card with central embossed panel. These cards are too thick to run through a laser printer; use the printer's output as camera-ready art and have the panel cards offset printed. Ask for a sample of the stock beforehand. Make sure to leave enough room for the $\frac{1}{2}$-inch (13-mm) thick border. Also called ANNOUNCEMENT CARDS.

Lorem Ipsum Dolor Sit amet

Consectet eisumod tempor incidum ut labor Velit 14, 1995

Lorem ipsum dolor sit amet consectetu tempor

Panel card

PANOSE SYSTEM a typeface classification system developed by ElseWare (located in Seattle Washington). The unusual name comes from the letters of the alphabet that are measured to determine the typeface's characteristics. The PANOSE system is used to identify and match existing type. Also, because the typeface's characteristics can be reduced to a numerical code, it can be used to to select a similar font automatically if the specified font is not available.

For example, let us imagine my client has brought to me an old brochure set by another typesetter. If he wants the same typeface, I'll have to identify it. I can consult my PANOSE manual to help me identify the typeface. I follow the number generator — this is a typeface with cove serifs, old style in its proportions, medium-low contrast in its stress, which is vertical. The letterforms best fit the *contact* category (the letterform comes in contact with all four sides of its visual dimensions) chart. This face has a standard MIDLINE with a pointed APEX and the X-HEIGHT is standard. There are illustrated charts to help me at each classification. The number I have generated is 1123-122. It's Granjon, which I don't have on my system. The PANOSE manual gives me references to similar typefaces; of these I have Baskerville (PANOSE number 1133-122). The contrast number is different, and the type does appear a little darker. The typefaces have a very similar appearance and, pending the client's approval, I think it will be an acceptable substitute.

The second application for PANOSE is letting the computer substitute fonts for you. Perhaps you have exchanged a file with your friend who has 4000 fonts and has used something a bit unusual to set the newsletter that you're supposed to edit. If your software is using the PANOSE system, it will get the identification number from the font's header and find the closest match.

When your software uses the PANOSE system to automatically substitute a font, it should definitely inform you. In most cases the substitute should be acceptable, but there are going to be exceptions.

PANTONE MATCHING SYSTEM (PMS) a color matching and calibration system designed by the Pantone company. There are a wide variety of products all keyed to the same numbering system. If you want a certain color, you can specify it by its Pantone number and be assured of consistent reproduction. Some software also utilizes the Pantone system. A competing system is TRUMATCH. *See* COLOR.

PAPER a substance composed of fibers from wood, rags, and, sometimes, recycled materials that is processed into thin sheets that are suitable for writing and printing upon. Paper is such a basic commodity in our society that we can hardly imagine life without it. Despite this, it is difficult to keep up with all the new types of papers — papers in rainbow colors, of all different thicknesses, with different textures, and coatings, and made of different materials. A trip to an office supply store or to the printer's office to choose paper for a project can be a mind-numbing experience.

1. Choosing paper for your laser or inkjet printer. You will need to keep two grades of paper at your office—one for drafts and a high-quality paper for final output. For drafts, 20-pound bond (LONG GRAIN) is usually acceptable. Don't buy the super cheap brand; your printer will squeal and tend to jam more. If there's any doubt about the quality of a particular brand, try just one ream. If it's acceptable, you might consider buying a whole case. Tinted paper is useful to have around sometimes.

The paper used for printing CAMERA-READY COPY should be a little heavier (24 pound) and should have a smoother finish than the draft paper. Some brands have a *kaolin* coating that makes one side of the paper look shiny; these papers are for laser printers and give excellent, crisp printouts. Paper for inkjets needs to be more porous to be able to accept the ink; look for a note on the label that will indicate if the paper is suitable for inkjet printers.

2. Choosing paper for a printing job. If you are lucky, you will have a vision of what you want the final piece to look like. But, so many times, when it's time to choose the paper, our ideas are unclear or unformed and the vast array of available paper products tends to confuse even the most seasoned desktop publisher. This is a good time to visit the printer.

First of all, describe the project. Is it a newsletter? a postcard? a booklet? In many cases, the nature of the final printed piece will dictate the proper type of paper to use. If there are HALFTONES to be printed, avoid colored papers; without a pure white for the highlight area, halftones look muddy. Special effects like DIE CUTS and EMBOSSING will need a sturdy paper that can tolerate the abuse. In some cases, you might want to choose a *cover stock* (a thick, sturdy paper) for a cover and have the inner pages printed on a lighter-weight paper. Remember to coordinate the choice of paper color with ink color.

The paper surface needs to be considered. For instance, photographs reproduce much better on a COATED STOCK. Some coated papers do not fold well; take a sample of the paper and test it. Letterheads look more elegant printed on a paper with a *laid* texture. Covers can be printed on papers with colorful fibers in the weave of the paper, gorgeous textures, and sophisticated colors. (The feel of a good quality paper can say a lot to the intended audience about the quality of the literature they are holding. That's why annual reports are always printed on obviously expensive papers.)

Investigate recycled papers; not only are they environmentally responsible, but most are quite attractive.

Finally, consider the cost. (Everything does seem to come down to money in the end.) Paper costs have steadily been rising as the paper mills comply with new antipollution legislation. The initial price quote of any printing job is quite likely to send you (and your client) into sticker shock. Compare costs between two possible choices; is the higher-priced product going to give you a proportionally better printed piece? It *may* be worth its higher price.

The printer should advise you of the availability of the paper you have chosen. Sometimes this will involve a quick phone call to the supplier. Make the printer aware of any time constraints you have. If you must deliver the printed pieces in one week, there may not be enough time to special order a paper from the distributor. Specify a second choice in case your first choice is unobtainable.

See also LASER PRINTER; INKJET PRINTER; COLOR; PRINTER.

PAPER SIZES *See* A4; DIN PAPER SIZES; ENVELOPE SIZES; FOOLSCAP; LEGAL SIZE; LETTER SIZE; OCTAVO; PAPER SIZES (ISO); QUARTO.

PAPER SIZES (ISO) a set of standard sizes of paper used in Europe, of which A4 is the best known. *See* A4. The sizes are shown in *Table 6*. Each size is made by cutting the next larger size in half, and all sizes have the same height-to-width ratio (1.414:1). A0 paper has an area of 1 square meter, and B0 paper is 1 meter wide. Note that A4 paper is usually mailed in C6 or DL envelopes. *See* ENVELOPE SIZES.

These standards are administered by the Inter-

Table 6 ISO paper sizes

Each size is made by cutting the next larger size in half.

	mm (exact)	inches (approximate)
A0	841 × 1189	33.1 × 46.8
A1	594 × 841	23.4 × 33.1
A2	420 × 594	16.5 × 23.4
A3	297 × 420	11.7 × 16.5
A4	210 × 297	8.3 × 11.7
A5	148 × 210	5.8 × 8.3
A6	105 × 148	4.1 × 5.8
B0	1000 × 1414	39.4 × 55.7
B1	707 × 1000	27.8 × 38.4
B2	500 × 707	19.7 × 27.8
B3	353 × 500	13.9 × 19.7
B4	250 × 353	9.8 × 13.9
B5	176 × 250	6.9 × 9.8

national Standards Organization (ISO). They were formerly a German industrial standard (Deutsche Industrie-Norm) and were known as DIN paper sizes.

PARA short for paragraph.

PARAGRAPH a group of sentences that form a whole; paragraphs are the basic building blocks of articles, stories, and reports. Be consistent: Choose a style of setting paragraphs for the document and stick with it. Here are some of the many correct ways to indicate a new paragraph:

- No indent; leave extra space between paragraphs.
- 1-em indent (or outdent), no extra space between paragraphs.
- 1-em indent *and* space between paragraphs.
- A FLEURON or PILCROW (¶) at the beginning of a paragraph in continuous text.

PARAMETERS specifications or instructions passed to a computer program either by the user or by another program.

PART TITLE the first page of a book after the end-papers; sometimes called a HALF TITLE. The part title contains the name of the book and nothing else. The next right-hand page will be the title page.

PASSWORD a secret word or phrase (it can contain numbers, too) that is required to use a computer system, thus preventing unauthorized persons from gaining access to the computer.

If you are using a password to protect your computer, do the following:

- Protect your password. Keep it a secret and don't share it.
- Don't choose an obvious password. Use some imagination and forethought. What would be hard to guess?
- Don't use a word in any language; some people crack computers by automatically trying every word in a dictionary.
- Change your password regularly.

PASTE to transfer material from a holding area (the CLIPBOARD) into the document or picture being edited.

PASTEBOARD the work area surrounding the page outline in a drawing program. It is often helpful to assemble complex objects on the pasteboard, then group them and move them into position on the page.

PASTE-UP to create a CAMERA-READY mechanical by fastening type and graphic images to a stiff piece of paper. It may horrify some people who thought that desktop publishing would make paste-up obsolete, but sometimes paste-up is necessary and preferable. By being willing to do some paste-up work, you can work on projects larger than the largest size of paper that your laser printer can handle. If you want to use some printed CLIP ART, you can leave a place for it, and simply paste it in. And sometimes, due to BUGS or short-sighted design, your software or hardware refuses to cooperate with you. Just get the type and graphics printed out separately and paste them up. (This is called out-smarting the computer.)

Ideally, you should have a drafting table or LIGHT TABLE for doing paste-up work. You'll also need a

T-square, and a triangle to help line things up. Although masking tape will work, invest in a roll of drafting tape; it won't tear the paper when you remove it. A graphics knife works better than scissors for cutting paper. A NONREPRO BLUE pen and a technical pen will round out your basic paste-up tools.

Commercially available paste-up boards have a grid of lines printed in nonrepro blue. Although these are nice to have, any white, stiff paper large enough for the project at hand will do. Illustration board is also a good choice. You should use a board large enough to leave a one inch margin around the image area. Mark all crop and fold marks in this margin. Also, identify the job and specify the color and tint of ink. By taping a piece of clear acetate at the top, you can position items that will be printed in a different color or tint.

Rubber cement can be used for occasional paste-up work. Make sure to clean all edges with a rubber cement pickup to avoid PASTE-UP LINES. If you find yourself doing a lot of paste-up work, you should investigate the purchase of a *waxer*, a machine that spreads a thin layer of wax on the back of a printout. Wax is easier to handle and clean up after.

Other adhesives suitable for paste-up work are spray adhesive and rub-down dry adhesive. Each method has its pros and cons; you'll have to evaluate which adhesive will work best for you.

PASTE-UP LINES smudgy lines caused by the shadow of a piece of paper on camera-ready artwork. The print shop can mask paste-up lines, or chemically remove them from the printing plate, but these are time-consuming procedures. The best way to fix paste-up lines is to prevent them:

- Don't paste up the artwork if you don't have to. Prefer digital clip art or use a SCANNER to get images into digital form. Ideally, the finished CAMERA-READY COPY should come straight out of the laser printer.
- Do not trim the artwork too closely. If possible, leave $\frac{1}{4}$ inch between any printed line and the edge of the paper.

- If you *have* to paste up, be neat. Keep your hands clean. Rubber cement is a good choice for doing limited amounts of paste-up. (If you find yourself doing a lot of paste-up work, you may want to investigate a waxer.) Do not bend or curl the edges of the paper. Any stray adhesive will attract dirt; use a *rubber cement pickup* to carefully clean the edge. Be gentle! Laser printer output is actually very fragile because the toner powder is so easily disturbed.

- Use a clean roller over the entire page to make sure everything is flat and solidly in place.

PATH

1. (draw program) a contour or outline. Most often encountered as FIT TEXT TO PATH, a command that lets you mold the baseline of a line of text to a specified shape (path).

2. specification of how to find a file on a disk that has more than one directory. In DOS, paths have either of two forms. For example,

`\AAA\BBB\CCC`

means, "In the root directory there is a directory called AAA. In AAA there is a directory called BBB. In BBB there is a directory or file called CCC." If the initial backslash is left out, the path starts at the directory currently in use rather than at the root directory. For example, the path

`AAA\BBB\CCC`

means, "In the current directory there is a directory called AAA. In AAA there is a directory called BBB. In BBB there is a directory or file called CCC."

3. command in MS-DOS (PC-DOS) that specifies directories where DOS can search for command files (.BAT, .COM, and .EXE files) if they are not found in the current directory. The PATH command is often included as part of the AUTOEXEC.BAT file so it will always be executed when needed.

See DIRECTORY; HARD DISK MANAGEMENT.

PCX a standard format for graphic image files developed by Zsoft, manufacturer of a program called PC

Paintbrush. PCX files store compactly, display quickly on PC screens and can be used by many programs.

PDD *see* PORTABLE DIGITAL DOCUMENT.

**Printer's error
(proofreader's mark)**

PE proofreader's mark for a printer's or typesetter's error. *See* PRINTER'S ERROR.

PEL picture element. A pel is the smallest unit of a bitmap. You can zoom in so much that the pels look like squares, but you cannot edit any unit smaller than the pel.
   This term is synonymous with PIXEL.

PEN a tool used to create lines. Sometimes a similar tool is shown as a pencil. Most programs allow control of the width of the stroke the pen makes, the shape of the "nib" of the pen, the MITER LIMIT, and the shape of the endcaps. These settings are usually under an *Attributes* or sometimes *Preferences* menu item. See your program's manual for details.
   The icon shown is from Corel PhotoPaint.

Pen

PERFECT BOUND a type of binding suitable for softcover books and magazines. After being folded and placed in order, the pages are literally glued to the spine of the book. Perfect binding is best for large press runs and publications too thick for stapling. For other methods of binding, *see* BINDING.

PERIPHERAL a device connected to a computer. Examples of peripherals include graphics tablets, tape drives, disk drives, and printers.

PERSONAL COMPUTER a computer designed to be used by only one person, either at home or in a business situation. Personal computers may be linked together by a NETWORK so that they can share files and peripherals.

PERSPECTIVE drawing techniques that give the illusion of depth. Rendering three-dimensional objects realistically in two dimensions (a screen or piece of paper) requires the use of perspective. Objects that are far away appear smaller and closer together. The sides of a large rectangular building will seem to converge on the horizon. The point where the two sides would meet is called the VANISHING POINT.

Perspective

Most drawing programs give you a lot of help with perspective renderings by letting you manipulate the vanishing point of an object. You can grab the vanishing point with the mouse and drag it wherever you want it to be. There are also draw and CAD programs whose strengths are perspective renderings and 3-D modeling.

Also remember that you can add the illusion of depth to a drawing by using *atmospheric perspective*, the effect you may have noticed on a hazy summer day — objects far away from you are lighter and slightly bluer.

PHOTOGRAPH   a continuous-tone image created with a camera. Because photographs closely reproduce what we are able to see with our eyes, we credit them with being more "real" than drawings. Photographs will make any document more interesting, and will convey much more information to the readers than words alone.

There are basically two ways to include photos in your work: have the photos stripped in at the print shop, or digitize them and use the laser printer output as your camera-ready art. Both methods have their pros and cons — sometimes you may prefer one method, and sometimes the other. You'll have to decide on a case-by-case basis.

The sharpest reproduction is achieved by using old-fashioned technology: simply leave a blank space or black box for the photo and have it stripped in by the printer. This way, a finer line screen can be used for halftoning the photo. *See* HALFTONE. All you will have to do is to indicate where the photo should be cropped, and the amount of reduction or enlargement. *See* SCALE. If the original photo doesn't have borders, mount it to a piece of white index paper or illustration board so you won't have to write directly on the photo.

Leave a place for the photo in your document. Either use an empty FRAME of the correct size or make a black rectangle. When your laser printer output is photographed by the copy camera, the black rectangle will become a clear area on the negative. The halftoned and sized negative of the photograph can be taped in place just before the printing plate is made.

What if the original photograph is deficient in some way? Or, what if you are sending the job to a DIGITAL PRESS? You'll have to get the photograph DIGITIZED so that you can work with it on the computer. If you don't have a SCANNER, find a local business that can scan the photo for you. It's best to scan the photo at the finished size and at the resolution of the output device (usually your laser printer). The contrast and brightness of the image can be adjusted while scanning it. You'll notice that photographs (especially color ones) create large files. A $3\frac{1}{2} \times 5$-inch color snapshot, scanned at 100%, 300 DPI, 24 bit (millions of colors) creates a 3.3-megabyte file. Transporting and managing files of this size can be quite a headache! Files of black and white photos are smaller; they don't have to include as much information.

Once the photograph is digitized, you can use a PHOTOPAINT program to alter it. Spots and flaws can be removed, distracting elements erased, backgrounds changed, or the over-all color balance adjusted. *See* RETOUCHING. Then import the digital photo into your page layout program. When you print the camera-ready copy with your laser printer, the photograph will be there. If it is a full-color photo, the computer will generate the CMYK color separations.

The disadvantages of this method are the resolution of the laser printer and the quality of the color separations. A 300-DPI laser printer can only produce the equivalent of a 50-LPI halftone. *See* RESOLUTION. This is coarser than a newspaper halftone. 600-DPI is obviously better (equivalent to 100-LPI)—if higher quality output is necessary, you'll have to send the file to a service bureau to be output on an imagesetter. Producing accurate color separations is sometimes a problem. The system must be properly COLOR CALIBRATED, and many factors beyond your immediate control may throw the color balance off. Some trial and error may be necessary.

When selecting photos for publication, look for sharply focused images with good tonal range. If the publication is to be printed in one color (usually black), you should ask for black and white glossy photographs. Color photos always look muddy when converted into black-and-white halftones. If you have to use a color photo, first make a photocopy to evaluate how the colors will convert to grayscale. Time and budget permitting, you could have the color negative printed onto black and white photographic paper. This will require locating a custom processing lab. The best results will be obtained by scanning the photo as color and letting your photopaint program do the grayscale conversion.

Avoid printing black and white halftone pictures of people in colored ink. At best, the people will look sickly. An alternative is to run the text in a colorful ink and having the photo print in black. You might also experiment with DUOTONES (overprinting a color halftone over the black one). *See* COLOR; DUOTONE.

Smooth paper will reproduce halftoned photographs best. Textured papers break up the halftone pattern and lose detail. *See* PAPER.

Finally, be careful when handling photographs. You must not bend them, spill liquids on them, or touch the image area. Any crack or flaw on the *emulsion* (the glossy coating) will be seen by the copy camera or scanner. If you need to indicate crop marks, mount the photo to index paper or illustration board; don't write directly on the photo. When shipping photographs, make sure that there is enough stiff cardboard in the mailer to protect them. Write "PHOTOS: DO NOT BEND" on the outside of the mailer.

PHOTOPAINT   a type of bitmap editing program with special tools and filters for manipulating photographs. You can also create illustrations from scratch with the drawing tools provided.

In many ways, photopaint programs are the professional versions of the limited paint programs that come with operating systems. They are proportionately difficult to learn and master. Be prepared to spend enough time reading the manual and experimenting.

PHOTOSTAT   a photographic print produced on special paper with a copy camera. Photostats are either proofs of phototypesetting work, line art, or screened continuous-tone artwork. The photostat (*stat* for short) is often used to indicate position and cropping on a mechanical.

PHOTOTYPE type produced by photographic means. *Contrast* DIGITAL TYPE *and* HOT TYPE.

PICA

1. a pica typewriter prints 10 characters per inch. So do most fixed-pitch computer printers.

2. a unit of measurement, commonly used in typesetting and desktop publishing. 1 pica equals approximately $\frac{1}{6}$ inch or 12 POINTS.

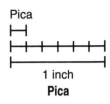

Pica

1 inch

Pica

PICK TOOL a cursor shaped like an arrow that is used to pick up or pick out objects.

The icon shown is from CorelDraw 3.

Pick tool

PICKUP a rubbery square which is used to clean excess rubber cement off a MECHANICAL.

PICTOGRAPH a picture that represents an idea. Computer icons are a type of pictograph.

PIECE FRACTION a fraction constructed of three characters: the small numerator and denominator separated by a slash or horizontal bar. You can use piece fractions to supplement the font's collection of CASE FRACTIONS. Some word processors have tools and macros that speed the building of piece fractions.

Piece fractions are also called SPLIT FRACTIONS.

$$\frac{1}{2}$$

Piece fraction

PIE CHART a type of chart that resembles a pie and graphically shows the relative size of different subcategories of a whole.

PIE WEDGE a section of a pie chart. Also called a *slice*. Each pie wedge is used to represent a different category of the whole.

Pie chart

PIF (Windows, OS/2) **P**rogram **I**nformation **F**ile. A file whose name ends in ".PIF" contains information about how to run an .EXE or .COM file—how much memory it requires, whether it can run in a window, whether it can multitask, and the like. Most software installation programs can do this automatically. You may need your local guru to set up a .PIF file for any old nonwindowed application programs that you wish to run.

Pi font

Pilcrow

Pipe

PI FONT highly stylized artwork stored and utilized in the same manner as a regular alphabet. Also called SYMBOL FONTS and DINGBATS.

PIG BRISTLES text with too many words hyphenated at the end of the line.

PILCROW the symbol ¶, which is used to mark the beginning of a new paragraph when the text is set with continuous paragraphs. The pilcrow may also be used as a footnote symbol. *See* FOOTNOTE.

PIPE the vertical bar character "|" that is the shift of the backslash key on an IBM PC compatible keyboard. It is not often used in regular text; the pipe occurs mainly in computer documentation.

PIRACY the unauthorized copying of software, which is forbidden by law. (*See* SOFTWARE LICENSE; COPY-RIGHT.)

It is in your own best interests not to use pirated software. You cannot get (nor should you expect) user support from the software vendor if you are running an illegal copy of "WhizzyWrite." You won't have a copy of the manual. You are at greater risk of VIRUSES. And if the software company isn't getting the revenues from sales of their program, they will not be able to maintain the program (i.e., fix the bugs) or to keep adding new features.

PITCH the number of characters per inch a typewriter or typewriter-like printer produces. The most common pitch is 10 characters per inch, but an elite typewriter has 12 per inch.

Typefaces are sometimes described as FIXED PITCH or PROPORTIONAL PITCH. A fixed-pitch typeface has all the characters the same width. This mimics the look of a typewriter. A lower case *i* occupies the same width as an upper-case *W*. A proportional pitch design allows variation in the widths of the letterforms. Most typefaces used on your computer *are* proportional pitch. Note: This is why it is important to use *tabs* to construct tables and columns. Otherwise, there is *no way* to get the type to line up!

PIXEL tiny dots that make up a picture on a computer monitor. For example, a 14-inch VGA color screen in

𝓗px   ⊢px   Hpx   **Hpx**

Figure 20   These samples are all set in 24 point type.

high-resolution mode consists of a 640 by 480 pixel array. You can draw pictures on the screen by controlling the color of each pixel. *See* GRAPHICS; PAINT PROGRAM; BITMAP.

The term PEL (for **p**icture **el**ement) is coming into wider use. It means essentially the same thing as pixel, but acknowledges that at high magnification you are working with a larger square instead of a dot on the computer monitor.

Pixelate

PIXELATE a photopaint filter that transforms the bitmap into larger blocks. Detail is lost because the new PEL (picture element) is much larger and coarser than before. This is a fun filter to play with. It's a useful one to remember when you want an image be obviously computer enhanced.

PLATE *see* PRINTING PLATE.

PLATEN the roller in a typewriter or printer against which the keys or pins strike.

PLATFORM equipment used as a base on which to build something else. So, you might describe your computer as a desktop publishing platform.

PLUG-IN an accessory program that provides additional functions for a main application program. Plug-ins have to be loaded at the same time as the main program; they then show up as an option in an appropriate menu.

PMS *see* PANTONE MATCHING SYSTEM.

PO *see* PURCHASE ORDER.

POINT a unit of measurement, used in typesetting. A point is equal to $\frac{1}{72}$ of an inch. The size of type is usually expressed in points.

Why, then, is some 10-point type larger than others? The answer lies in the way type was measured in "the good old days." The measurement was taken of the *wooden block* on which the metal type was mounted. This usually included some space at the top of the tallest capital letters and below the descenders. To this day, even digitized typefaces show some of the same idiosyncrasies. (*See Figure 20.*) Why haven't all the typefaces been regularized when converted to digital form? Basically, we are trying to be faithful to the original designs.

In a typical book-sized line of type, about 25 picas wide, legibility is greatest with 10-point type with 2 points of leading. This works out to 6 lines per inch. Longer lines would dictate a larger font. *See* LEADING; TYPEFACE; LINE LENGTH; TYPESETTING ERRORS.

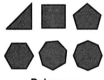

Pointer

POINTER a symbol that moves around a computer screen under the control of the user. For example, to execute a command on the Macintosh, use the mouse to move the pointer to the icon representing that command, and then click the button on the mouse. The appearance of the pointer will change depending on the software and the tool being used.

POINTING DEVICE a computer peripheral that allows you to control your computer in a graphical user interface (GUI). The most familiar pointing device is a MOUSE, but some people prefer TRACKBALLS, or GRAPHICS TABLETS.

Polygons

POLYGON a closed geometric figure with any number of straight sides. The sides may differ in length. Triangles, squares, pentagons (five sided), hexagons (six sided), heptagons (seven sided), and octagons (eight sided) are all examples of polygons.

POP-UP MENUS *see* DROP-DOWN MENU.

PORTABLE DIGITAL DOCUMENT a file format supported by Macintosh computers with QuickDraw GX. A document saved in this format can be viewed on any other Mac with QuickDraw GX, even if the computers do not have the same application software or fonts. *See* QUICKDRAW GX; ELECTRONIC PUBLISHING.

PORTFOLIO a collection of one's best work, maintained to display to prospective clients or employers.

Actual finished printed pieces are preferable to student work or self-promotion pieces. There should be around a dozen samples — most people don't feel up to viewing more than that.

Great care should be given to the physical presentation of your portfolio. An appropriate portfolio case, with or without acetate pages, should be purchased. Loose papers should never be presented; there is too much risk of damage to the samples. Brochures and pamphlets may be in clear plastic pockets so they can be removed and examined. Artwork should be matted or mounted. Very large works (signage, posters, or banners) can be photographed. Slides (in slide pages) are acceptable; if you prefer photographic prints, have them matted.

Portrait

PORTRAIT paper oriented so that it is taller than it is wide (like a portrait painting). Most printers can offer you a choice of portrait or LANDSCAPE orientation (which is paper turned sideways). Some software calls this "tall" instead of portrait.

POSITIVE an image that represents black as black and white as white; usually black graphics on a white background. *Contrast* NEGATIVE.

POSTCARD an inexpensive mailer, useful for return business communications, some forms of direct mail solicitation, and the proverbial "wish you were here" vacation notes. According to the United States Postal Service, postcards must be no smaller than $3\frac{1}{2} \times 5$ inches and no larger than $4\frac{1}{4} \times 6$ inches. The paper for postcards must be between 0.007 and 0.0095 inches thick.

POSTER TYPE specially designed fonts for large sizes. *See also* DISPLAY TYPE.

POSTSCRIPT a graphical command language for laser printers and other graphical output devices developed by Adobe Systems of Palo Alto, California.

A PostScript printer accepts not only characters to be printed but also commands to change the size of type fonts or to draw circles or lines in specific positions. In effect, a PostScript printer has a computer that understands a special programming language built inside of it!

An application program designed to work with PostScript will automatically send PostScript codes to the printer.

PostScript was introduced in 1985; Level 2 Post-Script, an extended version of the language, was introduced in 1991 and is now standard. *Encapsulated PostScript* (EPS) is a file format for using the Post-Script language to exchange graphics between programs. Notoriously, software that imports some EPS files does not necessarily understand the entire Post-Script language; many programs confine themselves to the Adobe Illustrator (AI) subset of EPS. So, if an .EPS file does not import well, try saving it as an .AI file in the application in which you created it.

POWER LINE PROTECTION measures that can be taken to insure the quality of electrical power supplied to computers. Several things can go wrong with the AC power supplied to a computer from the wall outlet.

1. Brief bursts ("spikes") of excessive voltage can damage the computer. These spikes come from lightning or from large electric motors switching off. They are easily absorbed by a surge protector (see SURGE PROTECTOR).

2. Power failures cause the computer to shut down or restart suddenly, losing the data that you were working on. A surge protector cannot prevent this. If the problem is frequent, you may want to invest in an uninterruptable power supply (UPS).

3. The computer can emit radio or TV interference through the power line. *See* RFI PROTECTION.

POWERLINES a feature available in CorelDraw 4.0 and up, which allows complex calligraphic effects to be applied to lines.

PREFACE brief introductory comments written by the author of a book. The preface is part of the *front matter* (items that usually precede Chapter 1 of the text). *See also* FOREWORD; INTRODUCTION.

PREFERENCES settings for a computer program to allow for individual differences. The preferences menu is sometimes a rather obscure catch-all for adjustments to mouse tracking, the double-click rate, the NUDGE rate and the MITER LIMIT. Take the time to become familiar with the "Preferences" settings in your software; sometimes a problem can be quickly solved by making a small adjustment.

PREPRESS actions that must be completed before sending a job to the printing press operator—specifically the production of the NEGATIVES and PRINTING PLATES from the CAMERA-READY artwork. This may entail STRIPPING in photographs, cleaning up paste-up lines, and preparing COLOR SEPARATIONS.

The newest generation of DIGITAL PRESSES eliminates this step by allowing the printer to print directly from a computer file.

PREPRINTED STOCK previously printed paper that can be used in a laser printer, photocopier, or offset press. This is a relatively inexpensive way to add the impact of color to a small job. There are basically two types of preprinted stock: commercially available and do-it-yourself.

There are several companies that specialize in manufacturing preprinted stock. There are a wide variety of brochures, letterheads, certificates, and business cards available. Sometimes these preprinted products are the only affordable way to get four-color printing. The main danger is that a competitor may choose the same paper that *you* did. If that possibility is unacceptable, you may choose to do your own preprinted stock. Plan a design that can have the color printed first. For instance, run the FLAG of the newsletter in color, leaving all the rest blank. Negotiate a quantity discount with the printer. Have them run a six-month supply of the newsletter stock. The print shop may even agree to store the preprinted stock in exchange for being allowed to print six editions of a monthly newsletter.

Letterheads lend themselves to being preprinted with a corporate logo. Individual business letters can then be printed on the laser printer.

PRESENTATION a talk or lecture with accompanying charts, notes and illustrations. Businessmen usually think in terms of sales presentations, but any project or seminar that needs to display and explain findings to an audience can be called a presentation.

PRESENTATION SOFTWARE a program or suite of programs that allow the user to create graphic images (drawings, charts, and texts) to accompany a talk or lecture. Examples of software include Persuasion (from Aldus), Freelance Graphics (Lotus), and PowerPoint (Microsoft). Typically, these programs include drawing tools and the ability to make charts out of data taken from a spreadsheet program. Users can create a complete show by arranging the images in the desired order and standardizing the color scheme for all of the images. By viewing miniature images (thumbnails) of the presentation all on the same screen, the user can obtain an overview of the finished product. Newer programs also allow sound, music, and animation to be used to enhance the presentation. *See* MULTIMEDIA.

PRESS

1. to depress the mouse button and hold it until you complete the mouse action. *Contrast* CLICK.

2. a printing press. *See* CAMERA-READY for tips on preparing your publication for the press. *See* PRINTER for suggestions on how to have a good working relationship with your printer.

PRESS APPROVAL final approval for a job given after viewing a PRESS PROOF.

PRESS PROOF a printed piece that is carefully examined for registration errors and color balance. It is recommended that the designer be on hand to check press proofs for PROCESS COLOR work and jobs requiring special inks or techniques such as METALLIC INK.

PRESSTYPE a type of lettering suitable for setting short headlines in decorative fonts. Also called RUB-DOWN LETTERING. Presstype comes on a plastic sheet. You mark a light line, preferably in NONREPRO BLUE, where you want the baseline of the type. You then proceed to carefully align and rub down (burnish) each letter. You will need to purchase a different sheet of lettering for each size of type that you need.

PREVIEW a viewing mode that displays the appearance of the finished document or drawing. In order to let you work quickly, many drawing programs show you only an outline of the objects on screen. (This is called WIREFRAME MODE.) When you want to see what the final printed piece would look like, you have to use the "Preview" command. Then all of the objects appear with their fills so that you can check whether they are layered correctly.

Most drawing programs will allow you to work in preview mode, but the time spent redrawing the screen after each action can be quite irritating. It is best to work with the wireframe and preview to check your work. Another method is to open two windows containing the same file; one in wireframe and the second in preview.

Some non-WYSIWYG word processors will also allow you to preview your document.

PRINTER

1. a device for putting computer output on paper or transparencies. *See* LASER PRINTER; INKJET PRINTER; DYE-SUBLIMATION PRINTER; WAX THERMAL PRINTER.

2. a person who helps desktop publishers produce multiple copies of their work. Here's some advice for getting the most from your friendly local printer:

- **Establish a good working relationship.** Take the time to get to know your local printer. Ask about equipment that may have special requirements. If you have any technical questions, don't hesitate to give the printer a call. If you are trying something with special inks or papers, bring the printer in as a consultant at the *design* stage. Twenty-four hours before the brochures are due at the client's office is a *very* bad time to learn that it is technically impossible to put metallic ink over varnish. Try to be easy to get along with; you may need a favor later.

- **Time considerations.** It's important for you to give the printer enough time to do the work. No matter how urgently you need the finished job, no matter how you beg and plead, printers cannot change the laws of physics. It takes time for the paper to run through the press, time for the ink to dry, time to do the BINDERY WORK. The printer has the headache of juggling all the other clients. Ask the printer to estimate how long your job will take when you're getting the cost estimate.

Don't make changes after giving the printer the camera-ready copy. Proof the job carefully. Get clients to sign that everything is OK. Make sure that they understand that this is the last chance to make changes. Tell them, "Up to now, we've been working on the computer, and it's been easy to make corrections. But now, I'm taking this to the printer and this has got to be the *final* version. At best, you'll keep delaying the start of your job. At worst, you will incur charges for PLATES that have to be redone."

- **Mistakes.** Most printers are very good about redoing jobs that they made a mistake on. In case of any disagreements, you have the option of reporting them to the Better Business Bureau in your area. Some areas have arbitrators to help settle disputes. Your last resort is small claims court.

  The best way to deal with mistakes, though, is to *prevent* them. (Remember Murphy's Law! "If anything can go wrong, it will.") Label everything that you give the printer. Put your name, address, and phone somewhere on each piece of camera-ready art. Number multiple originals "1 of 3," "2 of 3," etc. Be specific in your instructions. Don't just say "Print this green." Label it "Pantone 368." Use your laser printer to make a DUMMY to show how you want everything put together. Color jobs should be proofed either on a high-quality dye-sublimation printer or with a *color key* (a photographically prepared proof).

- **Money.** As usual, everything boils down to money. Remember that this is a business relationship. Be professional in your dealings with printers. Make sure you pay them promptly. Different printers will have different feelings on negotiating prices, but if you are sending work regularly, the printer may be able to give you a price break.

PRINTER'S ERROR a production or typesetting error made by the printer. Abbreviated *PE*.

PRINTING PLATE the object that transfers the image being printed to the paper. In OFFSET LITHOGRAPHY, printing plates are made of either metal, plastic, or even a specially coated paper. The image of the CAMERA-READY copy is photographically copied to the plate. After the plate is properly developed and treated, only the image area will hold ink. The plate is wrapped around a large cylinder, inked by one set of rollers, and prints the image onto the paper as the cylinder turns. (*See* illustration at OFFSET LITHOGRAPHY.)

Jobs with HALFTONES should be printed with metal plates; although they are more costly and take longer to prepare, a finer line screen can be used to give a more faithful reproduction of the art. Metal plates should also be used when the quantity to be printed exceeds 5000 copies. A plastic or paper plate will break down around 5000 impressions and have to be replaced.

PRINT MANAGER one of the Microsoft Windows system programs. Print Manager is in charge of overseeing the relations between the computer and the printer. It has to be provided with the specifics of your printer when Windows is installed. You will occasionally have to adjust the orientation or paper size; most of this sort of control is provided to Print Manager by the application program. Print Manager will also tell you if there are any files waiting to be printed, and it automatically handles SPOOLING the files to the printer.

If you are having problems with a document not printing correctly, it's a good idea to double-check the settings of the Print Manager. •

PRINT SPOOLER a program that accepts output from an application program and feeds it to the printer at the correct speed. Normally, a print spooler runs in the background. This frees the application program from having to supervise the print job so that you can keep on working.

PRO BONO WORK professional services donated to a worthy cause, usually a nonprofit organization or a needy individual. From the Latin phrase *pro bono publico*, meaning "for the public good."

Pro bono work can be an integral part of your business' contribution to a better world; there are many deserving organizations who need help designing and producing literature. Even so, the fair-minded desktop publisher will at some point have to turn down requests for help, simply because there are not enough hours in the day (given no bounds, *pro bono* work will expand to fill all available time). Saying "no" to a worthy cause is difficult; it may help to explain that you budget a certain amount of time each year for volunteer work and that you have already exceeded that limit.

For tax reasons, you should keep track of the hours spent on *pro bono* work. Seek your accountant's advice on the best way to handle the contribution.

PROCESS COLOR a method of printing that uses the combination of four inks (cyan, magenta, yellow, and black) to reproduce realistic pictures. You would want to use process color when reproducing color photographs or a full-color illustration. *See* CMYK; SPOT COLOR.

PROGMAN short for **Prog**ram **Man**ager (part of Windows).

PROGRAM a set of instructions for a computer to execute. You can write your own programs if you know a programming language, but most of us buy prewritten programs to do certain tasks, such as word processing or page layout. Programs are also called SOFTWARE.

PROGRAM GROUP in Microsoft Windows, a logical or useful grouping of application programs that can be reduced to a single icon. In many ways, a program group is similar to a SUBDIRECTORY or a Macintosh FOLDER. An application program can appear in more than one program group.

PROGRAM MANAGER a program supplied with Microsoft Windows 3 that allows you to organize and run your application programs. Program Manager by default takes over most of the screen and lets you control all the other applications from within it. Because of this, to many people, Program Manager *is* Windows. When you close the Program Manager, you end your Windows session.

In some ways, the Program Manager provides another layer of structure to the GRAPHICAL USER INTERFACE (GUI) as compared to the Macintosh environment. On the Macintosh, you work directly from the desktop, and all devices, folders and files can be manipulated in pretty much the same fashion. (You can open a drive, open a folder, or open the trash can. Each of these objects can contain others.)

In Windows, you usually work within the confines of the Program Manager. You *can* minimize your frequently used applications and have them appear on the desktop on startup, and then work pretty much in the same fashion as on a Macintosh. The big difference comes in dealing with the hardware. The disk drive is not the same thing as a PROGRAM GROUP to Windows. You have to use FILE MANAGER to view a directory. Deleting a file is an action to perform, not the elegant concept of the Macintosh trash can icon.

On the other hand, the Program Manager may provide better organization for application programs. By making specific the distinction between programs, files, hardware, and actions, Windows may provide a greater sense of control to the computer users.

PROMPT a symbol that appears on a computer monitor to signal to the user that the computer is ready to receive input. Programs that use prompts are usually of the pre-windowed generation of software, such as DOS.

PROOF

1. to examine work for textual accuracy, color balance, correct typography, grammar, and punctuation.

2. a test print, usually produced with a laser printer or a color printer. The proof should be carefully evaluated for all aspects of design and quality of the writing. If the laser printer will be the final output device, pay attention to the letterforms; some software and printer combinations will occasionally produce some bad characters. Proof the text for spelling errors (a spell checker can't catch everything!), grammar, punctuation, and readability.

For color jobs, the proof is especially critical for evaluating the color balance. Make sure the system (scanner, monitor, printer) has been properly CALIBRATED.

Photographic proofs pulled from the same negatives that will be used to prepare the printing plates are called *blueprints, bluelines* or just *blues*.

PROOFREADER'S MARKS a standard set of symbols and abbreviations used when proofreading text. *See Figure 21.* If a confusing situation arises, feel free to elaborate in the margins. When there is not enough margin to write in, you could use a tracing paper overlay or attach sticky notes to the proof.

PE and AA are only used when it is necessary to assign who should bear the cost of making the corrections.

PROPORTIONALLY SPACED TYPE *see* PROPORTIONAL PITCH.

PROPORTIONAL PITCH type in which different letters are of different widths. This contrasts with FIXED-PITCH type, which is normal for typewriters and dot-matrix printers. Proportional pitch fonts have more consistent spacing and present a more even color. Most fonts for your computer are proportional pitch. The notable exceptions are typefaces that purposefully mimic typewriters such as Courier and American typewriter. *See illustration at* FIXED PITCH. You should prefer proportional pitch fonts over fixed pitch. They look more professional.

Because the letters are of different widths, it is not possible to count letter spaces in proportional-pitch type to line up columns. Always use tabs.

Proportion wheel

PROPORTION WHEEL a circular device that helps compute the percentage of reduction or enlargement

Explanation	Mark in margin	Mark in copy
Delete	⌐	"What℘?" said Cathy.
Insert letter	⟨h⟩	"What?" said Caṱy.
Insert space	#	"What?" said⟨Cathy
Insert period	⊙	"What?" said Cathy⟨
Let it stand	stet	"What?" said℘ Cathy
Set in roman	rom	"⟨*What?*⟩" said Cathy.
boldface	bf	**"What?"** said **Cathy**
italic	ital	"What?" *said Cathy*
Capitalize	cap	"̲w̲hat?" said Cathy.
Upper and lower case	ulc	⟨"WHAT?" SAID CATHY.⟩
Lower case	lc	"What?" S̸aid Cathy.
Spell out circled word	spell out	⟨3⟩unicorns…
Equalize spacing	eq #	"What is that?" said Cathy.
Close up	⌒	"What?" said ⌐Cathy.
Start paragraph	¶	camp.⌐"What?" said Cathy.
Run in	NO ¶	"What?" said Cathy. ⌐ The three unicorns…
Move to point indicated		⌐ "What?" said Cathy.
Transpose	tr	"What?" ⟨Cathy said.⟩
Printer's error	PE	Used with other marks
Author's alteration	AA	Used with other marks

Figure 21 Standard proofreader's marks

of scaled artwork. Proportion wheels can be purchased at most office supply and art supply stores. To use a proportion wheel, measure the width of the original artwork using any convenient unit of measure (inches, picas, or centimeters). Locate the number on the inner ring of the wheel. Then, measure the width of the area that will hold the artwork in your document. Find this number on the outer ring of the proportion wheel. Now, match the two numbers by rotating the inner wheel. The percentage of reduction or enlargement will appear in the window of the proportion wheel. Then, measure the height (or depth) of the original artwork. Without turning the wheel, locate the height on the inner ring. Just opposite this number on the outer ring will be the new measurement for the height of the scaled artwork.

If you know beforehand the desired percentage of reduction or enlargement, the proportion wheel can tell you how large the artwork will be after scaling.

PUBLIC DOMAIN written or artistic works not covered by copyright. Items that are in the public domain may be reprinted without compensating the author. Always carefully check the copyright status of *any* artwork or text you are reproducing. Don't guess—be sure!

PUBLISH to create, print, and distribute printed materials.

PULL-DOWN MENU a menu that appears when a particular item in a menu bar is selected. A pull-down menu has to be held down by holding down the mouse button until the desired command is selected.

For picture, *see* WINDOW. *See also* MENU BAR.

Well-selected pull quotes can help the reader...

Pull quote

PULL QUOTE a provocative or representative quote, selected from the text. Pull quotes are set larger and in a distinctive type style to set them apart from the text. Horizontal rules are often used to block off pull quotes. Some designers like to use oversize quotation marks to add interest to the page.

Well-selected pull quotes can help the reader identify the author's main point. Make sure that the pull quote doesn't stray too far from where the reader will encounter it in the text. Ideally, the pull quote should be located on the same page and before the quoted material. Don't place the pull quote too close; it will create an unnatural echo.

PUNCTUATION the use of marks such as periods and commas to make sentences more readable. Punctuation marks are not mere decorations; they convey part of the meaning of the sentence.

Here are some rules for punctuating English; they presume that you already know the basics and have trouble only with the fine points.

1. **Parentheses** mark material that can be left out. The entire sentence must still make sense, and be correctly punctuated, when the parentheses and everything between them are removed.

   RIGHT: This is a sentence (without any errors).
   WRONG: This is a sentence (with an error in it.)
   RIGHT: This is a sentence. (This is another one.)

   In the second example, the period shouldn't be in the parentheses because it is still needed when the parenthesized material is left out.

2. Everything in the text is part of some sentence, even if it is a parenthesized attribution.

   RIGHT: "God is love" (I John 4:8).
   WRONG: "God is love." (I John 4:8)
   RIGHT: "God is love." (See I John 4:8.)

   Here the parenthesized attribution *I John 4:8* is not a sentence, so it has to be part of the sentence that precedes it. But *See I John 4:8* is a complete sentence and can be punctuated as such, with its own period.

3. A sentence that introduces a displayed formula can end with a colon rather than a period.

   RIGHT: The formula for force is:
   $$F = ma$$
   We also see that...

4. Periods within abbreviations take no spaces after them. Periods after abbreviations and initials are followed by single spaces. Examples:

   F.B.I.   U.S.A.   Ph.D.
   T. S. Eliot   Melody M. Covington

5. **Commas** mark breaks in sentence structure, *not* pauses in speech. Use them only where they make the sentence easier to read.

6. Commas can be used like parentheses to set off material that can be left out.

   RIGHT: Sicily, an island, has a mild climate.

   = Sicily (an island) has a mild climate.

7. Do not put commas around material that cannot be left out. Contrast these sentences:

   The student, who left, will come back.
   The student who left will come back.

   The first sentence implies that we already know which student is being talked about, and you are informing us that he left and is coming back. The second sentence means that the student who left is coming back, whoever that may be, and if you leave out *who left* you are no longer identifying the student.

8. Put commas around the year in a date and around the state or region in the name of a city:

   RIGHT: September 14, 1957, was the date.

   RIGHT: Valdosta, Georgia, was the place.

9. Put a comma in front of *and, or,* or *but* when joining two complete sentences.

   May 5 was the date, and Valdosta was the place.
   This is a sentence, and this is also a sentence.

   The comma can be omitted if the sentences are very short.

   Sentences should not normally begin with *and, or,* or *but.*

10. **Semicolons** are like commas but make a stronger separation; they can be used like commas to join phrases or numerals that have commas in them.

    The towns were Valdosta, Georgia, U.S.A.; Windsor, Ontario, Canada; and Macclesfield, Cheshire, England.

11. Complete sentences can be joined with semicolons (not commas).

    RIGHT: The coffee was bad; the tea was worse.

    = The coffee was bad. The tea was worse.

Often, the second sentence begins with a word such as *however:*

RIGHT: I saw it; however, no one else did.
= I saw it. However, no one else did.

12. **Apostrophes** mark points in a word where letters are left out:

it's	=	it is
'twas	=	it was
doesn't	=	does not
this 'n' that	=	this and that

Unlike quotation marks, apostrophes are oriented the same way (as ' not ') regardless of their position.

13. To form the possessive of a noun, add an apostrophe. Then add an *s* if the word does not end in *s* already.

SINGULAR		PLURAL	
PLAIN	POSS.	PLAIN	POSS.
dinosaur	dinosaur's	dinosaurs	dinosaurs'
lady	lady's	ladies	ladies'
man	man's	men	men's
sheep	sheep's	sheep	sheep's

Notice that the apostrophe always comes *after the complete word,* not inside it. The possessive of *Adams* is *Adams',* not *Adam's.* Examples:

Ansel Adams' photographs
Texas Instruments' new products
Athens' finest Greek food

If the possessive ending is pronounced as a separate syllable, it should be written *'s* even if there is an *s* before it: *Charles's Wain, James's house.*

There are no apostrophes in the possessive PRONOUNS *my, mine, your, yours, his, her, hers, its, our, ours,* and *theirs.* Notice that *its* is in this list.

14. Normal English plurals take no apostrophe: *one dog, two dogs.* But apostrophes sometimes mark the plurals of things that are not words:

There are three π's and two $\aleph$'s in that formula.
in the 1960's   (*or:* in the 1960s)

This usage of the apostrophe is confusing and not well established. Omit the apostrophe if you can.

15. **Quotation marks** surround a person's exact words. Periods and commas slide under the quotation marks and adhere to the words; otherwise, the punctuation within and outside quotes is whatever the logic of the sentence requires. Here are a few of the many combinations that arise; for others, see a grammar handbook.

    Sharon declared, "I am tired."
    "I'm tired," announced Sharon.
    "Where should I go?" she asked.
    Who said "I'm here" and who said, "What ho!"?

    In the last example, "What ho!" takes an exclamation mark, but the sentence that contains it is a question; both punctuation marks are necessary in order for the sentence to be understood.

16. "Scare quotes" are quotation marks placed around words that the author considers odd or inappropriate (the implication being "someone else uses this word this way, but I don't"):

    Their "lawyer" had never passed the bar exam.

    Some authors use too many scare quotes. Others use quotation marks as a vague form of emphasis. In either case the copy editor must remove the quotation marks, replacing them, if necessary, with clearer indications of what is actually meant.

17. **Poetry** is punctuated according to its sentence structure, just like ordinary text. Lines of poetry do not necessarily end with commas.

PURCHASE ORDER (PO) a business form used by some companies; a PO is used to track expenditures and reduce unauthorized purchases. *See* BUSINESS FORMS.

Q

QUARTO

1. a traditional size for printed books, made by folding an uncut sheet of paper in quarters (hence the name), and measuring about 8×10 to 10×13 inches depending on the paper used and the whims of the designer.

2. a traditional British paper size, 8×10 inches, now being superseded by ISO A4. *See* PAPER SIZES (ISO).

QUESTION MARK the punctuation mark (?) that indicates a query. Aldus Manutius is credited with simplifying the question mark to its present form in the 15th century.

?

Question mark

QUICKDRAW GX a new version of the Macintosh's graphics control language. Improvements include support for GX FONTS, transparent graphics, improved rotation and skewing, and allowing documents to be saved in a Portable Digital Document format (PDD). This means that any other Mac with QuickDraw GX can view the file, even if the other computer does not have the same application program or fonts.

See ELECTRONIC PUBLISHING; GX FONTS.

QUIT to clear an application program from memory; to EXIT (Macintosh) or CLOSE (Windows). Most software *will* prompt you to save changes to disk before quitting. Read all message boxes carefully.

" "

Quotes

QUOTES the punctuation marks used to indicate a quotation.

There is an important distinction between the way quote marks are typed on your computer and the way type is set correctly. The straight quote marks (") are a typewriter convention. If you want your work to look professional, always use proper open and closing quotes (" "). Take the time to learn how to do it in your word processor and page layout programs.

A single closing quote mark is called an APOSTROPHE.

See also PUNCTUATION.

Radial fill

Radio button

R

RADIAL FILL a type of FOUNTAIN FILL that radiates from a central point, blending the innermost color to the outermost.

RADIO BUTTON *See* OPTION BUTTON.

RAGGED a margin that is irregular. Type may be set FLUSH left, ragged right, or flush right, ragged left. *See* MARGINS, JUSTIFICATION.

RAISED INITIAL a display initial the shares the same baseline as the first line of the body copy. The raised initial extends above the block of type, helping to mark the beginning of the paragraph. *See* DISPLAY INITIAL.

RAM an acronym for **R**andom **A**ccess **M**emory, which is a description of the way the memory in your computer works. Any memory location can be found, on average, as quickly as any other location. A computer's RAM is its main memory where, it can store data, so the size of the RAM (measured in megabytes) is an important indicator of the capacity of the computer. *See* MEMORY.

RANDOM ACCESS MEMORY *See* RAM.

RASTER GRAPHICS graphics in which an image is generated by scanning an entire screen or page and marking every point as black, white, or another color, as opposed to VECTOR GRAPHICS.

A video screen and a laser printer are raster graphics devices; a pen plotter is a vector graphics device because it marks only at specified points on the page.

RASTER IMAGE PROCESSOR (RIP) a device that handles computer output as a grid of dots. Dot matrix, ink jet, and laser printers are all raster image processors.

RASTERIZE to convert an image into a bitmap of the right size and shape to match a raster graphics output device. *See* BITMAP; RASTER GRAPHICS; VECTOR GRAPHICS.

READ to transfer information from storage, such as a diskette or a hard drive, to memory.

READ-ONLY MEMORY *see* ROM.

REAM a package of 500 sheets of paper.

REBOOT to restart a computer—that is, to turn it off and then on again. (*See* BOOT.)

    Presumably, if you are rebooting, something has gone wrong. If your software has crashed and left your system unable to respond, there may be incorrectly saved or trashed files on the hard disk. After rebooting, use CHKDSK or a similar utility to clean up the mess. Try to figure out what went wrong. If you are the victim of a software bug, report it to the software developer.

REBUILD DESKTOP a housecleaning operation that needs to be periodically performed on a Macintosh. The Desktop system file is an invisible file that stores information about icons, comments from the "Get Info" box, and links to application files for all the document files. As this file grows larger, the computer's response will begin to slow to unacceptable levels. At regular intervals, the Desktop should be rebuilt. This will improve system performance.

    To rebuild the desktop, hold down the Command and Option keys during bootup. The Mac will ask if you're sure that's what you want to do (you'll lose your comments ...) and then take care of rebuilding the desktop file.

RECOVERING ERASED FILES the actions necessary to restore mistakenly erased data. When you *erase* a file on a computer disk, the space that the file occupied is marked as free, but the information is not actually overwritten until the space is needed for something else. If you erase a file accidentally, you can often get it back by using programs such as the Norton Utilities. If there hasn't been any new writing done to the disk, there's a good chance you can get your file back.

    This is an example of a superior feature of the Apple Macintosh. When you delete a file on the Mac, you take it to the "trash" icon, which then bulges to let you know it contains something. If you want to see what's in the trash, just double click on the trash can

—it opens like any other folder. If you see a file you need to keep, just drag it back to the desktop. That's how easy it is to "undelete" a file on the Mac. When you need disk space, you "empty the trash." At that point, however, you are in the same boat as the PC users if you want to recover one of the deleted files.

RECTO the front of a two-sided document; also the right-hand page of a book or magazine. Page 1 should always be placed on a recto. *Contrast* VERSO.

REDLINE a method of marking text that has been edited or changed. Use redlining in drafts or in frequently updated documents such as laws, regulations, or technical manuals; it is a electronic substitute for taking a red pen and marking blocks of text in the margin of the draft.

REDO to reverse the effect of the most recent UNDO command.

REFRESH WINDOW a command used to instruct the computer to update the material displayed.

This tends to bring up the question, "Well, why didn't the computer update the (list, drawing, window) *automatically?*" To save time, some screens are redrawn only on command, for instance, Microsoft Window's File Manager will only refresh the displayed directory *when asked*. (I mention this specifically because you can have a heart attack searching for a recently copied file if the window has not been refreshed.) Again, in a drawing program, you could spend all day watching the screen redraw itself if you have set the program to refresh the screen automatically after each step. One solution would be to do your editing in the WIREFRAME view. Or, divide the drawing into LAYERS and turn off the display of all but the current layer (not all drawing programs can do this). As a last resort, you could turn off the automatic refresh. *Be careful!* You could end up trying to move an object relative to an old position.

Register mark

REGISTER MARK a symbol consisting of a circle with a cross superimposed. Register marks are used to help the printer align the second (or third or forth) press runs to the first one. Also called BULL'S EYES.

REGISTRATION

1. the property of all color plates being correctly aligned in a properly printed piece. When colors are out of register, there are gaps between areas, type can be fuzzy, and MOIRÉS can occur. To help ensure proper registration, always include REGISTER MARKS on the CAMERA-READY COPY.

2. the act of actually filling out and mailing the postcards that come with new software. This makes sure that the company that produces the program has you in their database as one of their customers. You can then receive user support and upgrade offers (as well as large amounts of unsolicited mail). Remember to register your software. It may save you a substantial amount of money at upgrade time.

If you are horribly unhappy about getting junk mail, just request that your name *not* be distributed on any mailing lists.

REMOVE SPOTS a photopaint filter that erases spots from digitized photographs and pictures. Technically, it removes all pixel groups below a certain size; image detail may be lost.

REPAGINATE to allow the word processor or page layout program to work forward from the current cursor position, repositioning page breaks.

REQUIRED HYPHEN a hyphen that *does not* indicate a place where the word can be broken apart. For instance, phone numbers must not be broken across the end of the line. You need to let the computer know that the hyphen is *required* so that the number (or word) will not be split up. Different programs do this in different ways. You'll have to check your manual or help file for specific information. In WordPerfect, a required hyphen is typed by hitting the Home key and then the hyphen.

It would be a good practice to type all phone numbers with required hyphens. That way, they would not be broken up no matter how the text wraps.

REQUIRED SPACE a space that does *not* denote a place where words can be split apart at the end of a line. For instance, you would not want a company name (let's use "Happy Widgets") to be split if it falls at the end of a line. You need to let the computer know that the space is *required* so that "Happy" will not be at the end of a line and "Widgets" will not begin the next. Different programs do this in different ways. You'll have to check your manual or help file for specific information. In WordPerfect, a required space is typed by hitting the Home key and then the space bar.

RESEDIT (**Res**ource **Edit**or, or ResEdit) a program distributed by Apple Computer for configuring the operating system of the Macintosh and for editing resources of all types. *See* RESOURCE.

RESIZE to change the size or dimensions of; to SCALE.

To resize an object interactively with the mouse in most environments, select the object, then drag one of the HANDLES in the desired direction. Dragging a corner handle will keep the vertical and horizontal aspects of the object in the same proportion to each other (like reducing or enlarging something on a photocopier). Dragging one of the handles at the midpoint of the BOUNDING BOX will affect only one dimension of the object. This way, you can stretch or shrink the object to the desired shape.

RESOLUTION a measure of the sharpness of the images a monitor or printer can produce. For instance, many laser printers have a resolution of 300 dots per inch (DPI), meaning that they print characters using a grid of black or white squares each $\frac{1}{300}$ of an inch across. This is equivalent to 50 lines per inch (LPI). The human eye normally resolves about 150 lines per inch at normal reading distance, but a person examining a page critically can distinguish two or three times this much detail.

The resolution of a screen is given as the total number of pixels in each direction (e.g., 640 × 480 pixels across the whole screen). The equivalent number of dots per inch depends on the size of the screen. Present-day video screens resolve about 80 dots per inch; they are not nearly as sharp as ink on paper. A big advantage of draw programs, as opposed to paint programs, is that they can use the full resolution of the printer; they are not limited to printing what they display on the screen. However, some paint programs can handle very detailed images by displaying only part of the image at a time.

See DRAW PROGRAM; PAINT PROGRAM; VECTOR GRAPHICS.

RESOURCE (Macintosh and Windows) a modifiable part of an application program or of the operating system. Resources include menus, icons, and fonts.

RESTORE to make a window go back to its previous size after either being minimized or maximized. To restore a window, choose "restore" on its control menu. To see the control menu, click once on the control-menu box (if the window has been maximized) or on the icon (if the window has been minimized to an icon). See also WINDOW; MINIMIZE; MAXIMIZE.

Restore

RETOUCHING altering a photograph or illustration to eliminate flaws and unnecessary elements. The preferred software for this job would be a PHOTOPAINT program, which would have the appropriate tools and FILTERS to seamlessly correct digitized photographs.

There is currently quite a bit of debate over how much a photograph can and should be altered. It's agreed that there's no problem in removing dust specks or lightening a photograph that is too dark, but what about moving elements of a photograph around? What about changing or obliterating logos? It's easy to make a photograph lie.

The answer is of course, "It depends." Photographs intended to accompany news articles need to hold to the strictest standards of truthfulness (minimal to no retouching). However, an illustration of a fantasy world could have free rein. Advertisements should not mislead, but exaggerated comic effects are considered fun.

RETRY part of DOS's infamous "Abort, Retry, Ignore, Fail?" error message. If you can fix the immediate problem (by putting a disk in the drive or something of the sort), then choose "Retry." Otherwise, press or click on "Abort" or "Fail." Choosing "Ignore" is asking for trouble.

Reverse

RETURN KEY the "Enter" key. This harkens back to the good old days of the typewriter, where you either had to reach up and "return" the carriage with your own hand or let the electric motor return the carriage to the left margin. Specifically, the Return (or Enter, if you prefer) key inserts a special nonprinting code into your text that marks the end of the current line. *See also* SOFT RETURN; HARD RETURN.

REVERSE white letters on a black background. A reverse block of type can be a dramatic design element — however, legibility can become a factor. A large block of reverse text is difficult to read. Typefaces with hairline strokes do not reverse well. The COUNTERS of the letters may spread and fill in if the font size is too small. Always evaluate a proof of reverse type carefully.

Type may also be reversed out of a color or a tint. Check that there is enough contrast between the type and the background. *See* LEGIBILITY.

REVERT to reload from disk a previously saved version of the file, losing all intermediate changes. Revert is therefore a super-undo command. Save your file before attempting a potentially dangerous command (search and replace or applying a filter), and you will have the option of reverting to the older file in case something goes wrong.

RFI PROTECTION protection against radio-frequency interference. Computers produce the same kind of high-frequency electrical energy as radio transmitters. This often causes RFI (radio-frequency interference), also called EMI (electromagnetic interference). All computers interfere with nearby radio and TV reception to some extent, and sometimes the problem is severe. On rare occasions, the opposite happens—a strong signal from a nearby radio transmitter disrupts the computer, or two computers interfere with each other.

Here are some suggestions for reducing RFI:

• If possible, move the radio or TV receiver away from the computer, and plug it into an outlet on a different circuit.

- Supply power to the computer through a surge protector that includes an RFI filter (*see* SURGE PROTECTOR).

- Ground the computer properly (again, *see* SURGE PROTECTOR).

- Use high-quality shielded cables to connect the parts of the computer system together. Make sure all cable shields and ground wires are connected properly. This is especially important for the monitor cable and the printer cable. If possible, wind the cable into a coil to increase its inductance.

- Check that the computer has the appropriate approval from the FCC (Federal Communications Commission). Some computers are not approved for use in residential areas.

RGB   **r**ed, **g**reen, **b**lue. Your monitor makes combinations of colors by combining these three primary colors. Your software is responsible for translating this representation of color into a form understood by your printer. *See* CMYK; COLOR.

RISERS   the bars of a bar graph, particularly when the bars are rendered in three dimensions.

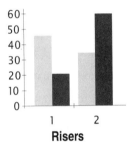

Risers

RIVER   a series of white spaces between words that appear to flow down the interior of a column of type. Rivers result from trying to justify type when the columns are too narrow or the available software or printer are not versatile enough. *See* JUSTIFICATION.

ROLLERBALL   a pointing device. A rollerball is sometimes described as "an upside-down mouse." You use it by rolling the ball with your fingertips; the on-screen cursor moves in the same direction as the ball. Some people prefer a rollerball to a mouse, especially if desk space is at a premium. Also called a TRACKBALL.

ROLL-UP MENU   a dialog box that stays open on screen while you choose among the settings it offers. The roll-up can be positioned anywhere you'd like and when you are finished with it, it can be "rolled-up" to just the size of its title bar. It is very similar in

Roll-up menu

concept to a TOOLBOX. The roll-up menu shown is from CorelDraw 3.

ROM (**R**ead **O**nly **M**emory) a memory storage device (either an IC chip or a CD) that contains instructions that do not need to be changed, such as permanent parts of the operating system or clip art files. The computer can read information from ROM, but can't store additional data there. *See* MEMORY; CD-ROM.

Handgloves
Roman

ROMAN a typeface design based on the designs perfected by the ancient Romans. A roman face has serifs and a distinct contrast between the thick and thin strokes. *See* TYPEFACE.

ROMAN NUMERALS the number system of the ancient Romans (*see Table 7*), used in Europe until Hindu-Arabic numerals were introduced by Gerbert of Aurillac around 1000 A.D., and still used for some purposes (outlines, clock faces, numbering the pages of the front matter of a book, and instances where they lend an air of dignity).

Roman numerals originated as tally marks (I for 1, II for 2, and so on). In prehistoric times someone hit upon the idea of abbreviating IIIII (5) as V, and by classical times the symbols X for 10, L for 50, C for 100, D for 500, and M for 1000 were also in use.

To further save space, some scribes used subtraction: instead of writing IIII they would write IV, which means V minus I, or 4. Likewise they wrote IX for 9, XL for 40, XC for 90, CD for 400, and CM for 900. Not everyone followed this practice.

Roman numerals never developed a symbol for 0, nor was there a standard way to write numbers larger than 3,999 (MMMCMXCIX), although in classical times a bar over a numeral (as in $\overline{VI}$) multiplied it by 1,000, so that 4,000 was $M\overline{V}$ and a million was $\overline{M}$.

Today the publishing industry uses lower-case roman numerals to number the pages in a book that precede page 1. All pages count, although not all of them bear numbers. In a typical book, the half title is page i, the back of it (blank) is page ii, the title page is iii, the copyright page is iv, and the first page of the

Table 7 Roman numerals

1	I	15	XV	50	L	700	DCC
2	II	16	XVI	60	LX	800	DCCC
3	III	17	XVII	70	LXX	900	CM
4	IV	18	XVIII	80	LXXX	1000	M
5	V	19	XIX	90	XC	1100	MC
6	VI	20	XX	99	XCIX	1776	MDCCLXXVI
7	VII	21	XXI	100	C	1970	MCMLXX
8	VIII	29	XXIX	101	CI	1980	MCMLXXX
9	IX	30	XXX	110	CX	1990	MCMXC
10	X	31	XXXI	200	CC	1996	MCMXCVI
11	XI	39	XXXIX	300	CCC	1997	MCMXCVII
12	XII	40	XL	400	CD	1998	MCMXCVIII
13	XIII	41	XLI	500	D	1999	MCMXCIX
14	XIV	49	XLIX	600	DC	2000	MM

table of contents (which is often the first page with a number actually printed on it) is page v.

ROTATE a drawing program command that turns an object around a specific center. By default, the center of rotation is at the center of the object itself. You can drag this center to wherever you want it to be and then rotate the object around it. Rotation can be done interactively with the mouse, or if you require more precision, you can use the DIALOG BOX to set the angle of rotation in degrees.

ROUGHS a layout design in its very early stages. Roughs are usually sketched to size with pencil. It sometimes helps to work on quadrille paper. Do several roughs when planning a new project, then take the best one to use as a guide when setting up the page layout on the computer.

ROW a horizontal line of entries in a chart or table.

RUBBER STAMP a paint program tool that duplicates a selected area of the drawing. Similar to the CLONE tool. The Rubber Stamp icon shown is from Adobe Photoshop.

Rubber stamp

RULERS a strip at the top (and sometimes the side) of the on-screen work area, marked in units of measurement. Like their physical counterparts, an on-screen ruler is used to help you measure things. Rulers can be found in word processors, drawing programs, and page layout programs. You have the option of displaying the ruler, or to hide it and give yourself some more working room. You can also have the ruler show units of measurement other than inches (PICAS might be more useful for many applications). A ruler is especially useful when using a high degree of zoom because it helps you keep your orientation.

In a word processor, the ruler can be used to set the TABS, MARGINS, and INDENTS.

Rules

RULES lines used to organize and emphasize. Rules are specified by their location, length, and thickness. Rules can be vertical, horizontal, or at any angle. Most page layout programs give you a dialog box to set all of these characteristics. The thinnest rule is called a HAIRLINE RULE.

RUNAROUND a block of body type with irregular margins that follow the shape of a nearby graphic. Also called SCULPTING.

RUNNING HEAD a small headline that appears at the top or bottom of each page. Running heads are usually there to remind the reader which chapter (or book) he or she is in. In a dictionary like this one, the running heads tell you the first and last entries on the page spread.

Handgloves

Rustic

RUSTIC a typeface that gives the appearance of being rough-hewn or old fashioned. Examples of rustic faces are Caslon Antique or Egyptian. These are specialty fonts, and you should limit the amount of text set in them. They are too hard to read as paragraph text.

S

SADDLE STITCHED; SADDLE STAPLED method
of binding in which the pages are opened and stitched
or stapled in the middle. The machine for doing this
resembles a horse's saddle.

SAD MAC the icon of a frowning Macintosh computer
that announces the Mac has found a hardware problem and cannot finish booting. Jot down the number
displayed below the icon, turn off the computer, and
make sure all the cables are secure. Try to boot the
computer again. If the Sad Mac appears again, it's
time to look up the number of the repair station.

Sad Mac

SANS SERIF a typeface that does *not* have serifs.
(*Sans* is French for "without.") Also called LINEAL.
Helvetica and Futura are sans-serif typefaces. *See
illustration at* SERIF.

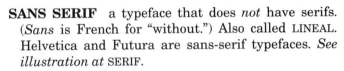

Handgloves
Sans serif

SATURATION the intensity of a color. A highly satu-
rated color is recognized as a vivid, brilliant color; to
dull a color (decrease its saturation), you add small
amounts of its *complement. See* HSB; COLOR.

SAVE to transfer information from the computer's
memory to a storage device, such as a disk drive.
Saving data is vital because the contents of the computer's memory are lost when the power is turned off.
The opposite process is LOADING or retrieving.

SAVE AS...
    1. to save a document or drawing under a differ-
ent name. The first time you save an untitled work,
you will use "Save as ..." instead of "Save."
    2. to save a file in a different format (e.g to save
a Corel Draw file as a Windows Metafile). *See also*
EXPORT.

SCALABLE FONT a font that can be used to print
characters of any size. Many newer laser printers include scalable fonts. To be fully scalable, the shapes
of the characters must be stored in the form of vector
graphics, as opposed to bitmaps. *See* FONT; VECTOR
GRAPHICS; TRUETYPE; TYPE 1 FONTS.

SCALE

1. to change the size or dimensions of an object, keeping the horizontal and vertical aspects in ratio to each other. To REDUCE or ENLARGE.

To scale an object interactively with the mouse in most environments, select the object then drag one of the corner HANDLES in the desired direction. Dragging in will reduce the size of the object; dragging out will enlarge it. *See* RESIZE.

2. to compute the finished size and the percentage of reduction or enlargement of a piece of art. To do this, you use a PROPORTION WHEEL (available at office supply and art supply stores). Measure the width of the original artwork using any convenient unit of measure (inches, picas, or centimeters). Locate the number on the inner ring of the wheel. Then, measure the width of the area that will hold the artwork in your document. Find this number on the outer ring of the proportion wheel. Now, match the two numbers by rotating the inner wheel. The percentage of reduction or enlargement will appear in the window of the proportion wheel. Then, measure the height (or depth) of the original artwork. Without turning the wheel, locate the height on the inner ring. Just opposite this number on the outer ring will be the new measurement for the height of the scaled artwork.

If you know beforehand the desired percentage of reduction or enlargement, the proportion wheel can tell you how large the artwork will be after scaling.

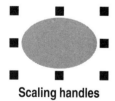

Scaling handles

SCALING HANDLES the black handles at the corners of a BOUNDING BOX. Dragging a scaling handle with the mouse will increase or decrease (SCALE) the size of the selected object, keeping the horizontal to vertical aspect constant.

SCANNER a device that enables a computer to read a printed or handwritten page. The simplest scanners give the contents of the page to the computer as a graphic image—a handy way of putting pictures into the computer (*see* DESKTOP PUBLISHING). There are three main types of scanners:

- **Hand-held scanners** are inexpensive and adequate for inputting sketches into a draw program. But they have some difficulty scanning images wider than they are; the image has to be scanned in two or more passes and then assembled into one file.

- **Flatbed scanners** are more convenient to use and usually come with superior software for the scanning process. This type of scanner is reasonably priced and generally suitable for all the desktop publisher's needs.
- **Drum scanners** are expensive, but give better results than the other types of scanners. Some service bureaus have drum scanners and can scan your artwork or photograph for you.

There are many nuances involved in scanning artwork. In some ways, it is quite similar to photography, and if you are comfortable with a camera, it will make the transition to working with a scanner very smooth. Scanners can adjust the contrast and brightness of the image. Controls for setting the *highlight* and *shadow* area are usually provided. Color images can be color-corrected at the scanning stage.

With appropriate software, scanners can read the letters of typewritten text, transmitting them into the computer as if they were typed on the keyboard (OCR). This process, however, is seldom 100 percent accurate. You will find it necessary to proofread scanned copy very carefully.

Several other kinds of electronic devices are called scanners, including bar code readers (*see* BAR CODE) and devices for scanning the radio spectrum.

SCATTERGRAPH a graph that shows points of data plotted on an X-Y coordinate system.

Scattergraph

SCISSORS a tool available in paint and photopaint programs that allows you to define an area of the bitmap that you wish to separate from its surroundings. The resulting CUTOUT may be resized (SCALED), STRETCHED, ROTATED, or moved.

Scissors

The scissors tool is one of several SELECTION TOOLS available to you. Others include the LASSO, MAGIC WAND, and the BOX SELECTION tools. To save space, these tools may be grouped together in your toolbox and only one may be visible at a time.

Screamer

The Scissors icon shown is from Corel PhotoPaint.

SCREAMER slang for the exclamation mark (!).

SCREEN

1. (v.) to apply a halftone screen to continuous tone artwork or a tint screen to an area of solid color.

2. a halftone or tint screen. The fineness of a screen is measured in *lines per inch* (LPI). The halftone screen produced by a 300 DPI laser printer is the equivalent of 50 LPI and is considered very coarse. A 600 DPI laser printer can produce the equivalent of up to 100 LPI screen; if you need greater resolution, the image files should be sent to a service bureau to be output on an IMAGESETTER.

3. the view that an application program will present to you as you work with it. At different points in the work session, the same application program may present a different screen to you.

SCREEN BURN-IN the phenomenon that occurs when an image is left displayed on a monitor for a long time. The ghost of the image is literally etched into the phosphors that line the cathode ray tube. If a computer is left running all day (without a screen saver program), an afterimage of the desktop screen will show through whatever the monitor is displaying.

SCREEN SAVER a program whose purpose is to prevent SCREEN BURN-IN. If a computer is left standing idle, the operating system will automatically run the screen saver after a specified period of time. The image a screen saver displays moves constantly, or else it blanks the screen. Windows provides some built-in screen saver programs, but you have the option of purchasing a separate program to use in their place. Many people use their screen saver to personalize their system or to provide comic relief.

New monitors with power-saving hardware actually turn themselves off under the control of a screen saver.

SCREEN SNAPSHOT, CAPTURE to cause an image of the current screen to be saved as a bitmapped image.

Snapshots of the screen are easy to get: for Macintosh users, hold down Command and shift, then press 3. This places a bitmapped image of the screen in a .PICT file in your root directory. For Windows, pressing the Print Screen key puts a copy of the entire screen onto the clipboard. Holding down Alt while pressing Print Screen saves a bitmap of the active window *only*.

SCRIPT a typeface design that mimics handwriting. The letters are usually slanted and join together. Some are definitely more formal than others.

SCROLL to move information across the screen as if the screen is a window or porthole through which you are looking. For example, all word processing programs can scroll vertically, and some can also scroll horizontally.

SCROLL BAR a bar on the side (and sometimes the bottom) of a window that enables you to scroll the window, i.e., look at different areas of the file or picture that the window is displaying. To scroll, click on the arrows at the ends of the scroll bar or use the mouse to move the scroll box along the bar. For picture, *see* WINDOW.

SCSI (**S**mall **C**omputer **S**ystems **I**nterface) a standard way of interfacing a computer to disk drives, tape drives, and other devices that require high-speed data transfer. Up to seven SCSI devices can be linked to a single SCSI port. Thus, a single SCSI adapter can interface a computer to one or more hard disks, a CD-ROM drive, a tape drive, and a scanner.

SCSI is especially popular with Macintoshes and UNIX workstations but is also used on some IBM PC-compatible computers, where it is supported by device drivers. Almost all SCSI hard disks use the same device driver, with no need for further settings to be made; that makes SCSI hard disks easier to install than any other type. Other SCSI devices such as CD-ROM drives require additional device drivers. This is often done in two layers: an ASPI (Advanced SCSI Programming Interface) device driver for the SCSI system, and various drivers that issue ASPI commands to specific devices. *See also* DEVICE DRIVER.

Handgloves

Handgloves

Handgloves

Script typefaces

SCULPTING making text flow around a graphic or crafting the text block into an interesting shape. Being able to sculpt text interactively is one of the most noticeable benefits of working on a computer. Previously, it was time-consuming, tedious, and expensive.

SEARCH AND REPLACE to work through a file, changing every occurrence of a particular sequence of characters into some other sequence of characters. (In Macintosh software, this is called "Find and Change.") Many word processing and page layout programs have very powerful search and replace features. (*See* EDITOR.) For instance, while drafting some copy, you could use abbreviations for some words or names. Then, by using search and replace, you could change all of those abbreviated forms into their full titles.

Be careful when using search and replace. It is a potentially dangerous command and you can end up outsmarting yourself. How so? Let's say I have the misfortune to often transpose the word "it" into "ti." If I tell the computer to convert every occurrence of "ti" into "it," the literal-minded machine will do so; including the "ti" in "information," "potential," "time," etc. The smart thing to do is to include the leading and trailing spaces when telling the computer what to search for and what to replace it with. Better yet, don't let the computer work automatically; examine each match yourself. It doesn't take much more time, and you will avoid this pitfall.

§

Section sign

SECTION SIGN the symbol (§) which is used to mark sections of text for reference (usually in legal documents). The section sign may also be used for a footnote symbol. *See* FOOTNOTE.

SELECT to tell the computer you are ready to work with an object or text. You can select one or more objects at a time. Usually, you select an object by clicking on it with the mouse. To select a group of objects, use MARQUEE SELECT or hold down the shift key while clicking on individual objects until they are all included in the bounding box.

SELECTION AREA an area marked by a bounding box. When scanning in an image, the selection area marks the only part of the page that will be DIGITIZED.

SELECTION TOOLS tools provided to define an area or choose an object to be worked with. Examples include the POINTER, LASSO, MAGIC WAND, AND SCISSORS.

SEND TO BACK in some graphical editing environments, a command that puts an object or window "at the back," so that other objects or windows are allowed to overlap it. *See also* OVERLAID WINDOWS; BRING TO FRONT.

SEND TO FRONT in a graphical editing environment, a command that brings the selected object to the front of all other objects. *See also* SEND TO BACK.

SERIF the short finishing strokes of the letterforms in a roman typeface. The type you are reading now has serifs. Some serifs are joined to the main stroke by a triangular BRACKET; others meet the main stroke at 90 degrees (SLAB SERIFS). Serifs can be pointed or rounded; noting characteristics about the serifs of a font can help you identify a typeface.

Serif

Serifs are actually artifacts of how the ancient Roman stonecutters finished their letters when carving inscriptions. It is thought that the horizontal nature of serifs help guide the reader's eye along the line of type.

SERVICE BUREAU a business that provides high quality output options for the desktop publisher. Not everyone can afford 2400 DPI IMAGESETTERS or DYE-SUBLIMATION PRINTERS. Just prepare your file, and send it by MODEM, disk, or tape to the service bureau. They can send back to you the slides, film, or printouts that you need.

When choosing a service bureau, it is best to find one that specializes in the same platform that you use. If you use a Macintosh, find a bureau that works with Macintoshes; similarly, if you are running a PC compatible computer, you need to find a service bureau that works from PCs. Find out what software the service bureau uses. It is best to send NATIVE FILES so that the software can adapt the file for the output device (printer, imagesetter, etc.). ENCAPSULATED POSTSCRIPT (EPS) files should be used when there is no common software.

Fonts can be a problem when sending a file to a service bureau. If they don't have the same fonts that you do, a substitution has to be made. This can adversely affect line breaks and generally wreak havoc on the typesetting. You will have to send along the necessary font files or convert the type to curves in a drawing program.

Files being sent to a service bureau are often huge —24-bit color bitmaps can easily exceed the capacity of a diskette. The file can be electronically transmitted by modem if the long distance phone charges are not excessive. (You can transmit about 3 megabytes per hour at 9600 baud.) Another option is to use TAPE. Always check beforehand whether the bureau has the proper equipment on their end to read your tape format.

SGML (**S**tandard **G**eneralized **M**arkup **L**anguage) a standard set of codes for marking boldface, italics, etc., in ASCII text files, which became the basis for HTML. *See* HTML.

SHADED a typeface design that has a shadow.

SHADOW the darkest area of a photograph or drawing that is being scanned. The image contrast can be adjusted by marking the shadow and HIGHLIGHT areas for the computer.

Shape tool

SHAPE TOOL in CorelDraw, the triangular tool that is used to edit the nodes that define the shape of an object.

SHARPEN a photopaint filter that sharpens the focus of a defined area. It's useful to enhance a slightly blurred image. (Don't expect miracles—the computer cannot compute information that is not in the original picture!) If overused, the sharpen filter can create an undesirable degree of PIXELATION, because it works by increasing the difference between adjacent pixels.

Sharpen paintbrush

SHARPEN PAINTBRUSH a retouching tool available in some photopaint programs allows blurred edges to be sharpened up (like touching up the focus on a camera). It works very similarly to the SHARPEN FILTER, except that the Sharpen Paintbrush works freehand on a small area at a time. Overworked edges tend to have a blocky look, so be prepared to UNDO or revert to a previously saved version of the file.

The icon shown is from Corel PhotoPaint.

SHORTCUT a faster way of getting something done. Many command shortcuts are combination keystrokes (Ctrl–D, Alt–X).

You may wonder why there is more than one way to do something in your operating system or application program. The most basic reason is that different computer users develop their own very individualized ways of working. Some prefer using menus; on the other hand, some old-timers still configure their word processor to recognize WordStar keystrokes. (*See* MACROS.)

In some ways, the menus you access by mouse are meant to be like "training wheels." The software designers expected that by the time you had (for the 1047th time) gone two menus deep to get to a particular command, you might be interested in knowing that a single keystroke could get the same effect. In many cases, the keyboard shortcut appears in the menu to the right of the command.

Have you ever noticed that some dialog boxes have certain letters underlined in the command buttons? Rather than move your hands from the keyboard to pick up your mouse, try typing "Y" for "**Y**es," "N" for "**N**o," "A" for "Yes to **A**ll," etc. In the same way, note that most menus have certain letters of the commands underlined. Typing the underlined letter is the same as selecting that command with the mouse —and it's a whole lot faster!

I don't recommend sitting down and trying to memorize all the keyboard shortcuts. Think for a moment about what you do *most* often: open a file, save it, duplicate an object, or go into text-editing mode. It would be worth your while to learn the shortcuts for those commands.

SHOW-THROUGH visibility of printed images from the back side of a piece of paper. Show-through is affected by two things: the *opacity* of the paper and the *ink coverage*. You will find that bold, dark designs, especially large blocks of reverse type, tend to show-through to the reverse side. Sometimes the problem is so severe that the reader has trouble seeing the text on the reverse side of the paper. The moral: For a big, bold design, use a thicker paper. Conversely, if you are limited to printing on a lightweight paper, keep that fact in mind during the design stage.

SHRINK to decrease either the vertical or horizontal dimension of an object. To use the mouse to interactively shrink a selected object, drag in one of the handles at the midpoints of the BOUNDING BOX. Contrast this with SCALE, which maintains the height-to-width ratio of the object.

SIDEBAR a short article that accompanies a major article in a magazine or newsletter. Sidebars run alongside, below, or above the main article, sometimes in a different typeface or inside a ruled or screened box for contrast.

SIGNATURE a sheet of printed book pages, that, after folding, trimming, and binding will form a group of 4, 8, 16, or 32 pages in a book.

SINKAGE extra white space allowed at the top of a page, usually to mark the beginning of a chapter or article.

SITE LICENSE a software license that allows unlimited copying of a computer program for use by a single organization at a specified site. A site license is often much cheaper than the purchase of multiple copies. *See also* SOFTWARE LICENSE.

SIZE *see* SCALE.

SKEW

Skew

SKEW a drawing program command that lets you alter the overall shape of an object. When you skew an object, you slide one side of its bounding box to the left or to the right. This will slant it or shift its bottom edge uphill or downhill. Skewing may be done interactively with the mouse, or, for more precision, the degree of skew may be specified in a dialog box.

Slab serif

SLAB SERIF a serif that does not have a triangular piece (BRACKET) joining it to the main stroke of the letterform. *See* SERIF.

SLANT to make the letterforms tilt. The most noticeable feature of an italic font is its *slant*. A BACKSLANT is a letterform that is slanted to the left. *See also* SKEW.

SLASH the character /. A slash is used to separate elements of a BUILT FRACTION (i.e. 3/4), to substitute for a comma (as in an address), or to separate either/or choices. Be careful not to confuse it with the backslash (\). Many computer commands are sensitive about using the correct one.

SLICE a portion of a pie chart. Also called a PIE WEDGE.

Slice

SLIDE a page setup option for creating a drawing or illustration that will be output to a 35mm slide. *See* SERVICE BUREAU.

SMALL CAPS a specially designed alphabet of capital letters that are approximately two-thirds the cap height of the font. Text set in small caps has the same visual texture as normal text, but gives the emphasis of setting text in all caps. The cross references in this book are set in small caps.

It is tempting to fake small caps by simply reducing the size of the font. This does not quite have the same effect; the proportions seem off and the stroke widths are obviously wrong. If you need small caps, you should choose a typeface that has a matching small caps font. (*See* EXPERT SET.)

SMEAR a retouching tool available in most PHO-TOPAINT programs. The Smear paintbrush drags color from one area over another, as if you had run your finger over a chalk picture. The Smear paintbrush works with the colors already present in the picture; *contrast* SMUDGE spraycan, which adds random mixed colors to the image.

Smear

The Smear icon shown is from Corel PhotoPaint.

SMUDGE a retouching tool available in most PHO-TOPAINT programs. The Smudge spraycan randomly mixes colors in an area. The Smudge spraycan adds texture to the image; with coarse settings, the effect achieved is rather impressionistic. *Contrast* SMEAR, SPRAYCAN.

Smudge

The Smudge icon shown is from Corel PhotoPaint.

SNAP POINT a point on an object that clings to the GRID or user-defined guidelines. Most objects have multiple snap points; generally speaking, they will be at every NODE that defines the shape of the object. *See* GRID.

SNAP TO GRID a draw program command that causes objects to have a "magnetic" attraction to a non-printing grid. Use "Snap to Grid" to solve precision alignment problems.

SOFT BRUSH a category of tools that include PAINTBRUSHES, and AIRBRUSHES (or SPRAY CANS). All of these tools leave "soft" edges and have transparent strokes. These tools may be grouped together in your toolbox and have similar dialog boxes for their settings.

Soft edge

SOFT EDGE a boundary between two areas that is diffuse and somewhat blurred. *Contrast* HARD EDGE.

SOFT FONT a description of a kind of type to be printed on a laser printer. Unlike a font cartridge or an internal font, a soft font consists of data transmitted to the printer by the computer before the text is printed. The availability of a wide variety of soft fonts provides users with great flexibility. *Contrast* FONT CARTRIDGE; INTERNAL FONT.

SOFT PAGE an invisible control code that indicates where the text will break at the end of a page. *Contrast* HARD PAGE.

SOFTWARE the set of programs that tell the computer what to do. The term contrasts with HARDWARE, which refers to the actual physical machines that make up a computer system. The hardware by itself is of little value without the instructions that tell it what to do. Software can be classified into systems software (*see* OPERATING SYSTEM) and APPLICATIONS SOFTWARE. For examples of common types of application software, *see* WORD PROCESSING, DRAW PROGRAM, PAINT PROGRAM, PAGE LAYOUT PROGRAM.

SOFTWARE LICENSE an agreement between the publisher of a computer program and the person who buys a copy of it. Some licenses specify that when you buy a copy of a program, you do not really own the copy but have merely bought the right to use it in certain ways. Licenses allow you to make a working copy of the program, which would otherwise be forbidden by copyright law (*see* COPYRIGHT).

Most licenses allow a single copy of the program to be used on only one machine at a time. It can be copied for backup purposes, and it can be moved from one machine to another, but it cannot be actually in use in two places at once. Thus you are forbidden to load the same program into more than one machine through a network. However, it is usually permissible for several people to use the same program on a multiuser machine with a single CPU.

A site license allows unlimited copying of a program for use by a single organization at a specified site. A site license is often much cheaper than the purchase of multiple copies. Another alternative for schools and colleges is the use of student editions of software; these are less powerful than the commercial version and are sold at much lower prices.

Many aspects of software licenses have not yet been tested in court. In particular, the license document is often packed where the user cannot see it until after buying and opening the software package. In such cases, it can hardly be described as a valid contract. When dealing with unclear or unreasonable licenses, users should make a good-faith effort to obey copyright law and to avoid depriving the publisher of income.

SOLID type set with no additional space added between lines. *See* LINESPACING.

SORT to place in alphabetical or numerical order. Many WORD PROCESSORS have a sort command; this allows you to alphabetize a list or to put numbers in order. Also, a convenient feature offered by some PAGE LAYOUT programs is the ability to rearrange the page order of a publication. Pagemaker calls this "Sort Pages"; in Quark Express the command is "Page — Move." Similarly, most PRESENTATION GRAPHICS programs have a "slide sorter" view that allows you to reorder the slides in the presentation.

SOURCE the place where information is coming from. For example, if I am making a backup copy of today's work, the original file on C: is the source and the TARGET (or DESTINATION) is the diskette in drive B:.

SPACE the character that is typed between words – the ASCII character 32. It appears to you as an empty area, but in actuality it is a character just like the printable characters. Other invisible characters include tabs, hard returns, and soft returns. Sometimes formatting problems are caused by extraneous or missing invisible characters. It is sometime necessary to examine the codes that the word processor has inserted automatically, and weed out the unnecessary ones. For example, if a headline is not centering properly, make sure that there is not an extra space at the end of the text.

When setting type, it is of the utmost importance to be consistent in your use of the space bar. There should be one, and *only* one, space in between each word. Although most people were taught to double space after a period when typing, this is not necessary. A single space is preferred for typesetting.

Do not attempt to JUSTIFY type by adding spaces yourself. If your software is not powerful enough to justify type, either stick to FLUSH left, RAGGED right type or go shopping for a new program.

Lastly, do not attempt to align type by using spaces. Set the tab stops where you want them and use the tabs. It is impossible to make proportional type line up correctly without tabs.

SPACE BAR the long key at the bottom of the keyboard that is used to insert a space in a document.

SPANISH the language of Spain and most of Latin America. Besides the regular alphabet, Spanish uses the following special characters:

Á á É é Í í Ó ó Ú ú Ü ü Ñ ñ ¿ ¡

Many typesetters omit the accents on capital letters, but not the tilde on Ñ, whose omission could lead to embarrassing misreadings (e.g., *ANO* for *AÑO*).

Spanish punctuates quotations with guillemets or dashes just as French does (*see* FRENCH). In addition, questions and exclamations are bracketed by ¿...? and ¡...! respectively. The question or exclamation may or may not be a complete sentence:

Por favor, ¿dónde están los servicios?

In hyphenation, the sequences *ch ll rr pl cl bl gl fl pr cr br gr fr tr* are never broken up.

SPECIAL CHARACTERS characters that cannot be typed directly from the keyboard, but require entering a special code or selection through KeyCaps (Macintosh) or the Character Map (Windows).

Windows software accesses these special characters by holding down the Alt key and typing a four digit code on the numeric keypad. Macintosh users can type special characters by holding down the option button while typing (here the option key acts like another shift key). You'll need to consult a keyboard map to find where the desired character is.

See also EXTENDED CHARACTER SET; EXPERT SET.

SPECING TYPE to give or determine the characteristics of the type for your document. Specing is short for "specifying type," and pronounced "spek-ing." Before desktop publishing, specing type was a distinct stage in the design phase. You already had the layout finalized and then you marked up the double-spaced manuscript for the typesetter. Now, with your computer to help you, specing type is a very fluid, interactive process. You can see on screen what adjustments need to be made and make the changes immediately. (*See* COPYFITTING.)

Here's what's involved in specing type: Choose the typeface. Set the point size. Set the line length. Choose the justification. Adjust spacing (between letters, words, and lines). Set the tabs. Now, take a look at what you've got. Do any adjustments need to be made? Are there any special problems? Now, decide how to set headings, subheads, SIDEBARS, and any other special elements in your layout.

If you are the author as well as the editor and typesetter, I *do* recommend that you make specing type a separate step. Otherwise, it's just too much to try and juggle in your head at the same time.

SPELL CHECKER; SPELLING CHECKER a program that checks the spelling of every word in a document by looking up each word in a dictionary. If the word does not appear in the dictionary, the user is alerted to a possible misspelling, and possible corrections are often suggested.

Many word processing and page layout programs include spell checkers. An effective spell checker needs to store a large number of words and it must be able to search the dictionary list quickly.

A spell checker will not recognize unusual proper names or specialized terms, but it will usually allow you to create your own personal dictionary of specialized words you often use. Be careful when adding words to your spell checker's dictionary; a dictionary of misspelled words is useless.

Spell checkers are valuable aids to proofreading, but they cannot catch the substitution of one correctly spelled word for another (such as *form* for *from* or *to* for *too*). Thus they do not guarantee that a document is free of spelling errors.

SPELLING the representation of words by standard sequences of letters. English spelling does not just represent pronunciation; it also indicates the history of words and the relationships between them.

Misspelled words distract the reader like noises during a concert. They may also indicate carelessness or lack of education. The writer who can't distinguish the spellings of *affect* and *effect* probably doesn't have a firm grip on the meanings either. *Table 8* lists some frequently misspelled words.

Computer spelling checkers are good at detecting random typing errors, but they do not detect substitutions of one correctly spelled word for another, such as *two* for *too*. Responsibility for choosing the words in a document rests with the author and (human) editor.

If you're a "bad speller," get a fellow human (not just a computer) to proofread all your work. Here are some other tips:

Never let yourself write a word misspelled, be-

Table 8 Frequently misspelled words.

compatible	(not -*able*)
copyright(ed)	(the *right* to *copy*; not from *write*)
Halloween	(not *hollow...*)
hobbyist	(= *hobby* + -*ist,* not -*est*)
it's	(= *it is*)
its	(possessive, like *his*)
lady's	'belonging to one lady'
ladies'	'belonging to ladies,' as in *ladies' clothes*
lens	(*one lens, two lenses*; not *len* or *lense*)
man's	'belonging to one man'
men's	'belonging to men,' as in *men's clothes*
tomorrow	(only one *m*)
viruses	(not *viri*; in Latin *virus* had no plural)
voilà	French for "look!"
you're	(= *you are*)
your	(possessive, like *our*)

cause if you do, it will soon "look right" to you even though it's wrong.

Pronounce words clearly. For example, pronounce *eternity* as *ee–turn–it–ee* (with *it* in the middle), not *uha–turn–uh–tee*; the clear pronunciation will help you remember the spelling.

Learn words, not just spellings. A word isn't really yours until you know how to spell, pronounce, and use it. There's no point in memorizing spellings without also learning the meaning and usage of each word.

Some words are spelled differently in Great Britain than in America. The British write *gaol, colour, humour, odour, centre, manoeuvre, judgement, acknowledgement, to practise* where Americans write *jail, color, humor, odor, center, maneuver, judgment, acknowledgment, to practice.* (But *humorous* is spelled the same way in both countries; so is the noun *practice.*) Some Britons write *itemise, finalise,* etc., in place of *itemize, finalize,* and other *-ize* verbs, but the

-ize spellings are now preferred even in Britain.

SPIRAL BINDING *see* BINDING.

SPLINE a curve that connects a set of points smoothly. *Figure 22* shows some examples. For details of computation, *see* B-SPLINE; BÉZIER SPLINE; CUBIC SPLINE.

$$\frac{1}{2}$$

Split fraction

SPLIT FRACTION a fraction constructed of three characters: the small numerator and denominator separated by a slash or horizontal bar. You can use split fractions to supplement the font's collection of CASE FRACTIONS. Some word processors have tools and macros that speed the building of split fractions.

Split fractions are also called PIECE FRACTIONS.

SPOOLING the process of briefly storing the computer output before sending it to the printer. This allows the user to proceed with other tasks on the computer, while the data is being sent to the printer at the proper speed.

SPOT COLOR the used of a specified color of ink. Spot color can be used for emphasis or to add interest to documents. It is less expensive than PROCESS COLOR and is often the preferred method of adding color to low-budget publications.

Using spot color adds a pass through the printing press. The black ink will probably be printed first, and then when it is dry, the paper will be run through the press a second time and the colored ink will be added. You will need to have REGISTRATION MARKS on your CAMERA-READY artwork to ensure that the two colors line up correctly. You may have as many different spot colors as you wish. Be aware that the cost savings over process color will disappear if you specify more than four colors.

There are many nuances to using spot color. The first consideration is carefully planning which color to use. You are *not* limited to the four process colors. Using a chart of available ink colors, pick which color is most suitable for your project. Do not rely on the colors displayed on your monitor; printed colors are richer and darker. (*See* CALIBRATION).

If the text is to be printed in black, you may use black plus a combination of the spot color to print

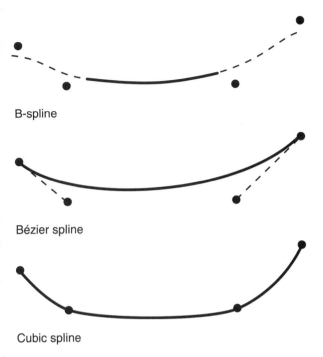

B-spline

Bézier spline

Cubic spline

Figure 22   Three types of splines.

DUOTONES. Some unusual and artistic effects can be achieved by combining two or more colors. Be careful not to exceed 240% total ink coverage.

SPRAYCAN   a tool found in various paint and photopaint programs that leaves a circular pattern of the selected color. To use it, you press and hold down the mouse button and drag the mouse. The center of the spray pattern will be solid, but the edges will feather out to the background color. If you need a dense, solid, color, move the mouse slowly; if you want a wispy trace of color, move the mouse rapidly. You will be able to change the size of the spraycan's coverage area — usually by changing the BRUSH SIZE.

A similar tool is the AIRBRUSH. Generally, a program will have either an airbrush *or* a spraycan tool, but not both.

The icon shown is from Corel PhotoPaint.

Spraycan

SPREADSHEET a table (usually) of numbers, arranged in rows and columns. Spreadsheets have long been used for business calculations. However, spreadsheet calculations can be very tedious; changing a single number can affect the results in many different rows and columns. Therefore, it helps greatly to have a computer perform spreadsheet calculations. Several software packages are available that turn the computer into an electronic spreadsheet. Some of the popular spreadsheet packages are Lotus 123, Excel, and Quattro. All of these programs can produce files that can be imported into page layout or charting programs.

Spur

SPUR the small pointed stroke that finishes large curved strokes in letters like C and G.

SPUR SERIFS serifs that come to points, like cowboy's spurs. *See* SERIF.

SQUARE SERIFS serifs that end bluntly, squared off. Also called SLAB SERIFS.

Spur serif

Square serif

STACKING ORDER the order in which objects are arranged in a drawing program. This determines which objects overlay others. Commands to reorganize the stacking order (Send to Front, Send to Back, Forward One, Back One) are usually found under an Arrange menu.

STANDARD GENERALIZED MARKUP LANGUAGE (SGML) a standard set of codes for marking boldface, italics, etc., in ASCII text files, which became the basis for HTML. *See* HTML.

STARTUP DISK any disk (either a hard drive or diskette) that contains enough of the computer's OPERATING SYSTEM for the disk to be used to BOOT the computer.

STAT *see* PHOTOSTAT.

STATISTICS the science of drawing conclusions from raw numerical data.

Statistics are often displayed in the form of a table or chart to help the reader understand their import.

Many pundits have drawn wry conclusions about the truthfulness of statistical data. It is true that different experts often draw different conclusions from the same set of data. Editorial responsibility demands great care in the interpretation and presentation of statistics.

STATUS LINE a line of information on the computer screen that gives valuable data about the current settings of the software and the current cursor position. The contents of a status line will vary depending on the software used; some programs give different information during the execution of different commands. It is a good idea to get into the habit of noticing what is in the status line. If you do not understand what you see there, take a moment to review the manual.

STET proofreader's mark for "let it stand." If you first marked a correction to the copy you are proofreading, and then later discovered that the original was correct, you would write "stet" in the margin and place a series of dots under the correction. *See* PROOFREADER'S MARKS.

Stet
(proofreader's mark)

STOCHASTIC SCREENING a new method of producing process-color halftone images that uses an irregular pattern of very fine dots. By eliminating the regular grid that composes traditional halftones, MOIRÉS are avoided.

STOCK on hand; readily available.

Stock photography is a collection of photographs that you can use much like clip art. You can purchase collections of photographs on CDs, or you can use the services of a stock photography agency. The agency will search for you to find a photograph that suits your needs. There is usually a fee for this search. You will then have to purchase the rights to reproduce the photo. This is more expensive than using a photo from a CD collection, but it is considerably less expensive than hiring a photographer and/or models to make a custom shot for you. Also, stock photography is the only practical way to get some one-of-a-kind images. You can't exactly cue a rainbow.

In printing, stock is a collective term for paper. You might hear the printer yell to the back room, "Have we got enough stock to run 500 copies of that newsletter?"

Stress

STRESSED letterforms that show a difference in the widths of the strokes. Noting the stress is one of the key items in recognizing and identifying typefaces. The opposite of a stressed typeface is a MONOLINE typeface.

STRESS, POINT OF MINIMUM the point where the stroke is thinnest. Noting the axis of this stress will help you identify and classify typefaces.

STRETCH to increase either the vertical or horizontal dimension of an object. To use the mouse to stretch a selected object interactively, drag out one of the handles at the midpoints of the BOUNDING BOX. *Contrast* SCALE, which maintains the height-to-width ratio of the object.

STRIPPING IN prepress production work involving assembling the negatives just prior to making the printing plates.

Even with all the advances in desktop publishing technology available to you, it may still give better results to have all photographs prepared by the printer and stripped in. It is still worthwhile to work with a low-resolution scan of the photo (marked FOR POSITION ONLY) to aid the correct positioning and cropping of the photographs.

STROKE the line created by the Pencil or PEN tool. Interesting and unusual special effects can be created in programs like Adobe Illustrator by merely adjusting the stroke attributes.

STUFFIT a popular data compression program by Raymond Lau for the Macintosh. Like ARC and ZIP on the IBM PC, StuffIt allows several files to be combined into one. StuffIt can also encode and decode BinHex files. *See* DATA COMPRESSION; ZIP.

Normal
Italic
Bold
Bold Italics
Condensed
Extended
Typeface styles

STYLE

1. the attributes of a font which make it different from other members of its typeface family; some descriptive terms used: normal, *italic*, **bold**, *bold italics*, condensed, or expanded. *See* FONT; TYPEFACE FAMILY.

2. the various layout, punctuation, and typographic decisions used for a particular publication.

Make sure that the style is consistent — you do not want to confuse a reader by constantly changing things.

STYLE SHEET settings and instructions given to the computer for the design of a particular page layout. A typical style sheet will have the margins and the base font set, and the number of columns specified. More sophisticated page layout programs have more intricate style sheets that may include TAGS for different levels of headings, and different MASTER PAGES for left- and right-hand pages. *See also* TEMPLATE.

STYLUS the pen-like part of a graphics tablet.

SUBDIRECTORY a disk directory that is stored in another directory. *See* DIRECTORY.

SUBHEAD a minor headline, smaller and less bold that the major headings.

SUBPATH part of a PATH.

SUBSCRIPT small type set below the baseline likethis. Subscripts are common in mathematical and scientific texts.

SUBTITLE the secondary part of a title that usually gives a fuller description of the publication's subject matter.

SUITCASE (Macintosh) a special kind of folder that contains system resources (fonts, sounds, desk accessories). You can manage your fonts by keeping them grouped logically in suitcases; some prefer to store their fonts in typeface families — special fonts used for a specific project could be in another suitcase.

SUITE a set of application software from a single vendor that attempts to span the basic uses of a computer. A suite usually has a word processor, a database, and a spreadsheet. The advantage to using a suite is compatibility; you are assured that all of the programs can accept data from any of the others and incorporate them in their own files. On the downside, the individual programs of a software suite sometimes lack desirable features. If additional software is purchased from another company, it may be difficult to get the programs to work together.

SUPERIOR CHARACTERS small characters printed above the normal baseline ^like this^. Also called SUPERSCRIPT.

SUPERSCRIPT small type that is set high ^like this^. Footnote references are set in superscript. Superscript is also common in mathematical and scientific texts.

SUPER VGA any video card incorporating all the functions of IBM's VGA plus additional modes with higher resolution and/or more colors usable at once. Many different companies make super VGAs that work in slightly different ways. Super VGAs typically offer resolutions of 800×600 and 1024×768 pixels, with up to 64K colors (65,536 colors) available in each. Not all resolutions are available with any particular combination of card and monitor.

Some super VGAs also incorporate *Windows accelerator* functions—that is, they take care of operations such as moving a window that would ordinarily require the full attention of the CPU.

Super VGAs are practical because operating systems such as Microsoft Windows and OS/2 Presentation Manager handle all graphical output. Thus, individual programs do not have to be modified to use special video modes; the user simply installs a device driver to support the super VGA card in the desired mode, and the operating system takes care of the details. That is why the great diversity of super VGA cards has not raised software compatibility problems. However, some device drivers are unreliable, and if software performs unreliably — even if the problem does not seem to be video-related—it is worthwhile switching to a plain VGA driver to see if the problem disappears. *See also* VGA.

SURGE PROTECTOR a device that absorbs brief bursts of excessive voltage coming in from the AC power line. These surges are created by lightning or by electric motors switching off. Early microcomputers were easily damaged by surges, but present-day personal computers usually have adequate surge protection built in.

Surge protectors do little good unless the power line is properly grounded. Always plug the computer into a three-prong outlet that meets modern wiring standards. Many surge protectors also incorporate RFI protectors to help reduce radio and TV interference emitted by the computer into the power line. (*See* RFI PROTECTION.) A surge protector cannot do anything about momentary power failures. *See also* POWER LINE PROTECTION; UNINTERRUPTIBLE POWER SUPPLY.

SWAP FILE a file used for swap space. In OS/2, the swap file is named SWAPPER.DAT and changes size as needed (provided enough disk space is free). In Windows 3.1, the swap file is hidden and does not appear in directory listings. It can be either permanent, and fixed in size, or temporary, and varying in size. Permanent swap files give faster execution.

Besides the swap file used by the operating system, there are also swap files used by particular applications, such as Corel Draw. *See* SWAP SPACE.

SWAP SPACE disk space that an operating system or program uses as a substitute for additional memory. *See* SWAP FILE.

SWASH a capital letter with a decorative flourish. Swashes are best when used sparingly.

Swash

SWIPE FILE a file of examples of excellent design or other good ideas. A swipe file is not meant for you to plagiarize ideas, but rather to provide inspiration on the days that you are short on creative invention. By examining the design of advertisements and brochures that appeal to you, you can learn about graphic design.

SYMBOL FONT highly stylized artwork stored and utilized in the same manner as a regular alphabet. Also called PI FONTS and DINGBATS.

Symbol font

SYS REQ KEY (also spelled SysRq) a key on the keyboard of PC-compatible computers. You type it by holding down Ctrl and pressing the SysReq key (labeled "Print Screen" on its top). This mysterious key was intended to allow the computer user a way to call the operating system (**Sys**tem **Req**uest), but little or no software has ever made use of it.

SYSTEM 7.5 the newest version of the Macintosh operating system, released by Apple in 1994.

System 7.5 continues in the tradition of its preceding versions by presenting an uncluttered and consistent user interface. Since the advent of the Macintosh in 1984, the goal has been to let the user do what he or she wanted to (within and sometimes beyond reason), and to let the computer deal with the housekeeping details. The elegantly simple idea of *choosing* an object and then telling the computer what to do with it has been carried through all versions of the Mac operating system, desktop accessories, third-party applications, and then the idea was even adopted by the PC world (*see* WINDOWS). Today, a person familiar with one operating environment can pretty much sit down at any computer, and within minutes, be doing productive work.

There are many new features in System 7.5: Apple Guide, a system help system that can assist you step-by-step through new procedures; the Apple menu may now contain submenus; electronic sticky notes can be stuck to the Desktop; windows may be rolled up to just their title bars to save space (WindowShade); the PC Exchange control panel (which allows the Mac to read and write to PC disks) has been improved; and QuickTime (multimedia support) has been improved. Most important to desktop publishers, a new internal graphics description language, called *QuickDraw GX* has been implemented. Immediate improvement in printout and display quality may not be obvious; application software will need to be updated to take advantage of the new infrastructure. But the groundwork has been laid for the Mac to add new graphics features and speed printing.

The greatest advantage QuickDraw GX will offer will be a new class of outline (SCALABLE) fonts. A GX font can contain up to 16,000 characters (compared to the current 256 character sets). This means a single font may contain not only the standard alphanumeric characters, but a full EXPERT SET (small caps, oldstyle figures, accented characters, ligatures), alternate characters, and swashes. These new fonts will be programmable—the computer will be able to mix in alternate characters, or find an appropriate place to use a swash.

QuickDraw GX also provides support for ELECTRONIC PUBLISHING by introducing a new file format called PDD (Portable Digital Document). A PDD file may be viewed by any other Macintosh running QuickDraw GX and still retain the appearance of the original document, including all formatting, graphics, and fonts.

T

TAB the key on the computer keyboard that is marked with forward and backward arrows. The tab key advances the cursor to a preset spot; shift-tab goes back to the previous tab stop. Most word processors and page layout programs let you set the TAB STOPS where you want them and otherwise provide a reasonable set of defaults, usually every $\frac{1}{2}$ inch.

Always use the tab key instead of the space bar to align type. When setting proportional type, it is impossible to get columns to line up by adding space characters; you *must* set the tabs.

TABLE numerical data presented in columns and rows. Tables are more precise than graphs; each cell has a specific value. There may be times when it is necessary to publish a chart and a table of the same data side-by-side. Tables are easier to typeset if they are set with a FIXED-WIDTH TYPE.

TABLE OF CONTENTS a listing of the subjects covered in a book or a listing of the articles that appear in a magazine or newsletter.

In most books, the Table of Contents comes on the first page after the Dedication or Epigraph (usually page V or VI). The rest of the front-matter, (FOREWORD, PREFACE, Acknowledgements, and Introduction) comes after the Contents, but before the main body of the text. Most page layout programs are able to generate a Table of Contents automatically from the TAGGED chapter heads and subheads. If you decide to include subheads in the Table of Contents, the listing may run to several pages, thus losing its usefulness as a guide to the reader. In that case, you may wish to have *two* Tables of Contents: The first should contain only the main chapter headings; the second could be an amplified version listing all the subheadings.

The Table of Contents of a magazine may have to vie with paid advertisements for placement. Try to place the Contents as close to the inside front page as possible. Many magazines group similar articles together in the Table of Contents, breaking with the book-publishing tradition of sequential listings. In a newsletter, the Contents may be reduced to a small box on the front page or left out entirely.

TABLOID a newspaper format that is usually about $11\frac{1}{2} \times 13\frac{3}{4}$ inches (half the size of a normal newspaper sheet). Tabloids are often used for special advertising sections.

TAB STOPS adjustable markers that indicate the next horizontal position of the cursor when the tab key is pressed.

TABULAR material arranged in a table.

TAIL

    1. the DESCENDER of the Q or of the g, which is also called a LOOP.

    2. the bottom edge of a piece of paper. The top is called the HEAD. When printing on both sides, you should specify whether the printing is to go HEAD-TO-HEAD (both sides up) or HEAD-TO-TAIL (back side upside down).

TALL paper oriented so that it is taller than wide; also called PORTRAIT orientation.

TAPE magnetic means of storing backup information. A tape cartridge for a computer looks like a fatter version of an audio cassette tape. It is cheaper to store information on tape than in the computer's hard drive or on a disk, but a longer time is required to locate a particular file if it is stored on tape.

    Tapes are an excellent way to make backup copies of your files and to transport large files (greater than the capacity of a high-density disk) to a service bureau. You will need to verify that the service bureau has the equipment to read a tape from your particular tape drive; there are a large variety of formats and sizes available.

TAPE DRIVE a device that reads and writes information stored on magnetic tape for a computer. If you have enough bays open in your computer system, you can have the drive installed internally, or it can be an external peripheral and sit beside the computer on the desk.

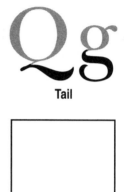

Tail

Tall

Task list

TARGET

1. the place to which information is to be copied (e.g., the "target disk" when copying disks). *See* SOURCE.

2. something that is being searched for (as when searching for a word in a document).

TASK LIST (Windows, OS/2) a menu of open (running) and minimized software, some of which may be hidden by overlaid windows. Access the Task List by double-clicking on the desktop.

A similar feature for Macintosh users is the AP-PLICATION MENU, which is located at the far right end of a window's title bar.

TEASER

1. a short phrase, set in small type, that runs above the main headline. Also called a KICKER.

2. a short cover reference crafted to catch a potential reader's interest. Many magazines make extensive use of teasers; some publications even use pictures along with the words.

TEMPLATE a particular pattern for a page layout program or a word processing program that is frequently used. Therefore, storing the template as a file will save you from having to reconstruct the format each time. *See* STYLE SHEET.

TEX (pronounced "tek") a computer typesetting program by D. E. Knuth, used by the American Mathematical Society and many book publishers and educational institutions. Unlike most desktop publishing systems, TEX does not attempt to show you the appearance of the finished document on the screen as you edit it (though screen previews can be generated). Instead, you type a document with codes in it that indicate boldface, italics, special characters (e.g.. "\S" for §), and the like.

The rationale is that correct typesetting relies on distinctions that are too subtle to see on a computer screen. A user who wants an em dash rather than an en dash should say so with explicit codes, rather than try to make a mark that appears the right length on the screen. Likewise, large-scale aspects of design should be automated; you should be able to give just the title of a chapter, and let the computer take care of numbering the chapter and putting the title in the right place on the page.

TEX is generally considered the most sophisticated computer typesetting system, as well as (for an experienced user) one of the easiest to use. It sets a standard that other desktop publishing systems try to emulate. This book was typeset with TEX.

TEXT BOX

1. an area in a dialog box in which the user can type or edit characters. For picture, *see* DIALOG BOX.

2. a special type of non-printing box that contains textual material. Also called a FRAME. Text boxes can be linked together to allow an article to be continued on a following page.

TEXT EDITOR   an editor designed primarily or exclusively for handling textual material (letters, manuscripts, etc.) rather than programs. *See* EDITOR; WORD PROCESSING.

TEXT FILE   a file that contains written information that can be sent directly to the screen or printer by using ordinary operating system commands.

The files produced by word processors are usually not text files. Although they contain text, they also contain special codes (for margins. underlining, etc.) whose meaning is known only to the word processing software. Many word processors can, however, produce text files (sometimes called "nondocument mode" or "DOS text files").

On machines that use the ASCII character set, text files are often called ASCII files.

To create a text file on the Macintosh, save a document as "Text only."

TEXT OUT   *see* EXPORT.

TEXT WRAP   *see* WORD WRAP.

THEIR   the possesive form of the pronoun *they*. Because it is commonly confused with *they're* and *there*, you should make sure that you have the right word when proofreading. *See* SPELLING.

THERE in that place; the opposite of *here* (which it is spelled like). This word is often confused with *they're* or *their* even though their meanings are very distinct. This trio of words should be like a red flag when proofreading — make sure you have the right word! *See* SPELLING.

THERMAL-WAX TRANSFER PRINTER a printer that uses heat to bond waxy pigment to paper. The color saturation is much superior to color laser or color inkjet printers. Thermal-wax transfer printers typically have a resolution of 300 DPI; however, the effective resolution looks coarser because the colors tend to bleed together as they overprint and form *super pixels* about five dots across. The printouts must be made on a special type of paper and the waxy ink tends to flake easily. The other drawback is speed; the print head must make four passes over the image area, allowing time for the wax to cool between passes. Still, thermal-wax printers are suitable for proofing color files.

THESAURUS a reference work, available in either book form or as a computer program, that contains lists of synonyms and antonyms.

THEY'RE a contraction for *they are*. *They're* is commonly confused with *their* and *there*. Remember, a spell checker will not catch a misused word if it is properly spelled! Try substituting "they are" in the sentence; if it reads right, you want *they're*. *See* SPELLING.

THREE-DIMENSIONAL GRAPHICS Computer drawings that give the illusion of depth due to the use of PERSPECTIVE. Traditionally, CAD PROGRAMS (**C**omputer **A**ided **D**esign) give more help in constructing three-dimensional models.

THREE UP to print three items on a single sheet of paper. This is an efficient way of reproducing small items such as tickets or coupons. *See* GANG UP.

THUMB the box on an elevator bar. The position of the thumb gives a graphical representation of the window's current position in the document or list.

The thumb can be dragged with the mouse to scroll rapidly around the page. *See* WINDOW for illustration.

THUMBNAILS (thumbnail sketches) small drawings done by hand in the earliest stages of planning a project. This is the time for trying new things and being creative. Do you want one column or two? Should you run the type around the illustration? Are you after an avant garde look, or a refined, classical feel? A few minutes of sketching before going to the computer can give you creative insights into the graphical problem you're trying to solve.

Thumbnails

Image library programs often display digital thumbnails of drawings or artwork to help you find the correct file.

TIFF **T**ag **I**mage **F**ile **F**ormat; developed by Microsoft, Aldus, and several other companies as a standard format for recording bitmapped images on disk. TIFF files can store images of any size with any number of colors, using several kinds of data compression. For comparison, *see* PCX; GIF. *See also* BITMAP.

TIGHT LETTERSPACING type set so closely that the letters almost touch. *See* LETTERSPACING for illustration.

Some typefaces actually look better set tight. At small sizes (less than 8 points), all typefaces benefit from increasing the letterspacing (making it looser).

TILDE the character ˜. *See* ACCENTS; SPANISH.

~

Tilde

TILE

1. a command that causes the displayed windows to divide the screen into sections without overlapping one another. *See picture. Contrast* OVERLAID WINDOWS; CASCADED WINDOWS.

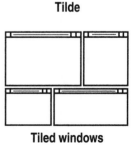

Tiled windows

2. to print a large page (larger than your printer can handle) by having the page broken up into a series of overlapping regular size sheets which can then be fastened together.

3. to create a pattern with a simple design by repeating it over and over. Many draw and paint programs have a library of tile designs; you may also design your own.

Handgloves

Times Roman

TIMES ROMAN a highly legible typeface designed by Stanley Morison in 1931 for *The Times* of London. Times Roman and its many varieties reproduce well at low resolutions, and this probably led to its current popularity as a laser printer font. *See* TYPEFACE.

TINT a color that is reduced in intensity by means of a HALFTONE SCREEN. Tints are specified by the percentage of ink coverage. A tint of 10% black is quite light; a 90% black tint is virtually indistinguishable from 100% black.

Be careful when printing black text on top of a gray tint or a tint of a second color. It is hard to read text when there is not enough contrast between the letters and the background.

TITLE BAR the label at the top of a window, usually identifying the program or file to which it belongs. *See* WINDOW.

TO the opposite of *from*. One of the most common words in the English language, this preposition and its homophones *too* and *two* form a trio that proofreaders must notice. *See* SPELLING.

TOC Table Of Contents.

TOGGLE to switch something back and forth from one state to another. For instance, in some editors, the Ins key "toggles" insert mode; that is, it turns insert mode *on* if it is off, or *off* if it is on.

TONER the black powder that is used by laser printers and photocopy machines to create the image on paper.

TONER CARTRIDGE replaceable assembly of a laser printer that contains the toner (a powdery ink) that will be used to make marks on the paper. Most toner cartridges actually contain parts that are likely to wear out (i.e. the electrophotographic drum) and replacing the cartridge replaces quite a bit of the inner workings of the laser printer. (This undoubtedly contributes to the cost of the toner cartridge.) Some types of toner cartridges are recyclable and refillable; however, please consult your printer's manual to see if your particular machine can safely use recycled cartridges. You will probably find that the image quality is not as good with a recycled cartridge as with a new one — not acceptable when you're trying to produce camera-ready copy!

TOO also or excessively. Easily confused with *to* and sometimes *two*, the sight of this word should alert you to double check it when proofreading. If you can substitute "also" or "excessively" and have the sentence read right, you should use the word *too*. *See* SPELLING.

TOOL a specialized function or command. Tools in a computerized environment can be analogies to real-life tools (a spraycan, a pencil), or abstractions (a text tool). Each tool fundamentally changes how the computer behaves and how the cursor looks.

TOOLBAR a row of small icons usually arranged across the top of the workspace on screen. Each icon represents a commonly used command; many programs allow you to customize your toolbar to suit your personal taste. Also called a BUTTONBAR.

TOOLBOX a collection of icons that represent frequently used commands. The toolbox may be displayed across the top or side of the screen or you may be able to relocate the toolbox(es) by dragging them with the mouse. The more complicated paint and photopaint programs sometimes have several toolboxes, with similar tools grouped together. *See picture.*

The toolbox shown is from Corel PhotoPaint.

TOUCHING type set so that the letters touch. This is best restricted to display type, as the legibility will suffer somewhat. *See* LETTERSPACING.

TOWER a computer enclosure that is tall like a skyscraper. Often a tower will have more space available for add-in cards, extra drives, and memory. A tower also has a smaller FOOTPRINT than a horizontal box and can either sit on your desktop beside the monitor or on the floor.

TRACE to create a path or outline around the contours of a bitmapped shape. It is necessary to trace bitmaps to convert them into VECTOR GRAPHICS. Tracing can be done by a separate utility program or from within the drawing program.

Toolbox

touching
Very tight letterspacing

TRACKBALL a computer pointing device similar in function to a mouse. Instead of rolling the mouse around the desktop, the user rotates the ball on the trackball in the direction desired. The trackball unit itself does not move, which is an advantage if there is not enough desktop space to operate a mouse conveniently. Sometimes called a ROLLERBALL.

TRACKING letterspacing; "Tighten the tracking on all the major headings." *See* LETTERSPACING for more detail.

TRADEMARK a symbol or word set in a special typeface that is used to represent a company or its products. *See* LOGO.

An R in a circle is used by the owner of a trademark to show that the trademark has been registered with the government. A superscript TM (^{TM}) is sometimes used in commercial writing to indicate that a particular name is a trademark, but there is no legal requirement to do so.

TRANSFORM a menu heading for a category of tools and commands that change a selected area, object, or picture.

Handgloves

Transitional

TRANSITIONAL a kind of typeface that was developed in the early 1700s in transition from the GAR-ALDE to the DIDONE styles, and incorporating elements from each style. A transitional typeface has a vertical stress or else the stress is very sightly inclined to the left. Serifs are bracketed and on the lower case ascenders, the serifs are finished at a slant. Baskerville and Janson are considered transitional typefaces.

TRANSPARENT

1. able to be seen through. This is a very simple thing, but by the very nature of computer drawing programs, it is *hard* to render transparent objects in a drawing. You have to resort to all sorts of trickery and subterfuge, combining multiple layers of objects and joining them together, *because each object is an opaque color!* The latest releases of some major drawing programs include special tools to create the effect of transparency. *See* LENS.

It is easier to get transparent effects with a paint program because you can define the area you want to work on and apply the necessary filters. Some paint programs (Fractal Painter, for example), have the ability to let you draw in NATURAL MEDIA, and you can get some nice transparent effects. Essentially, you are confronting the same problem that natural media artists have struggled with for centuries. To learn how to render transparent objects, you may have to sit down with a good art history book to try to figure it out.

2. Computationally, something is transparent if it has no visible effect. For instance, if a print spooling program is working properly and does its job quietly, without slowing down the other programs, and without causing any conflicts for the computer's resources, the print spooler is said to be "transparent" to the computer user. This, of course, is highly desirable.

TRANSPOSITION a common typing error caused by the typist striking the keys in the wrong order. Most transpositions are easily caught by using a spell checker on all your documents.

TRAP a slight amount of overlap that is necessary to ensure that two adjacent colors will not have a white gap in between.

If you are using only one color, you will not have to worry about creating trap. However, if you are using two or more spot colors, you will have to plan ahead for when the piece is printed. Look carefully at the design. Is there any place where the two colors have a common edge? If so, you will need to overlap the edges of the two objects to give the printer some play in getting the colors in correct registration.

TRAY the shelf-like support that holds the paper supply for a laser printer.

TRI-FOLD A common type of brochure, made by folding a piece of letter size paper ($8\frac{1}{2} \times 11$ inches) in thirds, giving a finished size of $3\frac{2}{3} \times 8\frac{1}{2}$ inches. Many companies offer preprinted stock for tri-fold brochures, suitable for laser printing or copiers.

TRUETYPE FONT an outline font format (originally

developed in 1991 by Apple as a competing format to PostScript fonts). TrueType fonts are sets of mathematical descriptions of the letterforms as B-spline curves. What this means in practical terms is that it is possible to SCALE or size the type to practically any point size. *See* VECTOR GRAPHICS. A common competing type format is Adobe's Type 1 font format. If your computer system is set up for TrueType fonts, you will not be able to use Type 1 fonts.

There is a slight difference in the TrueType formats for Macintosh and PC platforms; conversion utilities can convert one to the other.

TRUMATCH a color matching and calibration system developed and distributed by Trumatch, Incorporated, New York, New York.

TWO the number 2 spelled out. Be careful not to confuse this word with *to* or *too*. *See* SPELLING.

TWO UP printed with two items on a single sheet of paper. This is an efficient way of reproducing small items such as notepads or receipts. *See* GANG UP.

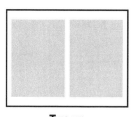

Two up

TYPE

1. to input information to the computer using the keyboard. For advice on good typing practices, *see* ERGONOMICS; TYPESETTING ERRORS.

2. the representation of letters, numbers, and other special characters. Type can be made either of metal, wooden blocks, photographic film, or digital information. A typeface is a set of all these characters in a similar design and weight.

Figure 23 illustrates some of the specialized terminology used to talk about type.

TYPE 1 FONT an outline font format developed by Adobe Systems. Type 1 fonts are sets of mathematical descriptions of the letterforms as BÉZIER SPLINES. In practical terms this means that it is possible to SCALE or size the type to practically any point size. *See* VECTOR GRAPHICS. TrueType fonts are a competing format to Type 1 fonts.

TYPEFACE a particular design of lettering, in a consistent weight and style. Traditionally, a FONT was

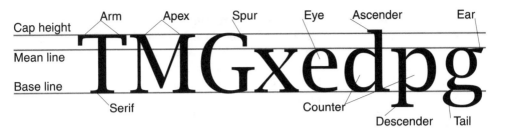

Figure 23 Anatomy of letters

Fujiyama Light

Fujiyama

Fujiyama 2

Fujiyama Bold

Fujiyama ExtraBold

Fujiyama Light Italic

Fujiyama Italic

Fujiyama 2 Italic

Fujiyama Bold Italic

Fujiyama ExtraBold Italic

Figure 24 An extended typeface family

a typeface in one particular size. Since the advent of SCALABLE FONTS has made one description of the design able to generate type of any practical size, *typeface* and *font* are used almost interchangeably. To be more precise, you should use the word *font* to refer to the digital files that describe the letterforms.

TYPEFACE FAMILY a group of related typefaces, basically the same design in different weights, with matching italic versions. A common typeface family will include the plain or normal typeface, the normal-weight italic, a bold, and a bold-italic. Some typeface families are more extensive and have more varieties available. *See Figure 24* for illustration.

TYPEFACES, CLASSIFICATION OF grouping and naming groups of typefaces according to their shared characteristics. There are many different methods of classifying typefaces, some more formal than others. The important thing to remember is that some typefaces can be placed in more than one category. Sometimes this is a judgement call on the part of the classifier, but sometimes you run into a typeface whose designer delighted in combining some unusual characteristics.

Here is a simplified classification system that has four main classes: ROMAN, SANS SERIF, SCRIPT, and DECORATIVE.

Roman typefaces are historically based on the letterforms inscribed into the Trajan column by the ancient Romans. The serifs are the stonecutter's method of finishing a stroke. (Further classifications of serif typefaces can be made on proportions, contrast and minute distinctions of design details. For now, we'll group them together.) These roman typefaces are our workhorses. They give us maximum legibility and reproducibility. Each typeface family usually includes italic, bold, and bold-italic members.

The sans-serif (without serifs) typefaces were designed in the 19th century. Sans-serif typefaces are considered to have a modern look. Most of the sans-serif designs are available in families of various weights and proportions.

Script fonts are based on handwriting. They are sometimes called CURSIVE. Scripts can look as if they were drawn with brushes or engraved on copperplate. They can look elegant or informal. Since they are usually slanted, they don't have related italics. Script fonts seldom have a bold version.

Decorative typefaces are a catch-all category. Here is where we put the typefaces that are somehow unusual or very distinctive. Fonts in this category have a lot of character and sometimes selecting a typeface for a headline is not unlike casting a part in a play. Decorative typefaces should *not* be used to set text. They need to be set large enough for their personality to show.

Figure 25 shows some examples of our simple classification.

The BRITISH STANDARDS 2961:1967 SYSTEM is detailed for you under that entry. It is a very precise and methodical typeface classification and will aid you in

Roman	AaBbCcDdEeFfGgHhIiJjKkLlMmNn&?")	
		Aldine 401
Sans serif	AaBbCcDdEeFfGgHhIiJjKkLlMmNn&?")	
		Zurich
Script	AaBbCcDdEeFfGgHhIiJjKkLlMmNn&?")	
		Park Avenue
Decorative	ABCDEFGHIJKLMNOPQRST&UV?	
		Bravo Engraved

Figure 25 A simple classification of typefaces

learning about typography. The ADOBE CLASSIFICA-
TION SYSTEM is a variation of the British Standards.

The most rigid and mechanical method of classification is the PANOSE system. PANOSE actually as-
signs a 7-digit classification number to each typeface.
You can use these identification numbers to identify
and match typefaces; it is even possible for some software to read the PANOSE number in the font's digital header and make automatic font substitutions.
PANOSE falls apart when classifying decorative and
script fonts; it is intended mainly for classifying roman fonts. *See* PANOSE.

TYPE GAUGE an engraved metal ruler with mark-
ings to measure the point size of type as well as linespacing. A good type gauge should be engraved rather
than screen printed; the process of screen printing is
intrinsically not accurate enough to mark the tiny
increments.

TYPESETTING ERRORS errors in setting type (as
opposed to typing errors or writing errors made by the
author). The following pointers will help you avoid
common mistakes setting type.

- Notice the differences between typesetting and
  the typewriter:

- Left and right quotation marks are different characters ("like this").
- A dash (—) isn't two hyphens (- -).
- Underlining is rarely used. Where you would underline on a typewriter, use italics (or possibly boldface) in type.

- Your type is proportionally spaced; letters are not all the same width. You can't count letter spaces the way you do on a typewriter, but must use other means of aligning.

- Always align columns with the tab key, not the space bar.

- Type carefully. Be sure not to hit the space bar more than once between words. It's hard to tell the difference between one space and two spaces by just looking at the screen.

- Don't justify everything. Justified type looks good only when the columns are wide enough. Flush left type with a ragged right margin is easier to read if the columns are narrow; with narrow columns, justification puts excessive space between words. (*See* JUSTIFICATION.)

- Don't use more than one or at most two typeface families in a document. Multiple-font documents are almost always ugly. Be sensitive to which typefaces are suitable for text. Unusual typefaces (such as Old English) are very hard to read.

- Make sure your document is not missing any essential features such as adequate margins or page numbers. If in doubt, find a well-designed document or book and imitate it.

- Use appropriate features of your software. When you type a footnote, use the footnote instruction if there is one, rather than just moving the cursor to the foot of the page. That way, if you change the layout later, the software will probably still handle the footnote correctly.

- Standardize. Don't face each document as an original design problem. Develop a standard format that you like, and stick with it.

TYPOGRAPHY the art and science of using type well. The best typography is often not noticed—if the typography is doing its job well, the reader is focusing on the message, not the medium. A certain amount of satisfaction can be yours by simply knowing that your work has helped an important idea be communicated to many people.

Using computers to set type can be a great aid to a typographer; it can also be a mighty hindrance. The trick is for the human to use the computer rather than for the computer to impose limits on the human. Stay abreast of new developments in software and hardware. Try hard to understand as much of the technical underpinnings as you can. Explore your software and learn to exploit its strengths and avoid its weaknesses.

It's good to have a vision of what you're trying to accomplish. Try to analyze what makes a good design appealing. Keep a SWIPE FILE of printed pieces that you admire. You may find that a taking a course on some aspect of desktop publishing at a local community college will help you set type better — or you may be more comfortable learning on your own. This continual self-training will help you solve typesetting problems when they arise.

TYPOS typing mistakes. Spell checkers are excellent for catching most typos. Always run a spell check on all textual material.

See TYPESETTING ERRORS for a discussion of the finer points of typography.

U

Handgloves
Ultra bold

Ö
Umlaut

ḣaꞏꝺꝺꞁoᴠes
Uncials

ULC a proofreader's abbreviation meaning "Set this in upper and lower case." Also written c/lc (caps and lower case). Ulc is the normal method of setting type; *contrast with* CAPS.

ULTRA extrabold. Very dark, heavy looking, and emphatic, ultrabold type should be used sparingly. I suggest using it for headlines only—never for text.

UMLAUT *see* ACCENTS; GERMAN.

UNCIALS rounded capital letters based on one style of medieval manuscript writing. Modern lower case letters were developed from uncials.

UNDERLINE type set with a line under each letter. This is a typewriter-style convention for italics. Always use the italic font for emphasis rather than underlining.

UNDERSCORE *see* UNDERLINE.

UNDO a command that allows the computer user to reverse the effects of the most recent operation. If "Undo" is DIMMED (printed in gray), it is not possible for your program to undo that command (perhaps you have performed an intermediate step — or perhaps that most recent command was a complex operation that cannot be undone). For this reason, it is wise to save different versions of the file as you work so that you will have a recent version to REVERT to in case of disaster.

UNERASE *see* RECOVERING ERASED FILES.

UNGROUP to cause a grouped object to be broken down into its component objects. You will have to ungroup sometimes to change the attributes of a single object or to change its shape.

Uniform fill

UNIFORM FILL a fill that is one solid color or tint, with no gradations. Contrast FOUNTAIN FILL.

UNINTERRUPTIBLE POWER SUPPLY a power supply that uses batteries to continue providing electricity to a computer for a few minutes in the event of a power failure. This makes it possible to shut down the computer in an orderly way without losing data.

If you are in a position where you cannot afford to lose your work, you must have an uninterruptable power supply; it's as vital a part of your system as the printer.

UNLINK to break the connection between linked text FRAMES. *See* LINK, definition 3.

UPLOAD to transmit a file to a central computer from a smaller computer or a computer at a remote location. *Contrast* DOWNLOAD.

UPPER CASE the capital letters. The term "upper case" goes back to the early days of letterpress printing. The metal type was kept in divided drawers called cases; the capital letters in the upper drawer, and the small letters in the lower.

UPS *see* UNINTERRUPTIBLE POWER SUPPLY.

USER INTERFACE the way a program communicates with the person who is using it. There are three important types of user interfaces:

- **Command languages**. An example of this would be the way you interact with DOS. At the prompt, you type in the command you wish the computer to execute. Command languages work well only if they are used constantly so that the user never forgets the commands.   .
- **Menus**. The user chooses an item from a displayed list. Menus are ideal for software that is seldom used or has a bewildering variety of commands, but experienced users may find them too slow.
- **Graphical environments**. The user performs operations by selecting icons (pictures) with a mouse. Environments of this type can be highly productive. For examples, *see* MACINTOSH; WINDOWS. A drawback is that there is no simple way to describe how something is done; you almost have to see someone else do it. This can be improved by extending your vocabulary to be able to describe what is happening on the computer screen.

US LEGAL *see* LEGAL SIZE.

US LETTER *see* LETTER SIZE.

UTILITY a program that assists in the operation of a computer but does not do the main work for which the computer was bought. For instance, programs that compress data or defragment disks are utilities. *See* DATA COMPRESSION; FRAGMENTATION. By contrast, word processors, drawing programs, page layout programs, and other programs that do actual work for the user are called APPLICATION PROGRAMS.

V

VACCINE a computer program that offers protection from VIRUSES by making additional checks of the integrity of the operating system. No vaccine can offer complete protection against all viruses. Also known as anti-virus or VIRUS PROTECTION software.

VANISHING POINTS the points on the horizon on which parallel lines seem to converge. *See* PERSPECTIVE.

Vanishing points

VARIABLE PITCH a typeface design in which the letters are allowed to be different widths; the *I* for instance will be much narrower than the *W*. The opposite of variable pitch is FIXED PITCH. *See illustration at* FIXED PITCH.

VARIABLE WIDTH *see* VARIABLE PITCH.

VARNISH a clear glossy coating applied over printing for protection and esthetic reasons. A subtle black-on-black effect can be achieved by printing a varnished design over an area of solid matte black.

VECTOR GRAPHICS a method of creating pictures on a computer by telling it to draw lines in particular positions. An advantage of vector graphics is that a picture can be moved easily from one output device to another, since it makes no assumptions about the exact way the lines are drawn. For the same reason, a vector graphics picture can be enlarged or reduced without loss of sharpness. It also needs less disk space to store a vectored drawing than a bitmap. By contrast, *see* BITMAPPED GRAPHICS. *See also* DRAW PROGRAM; PAINT PROGRAM.

VELO a plastic binding material. Velo binding pierces the papers in the left margin, anchoring itself with thin plastic strips that run the height of the booklet. Velo binding shares many of the disadvantages of staples (the book will not open fully or lie flat), but it is an economical and durable method of binding a small quantity of booklets.

VELOX a halftoned photographic print that may be used as CAMERA-READY ART. "Velox" is actually

Handgloves
Venetian

Kodak's trademark for the glossy paper formerly used to print the images; sloppy usage over the years has almost turned it into a generic term. *See* PHOTOSTAT.

VENETIAN typefaces closely derived from 15th century handwriting; Centaur and Venetian 301 are good examples. The cross stroke of the *e* is slanted, stress is to the left and the contrast between the thick and thin strokes is low. Also, the lower case ascenders are finished with oblique serifs. This classification is sometimes called HUMANIST.

VERSO the back side of a sheet printed on both sides; also the left-hand page of a book or magazine. *Contrast* RECTO.

VERTICAL up and down. HORIZONTAL is side-to-side or across.

VGA the video system introduced by IBM on the PS/2 computers in 1987, and also available on cards for use in conventional PCs. VGA originally stood for **V**ideo **G**ate **A**rray but nowadays is usually interpreted as **V**ideo **G**raphics **A**dapter.

The VGA provides a maximum resolution of 640×480 with 16 colors. It also supports all the video modes of the earlier IBM video adapters (MDA, CGA, and EGA). *See also* SUPER VGA; XGA.

VIDEO CARD (video adapter) a plug-in circuit board that enables a computer to display information on a particular type of monitor (screen).

VIRGULE a slash.

/
Virgule

VIRUS a computer program that automatically copies itself, thereby "infecting" other disks or programs without the users knowing it, and then disrupts the operation of the computer.

Viruses have existed as academic pranks since the 1960s, but 1987 saw the first malicious viruses, apparently the work of disgruntled programmers trying to sabotage their competition. The best protection against viruses is to obtain all your software from reliable sources, make regular backup copies of your work, and write-protect disks that do not need to be written on. Make sure there is not a diskette in drive

A when you start your computer; this is how a *boot-sector virus* spreads. If you frequently exchange data diskettes with others, you may want to invest in an anti-virus program.

Knowingly spreading a computer virus is a crime under common law and under specific laws in various states. *See also* VACCINE.

VIRUS PROTECTION SOFTWARE a computer program that offers protection from VIRUSES by making additional checks of the integrity of the operating system. No vaccine can offer complete protection against all viruses. Also known as anti-virus software.

VISION the act of seeing. Computer displays rely on many special properties of human vision, among them the following:

- The eye blends together images that are less than $\frac{1}{30}$ second apart. Most computers redisplay the screen image every $\frac{1}{30}$ second or so, and the human viewer does not see any flicker.

- Movements that are made in steps lasting $\frac{1}{30}$ second or less appear to be continuous. A moving image is actually a series of still images presented in very rapid succession.

- Colors can be simulated by mixing other colors. For example, yellow on a computer screen does not contain any yellow light; instead, it is a mixture of red and green light. *See* RGB MONITOR; PLANE; COLOR.

Working with a computer screen can be tiring to the eyes, especially if the display is blurry or glare is a problem, but no permanent harm results. Eyeglasses designed for the proper working distance can make computer work much easier. *See* EYEGLASSES FOR COMPUTER USERS.

Watch

Wedge

Š
Wedge

Light
Normal
Bold
Extra Bold
Weight

W

WARP version 3.0 of OS/2. The term comes from "warp speed," a concept used in science fiction to defy the laws of physics. Version 3.0 runs faster than version 2.1 but is otherwise very similar.

WATCH the icon that appears when the Macintosh is too busy to accept new input from the keyboard or the mouse.

WEB *See* WORLD WIDE WEB.

WEB BROWSER *See* BROWSER.

WEDGE

    1. part of a pie chart, also called a SLICE.

    2. an accent mark which is also called a CHECK, HÁČEK, or CARON, as in š. *See* ACCENTS.

WEIGHT refers to the width or heaviness of the stroke of a letterform. Most typefaces have a normal and bold weight; some typeface families have an extensive range of weights available.

WHITE SPACE the area of a page not covered with type or illustrations. Also called *negative space*. In their zeal to cram as much information as possible into the space available, novice desktop publishers often try to do away with white space. This can be a mistake, for good layouts use areas of white space to their advantage. White space can be dramatic and can create emphasis and a mood of calm and serenity. It is the designer's greatest tool for organizing complicated material.

    The rule of thumb is: Throw the white space to the outside. Don't let it get trapped inside the page. This is why wide gutters between columns look amateurish. *See* MARGINS; COLUMNS; GUTTERS.

WIDOW the first line of a paragraph that appears by itself as the last line of a page or column. Some word processors automatically adjust page breaks so that there are no widows. *See also* ORPHAN.

WINDOW an area of the screen set aside for a special purpose. On the Macintosh and in Microsoft Windows, the screen is divided into windows for differ-

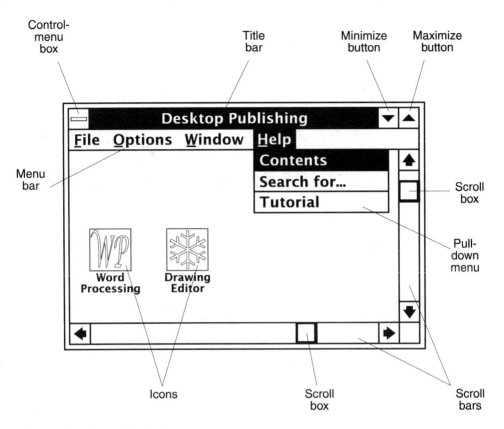

Figure 26 A generic window

ent pieces of software. The user can control the size, shape, and positioning of the windows. The active window is the one in which you are currently typing.

Figure 26 shows the main parts of a generic window. To move the window, place the mouse pointer on the title bar, hold down the left button, and move the mouse. To change the size of the window, do the same thing but with the pointer on the left, right, or bottom border of the window. To close the window, double-click on the control menu box. *See also* ICON; SCROLL BAR; MENU BAR; PULL-DOWN MENU; TITLE BAR; MINIMIZE; MAXIMIZE.

WINDOWS ACCELERATOR *see* SUPER VGA.

WINDOWS, MICROSOFT the name of three graphical operating systems produced by Microsoft Corporation of Redmond Washington:

1. *Microsoft Windows* for PC-compatible computers, which runs on top of MS-DOS (although a later version will be a complete operating system).

2. *Windows for Workgroups* (WFW), which is Microsoft Windows with network support added.

3. *Windows NT*, an operating system for a variety of CPUs, including not only PC compatibles but also the DEC Alpha and the PowerPC. Windows NT provides high performance but is only partly compatible with Microsoft Windows.

Of the three, Microsoft Windows is the most popular, and the rest of this article will concentrate on it.

As an extension to MS-DOS, Microsoft Windows provides a graphical user interface, extended memory, and multitasking. The screen is divided into windows, and the user uses a mouse to start programs and make menu choices. Windows can run not only Windows software (which use the graphical user interface) but also ordinary DOS software. In fact, Windows includes several application programs, including a word processor, a text file editor, a paint program, and a terminal emulator.

To run in enhanced mode with multitasking, Windows requires an 80386, 486, or Pentium CPU with at least 4 megabytes of memory. In this mode Windows can run several DOS and/or Windows application programs concurrently, each in its own window.

Under Windows, screen and printer output is handled by device drivers. Thus, all Windows applications run correctly on whatever screen and printer Windows is configured for. To use a new printer or video card, it is only necessary to reconfigure Windows, not the application software.

Like OS/2, Windows can use a disk file as swap space to substitute for extra memory. Unlike OS/2, Windows relies on cooperation between the programs that run concurrently; an improperly written program can stop the machine.

The newest version of Windows (Windows 95, formerly known as "Chicago") is scheduled to be released in the fall of 1995.

See also MULTITASKING; OS/2; DEVICE DRIVER.

WIREFRAME a method of displaying a drawing in outline form that speeds the time spent redrawing the screen. It is customary to work on a complex drawing in wireframe mode to save time. To see how the finished drawing will look, drawing and CAD programs provide a preview mode. Some programs will allow you to edit the drawing in preview mode, but it is always faster to work with the wireframe.

Wireframe

WIZARD a help feature that displays tips and other helpful information automatically. For example, a wizard will accompany a DIALOG BOX to help you understand the purpose of all the possible settings. Wizards can be very useful for novices; more advanced users can turn them off. Similar program features are called COACHES, CUE CARDS, or BALLOON HELP.

WORD PROCESSING the process of using a computer to prepare written documents (letters, reports, books, and the like). The boundary between word processing and *desktop publishing* is not sharp, but in general, word processing is the preparation of clearly worded, readable text, and does not include elaborate design or typography.

Word processing makes it easy to change or correct a document and then print it out without introducing new errors. More importantly, word processing lets you turn a rough draft into a finished report with no retyping and no wasted effort. You can start with a rough, fragmentary outline of what you want to say, then fill in the pieces in any convenient order. You don't have to finish page 1 before writing page 2. Many writers find this very convenient; you can get a document almost finished while waiting for information that you will fill in at the last minute, and if you have to produce many similar documents (letters, for instance), each one can be a slightly altered copy of the previous one.

Many word processors include spelling and grammar checkers. Take their advice with a grain of salt; they don't understand English and they don't know

WORDSPACING

what you are trying to say. A spelling checker simply looks up each word in a dictionary, and complains if it can't find it; it does not catch substitutions of one correctly spelled word for another, such as *to* for *too*. Grammar checkers catch some common errors, but they also complain about some combinations of words that are not ungrammatical. There is no substitute for careful reading by a human being.

Almost all word processors have all the features needed for office work and student term papers. Not all of them handle mathematical formulae, chemical symbols, foreign languages, long footnotes, or complicated formatting; if you will be typing academic or technical material, choose software that meets your specific needs. *See* DESKTOP PUBLISHING; TYPESETTING MISTAKES.

WORDSPACING   the spacing between words. The amount of wordspacing is adjustable in most word processing and page layout programs. If the text is being set JUSTIFIED, the program will insert very tiny amounts of space (called MICROSPACING) between words until the line of type is the correct length.

WORD WRAP   a feature of word processing programs that starts a new line when a full line has been reached. This means that it is not necessary to hit the return key at the end of each line. If new text is added, it pushes the existing words ahead of the cursor, rearranging the placement of words as necessary to avoid breaking a word.

WORKBOX   *see* TOOLBOX.

WORLD WIDE WEB   (WWW) a loosely organized set of computer sites that publish information which anyone can read via the Internet, mainly using HTTP (Hypertext Transfer Protocol). Each screenful (*page*) of information includes menu choices and highlighted words through which the user can call up further information, either from the same computer or by linking automatically to another computer anywhere in the world. Thus, the information is arranged in a web of tremendous size, and the links are created by the author of each page. *See* INTERNET; HTML; BROWSER.

WRAP to flow text from one line or column to the next; or to flow text around an illustration.

One advantage that computerized typesetting has over traditional typesetting is the ability to quickly and accurately arrange text around an irregular contour. This is made possible by the computer's ability to treat the copy as if it were fluid, pouring it in until the column is filled. *See* RUN AROUND; SCULPTING.

WRISTWATCH *see* WATCH.

WRITE to record digital information onto a disk or tape.

WRITE PROTECT to set a disk or tape so that the computer will not write or erase the data on it. Write-protecting a diskette can keep a computer virus from being copied onto it. However, write-protecting will also block the operation of any software that normally writes on the diskette. To write-protect a $5\frac{1}{4}$ inch diskette, place an opaque cover on the notch on the side. To write-protect a $3\frac{1}{2}$ inch diskette, slide the movable tab so that the hole is uncovered.

Any disk sent to a service bureau should be write-protected so that VIRUSES cannot be written on the disk.

WRONG-READING mirror-imaged type. *See example at* FLIP.

WWW *see* WORLD WIDE WEB.

WYSIWYG an acronym for "What you see is what you get." (Most people pronounce it "wizzy wig.") With a word processing program, this means that the appearance of the screen almost exactly matches the appearance that the document will have when it is printed.

X

X-AXIS the horizontal axis in an X-Y coordinate system.

XGA a super VGA card marketed by IBM for the PS/2. The original XGA, introduced in 1991, offered 1024×768-pixel images with 256 colors (with the IBM 8514/A monitor) and 640×480 images with 65,536 colors (with 8514/A and plain VGA monitors). XGA stands for **E**xtended **G**raphics **A**rray. *See* SUPER VGA.

X-height

X-HEIGHT the height of the *body* of the lower case letterforms (such as the small "x" of a typeface).

   Sometimes the x-height of a font has more to do with its apparent size than its point size. A typeface with a large x-height (Century Schoolbook) appears larger than the same size type in a font with a small x-height (such as Times Roman). (*See diagram at* LEG-IBILITY.) You may need to take this into consideration when choosing a typeface for a long text. At smaller sizes (8 points or below), the typeface with the larger x-height will be the better choice.

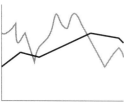

X-Y graph

X-Y GRAPH a graph which plots y as a function of x. This is a very common graph in academia and one that is not supported by most business charting software.

Y

Y-AXIS the vertical axis in an X-Y coordinate system.